"With *LAbyrinth,* Randall Sullivan offers a heretical view of Rampart and much more. . . . *LAbyrinth* is a jeremiad, leveling everything in its path. . . . *LAbyrinth* gleefully wants to provoke a discussion. Well, a knockdown brawl, but still." —R. J. Smith, *Los Angeles Magazine*

"A fascinating read." —Mark Brown, *The Rocky Mountain News*

"One of the most exhaustive, compelling studies of hip-hop culture ever published." —Meghan Sutherland, *Paper*

"Sullivan makes a strong case for thinking that the murders of Tupac Shakur and Biggie Smalls are connected, and the LAPD Ramparts Division scandal is connected to them. . . . You haven't got the goods on any of these notorious cases until you read this intricate showbiz true-crime thriller." —*Booklist*

"Sullivan strikes again. . . . Sullivan's reportorial writing style accurately reflects the investigative work of homicide gumshoe Russell Poole while building the drama within the truly labyrinthine political cover-ups, cop-to-criminal crossovers and the breaks in the LAPD's code of silence." —*Publishers Weekly*

"Compelling . . . Augmented by a roster of more than 130 key players, a detailed timeline of events, and reference to 224 supporting documents, the book offers a blueprint for federal authorities to investigate the grave injustices it alleges. . . . No single source presents so complete or damning a record as *LAbyrinth.*" —Evan Serpick, CNN.com

"Knowing a scandal when he sees one, Sullivan names names and sets scenes piled high with drugs, guns, cash, fab cars, and corpses." —Anneli Rufus, Eastbayexpress.com

Also by Randall Sullivan

Untouchable

The Price of Experience

LAbyrinth

A Detective Investigates the Murders of
Tupac Shakur and Notorious B.I.G.,
the Implication of Death Row Records'
Suge Knight, and the Origins of the
Los Angeles Police Scandal

RANDALL SULLIVAN

Grove Press
New York

Permission to quote from Notorious B.I.G.'s "Somebody's Gotta Die" by Hal Leonard Corporation. Words and music by Sean Combs, Christopher Wallace, Nashiem Myrick, Carlos Broady, and Tony Hester. Copyright © 1997 EMI April Music, Justin Combs Publishing Company, Inc., Big Poppa Music, EMI Longitude Music, Nash Mack Publishing, and July Six Publishing. All rights for Justin Combs Publishing Company, Inc., and Big Poppa Music controlled and administered by EMI April Music, Inc. Contains elements of "In the Rain." All rights reserved. International copyright secured. Used by permission.

PHOTO CREDITS: page 1, bottom right, Robert Yager; page 3, top, Ted Soqui/CORBIS Sygma; page 4, bottom left, CORBIS; page 4, bottom right, Simone Green-English; page 5, top left, AP/World Wide Photos; page 5, top right, Bill Jones; page 5, lower left, AP/World Wide Photos; page 5, lower right, George De Sota/Newsmakers; page 7, top right, Robert Yager; page 8, top, Robert Yager.

Published simultaneously in Canada
Printed in the United States of America

Library of Congress Cataloging-in-Publication Data

Sullivan, Randall.
    Labyrinth: a detective investigates the murders of Tupac Shakur and Notorious B.I.G., the implication of Death Row Records' Suge Knight, and the origins of the Los Angeles Police scandal / Randall Sullivan.
       p. cm.
     ISBN-10: 0-8021-3971-X
     ISBN-13: 978-0-8021-3971-9
     1. Murder—California—Los Angeles—Case studies. 2. Police misconduct—California—Los Angeles—Case studies. 3. Police corruption—California—Los Angeles—Case studies. 4. Shakur, Tupac, 1971– 5. Notorious B.I.G. (Musician). 6. Knight, Suge. I. Title.

    HV6534.L7 S848 2002
    364.15'23'0979494—dc21   2001053709

Grove Press
an imprint of Grove/Atlantic, Inc.
841 Broadway
New York, NY 10003

Distributed by Publishers Group West

www.groveatlantic.com

12 13 14 15   11 10 9 8 7

To M.D., who talked me into this.

CONTENTS

"Every society gets the kind of criminal it deserves. What is equally true is that every community gets the kind of law enforcement it insists on."

—Robert F. Kennedy

Retaliation for this one won't be minimal
   Cuz I'm a criminal
   Way before the rap shit
   Bust the gat shit
Puff won't even know what happened,
   If it's done smoothly

—from "Somebody's Gotta Die," Notorious B.I.G.

PROLOGUE

March 18, 1997, North Hollywood, California

Even people in passing cars could see that this was an occasion for steering clear. It was just past four in the afternoon, the beginning of rush hour in Los Angeles, when two men, one white, the other black, became embroiled in what appeared to be an overheated traffic dispute. Both combatants were dressed to display their muscular builds, although in styles at considerable variance. The white man, who drove a battered Buick Regal, wore a pale gray tank top that showed off his bulging biceps and with it a baseball cap bearing the insignia of a marijuana leaf. He sported a bushy Fu Manchu mustache and his long, silver-streaked hair was tied back in a ponytail. The black man, who drove a shiny green Mitsubishi Montero, had a shaved head and a goatee, while the breadth of his bare chest showed beneath a green Nike jacket worn open nearly to the navel.

The Buick had just stopped in heavy traffic at the intersection of Ventura and Lankershim Boulevards when the Montero pulled up on the left, rap music thumping through its open windows. The black man began staring in the direction of the Buick and shaking his head. The white man thought he must be looking at someone on the sidewalk and turned to check, but the sidewalk was empty. The white man rolled down his window and asked, "Can I help you?"

"Roll that window up, you punk motherfucker!" the black man shouted back. "Get out of my face or I'll put a cap up your ass!"

"What's your problem?" the white man asked.

"I'm *your* problem, motherfucker!" the black man shouted. "Pull over right now and I'll kick your motherfucking ass!"

"Yeah, sure," the white man replied.

The black man became so enraged that his eyeballs bulged. "I'll cap your ass, motherfucker!" he screamed. "Pull over right now!" The man in the Montero punctuated his threat with a series of curious hand gestures, then pointed to the side of the road.

The white man nodded and said, "All right, let's go. Pull over."

It looked as if the two were going to climb out of their cars and go at it right there, but as soon as the Montero parked in a red zone on the other side of the intersection, the Buick sped away, veering south on Cahuenga Boulevard. Screaming curses out his window and pounding on his steering wheel, the enraged black man forced his way back into traffic and took off after the Buick, slaloming between cars, even veering into an oncoming lane at one point.

The Montero finally caught up when the Buick was stopped by a red light at Regal Place, four car lengths from an on-ramp to the Hollywood Freeway. As the SUV pulled up next to the sedan, other motorists heard the black man screaming through his passenger-side window, then saw him lean toward the Buick and extend his right arm. The white man, who had been shouting back, suddenly ducked his head, banged his chest against the Buick's steering column, and let his foot slip off the brake as the car lurched slightly forward. The Montero's windows were tinted almost to opacity, and witnesses weren't sure whether the black man had a gun, but the hand that came out of the Buick's open window a moment later, as the white man sat up straight again, definitely was filled with an automatic pistol. A woman in a Mercedes sedan who was a long way from her home in Pacific Palisades remembered that the white man wore "this very determined, focused expression" as he fired off one shot, then a second.

The first bullet passed through the passenger-side door of the Montero and lodged in a gym bag. The second shot struck the black man on the right side just below his armpit, punctured his heart, and stopped in his left lung.

Though only seconds from death, the black man managed to swing his Montero into the left lane and make a U-turn. A woman working in an office across the street looked up when she heard the gunshots and saw, through the SUV's open window, "the full face of this black man smiling and grinning, a sarcastic laugh-grin . . . holding the steering wheel with his left hand and pumping his right hand." The black man disappeared from the woman's sight as his Montero coasted into the parking lot of an *am-pm* mini-mart and came to rest against the store's front wall. The Buick, now following the Montero, pulled into the same parking lot moments later.

Behind the store were two California Highway Patrol officers who had just finished a coffee break when they heard gunshots. The CHP officers swung their separate patrol cars around the west side of the building just in time to see a white male wearing a cap with a marijuana leaf on it pointing a handgun at a black male who was slumped forward in the seat of a green SUV. The CHP officer in the lead braked to an abrupt stop, swung open his car door, and crouched behind the vehicle as he drew his sidearm and ordered the white male to drop his weapon. "I'm a police officer," the marijuana guy shouted back, and pulled on a chain around his neck to lift the gold shield of a Los Angeles Police Department detective above his tank top.

He was Frank Lyga, an undercover narcotics cop assigned to the Hollywood Area Field Enforcement Section. He had never seen the dead man before, Lyga said.

By the time detectives from the LAPD's elite Robbery-Homicide Division arrived on the scene, however, they knew not only the dead man's identity but also what it meant. The deceased was Kevin Gaines, an LAPD officer for the past seven years. Currently assigned to the department's Pacific Division, Gaines was off duty at the time of his death.

"As soon as we found out that the dead guy was a black police officer, we knew we were stepping into a political minefield," recalled Russell Poole, who would become lead detective in the LAPD's criminal investigation of the shooting. What Poole couldn't begin to imagine was how widespread and well concealed those mines were laid. The detective began to experience a distinct sense of foreboding, however, when a computer check revealed that the Montero was registered to the address of a production company owned by Death Row Records. Knightlife, it was called.

PART ONE

THE RACE CARD

Detective Poole is an absolutely outstanding detective. He now has 9½ years of homicide experience and has handled every possible situation. He is hard-working, loyal, productive, thorough and reliable. His contact with the public is always courteous and professional. He is a definite asset to the Los Angeles Police Department.

—From the final "Performance Evaluation Report" filed on Detective Russell Poole before his transfer to the LAPD's Robbery-Homicide Division in late 1996

CHAPTER ONE

It was after dark by the time Russell Poole arrived at the shooting scene. Cahuenga Boulevard, the main thoroughfare linking downtown Los Angeles to the San Fernando Valley, was closed off in both directions by yellow police tape and patrol cars with flashing lights. The enclosed area was crawling with brass, captains as well as lieutenants. Poole's squad leader, Lt. Pat Conmay, his partner, Detective Supervisor Fred Miller, and the members of the LAPD's Officer Involved Shooting team were all standing in a group. The Internal Affairs investigators, as always, kept to themselves.

Frank Lyga was still at the scene and had been informed that the dead man was a police officer. "Lyga was very confident at that time," Poole recalled. "He felt certain he had done nothing wrong. I don't think he realized that the fact Gaines was black was going to be as much of a problem for him as it was."

The OIS team drove Lyga back to the North Hollywood station to take his statement. Poole was informed that his assignment would be to investigate a possible charge of assault with a deadly weapon against the undercover detective. Poole was collecting spent cartridges and making measurements of the shooting scene when he and Miller received a tip that Gaines, although married, had been living with a girlfriend at an address in the Hollywood Hills. The two detectives drove to the Multiview Avenue address and found themselves at the gated driveway of a mansion belonging to the notorious gangsta rap mogul Marion "Suge" Knight, CEO of Death Row Records. Gaines's girlfriend was Knight's estranged wife, Sharitha.

Sharitha Knight already had been informed of Gaines's death, and was cried out by the time Poole and Miller interviewed her. Sharitha's mother, who introduced herself as Mrs. Golden, did most of the talking at first, explaining that her daughter was married to but separated from Suge Knight, and that Kevin was her boyfriend. They had seen Kevin only a few hours earlier, Mrs. Golden told the detectives. He said he was going to the gym and intended to pick up new tires for the Montero on his way home. "Sharitha did say that Kevin had done some 'security work' for Death Row, but she gave no details," Poole recalled.

Sharitha Knight had met Gaines in 1993 at a gas station on La Brea Avenue just south of the Santa Monica Freeway. Gaines (who had been reprimanded repeatedly for attempting to pick up women while on duty) pulled up in his patrol car next to her Mercedes, Sharitha said, and began a casual conversation that grew more animated when she told the officer who she was and described her mansion in the hills above Cahuenga Pass. Gaines bet the woman dinner that she was exaggerating, and the two began dating exclusively after he paid off. Gaines soon took up residence in the mansion, separated by twenty-five miles and two million dollars from the house in Gardena where his wife, Georgia, and their two children lived. Sharitha was working at the time as Snoop Dogg's manager, and obtained work for Gaines as the rapper's bodyguard.

Poole and his partner made no protest when Sharitha Knight cut the interview short after less than half an hour. "This was her boyfriend and she was distraught," Poole explained. "It was a delicate situation."

As he drove back down Cahuenga Pass toward the LAPD's North Hollywood station to interview Frank Lyga, Poole recalled, "I thought to myself, 'This case is going to take me to places I've never been.'"

* * *

Poole already had been to places that few people raised in the suburbs ever see. Now a burly forty-year-old with a sunburnt squint and glints of silver in his reddish-blond hair, Poole had been a slim twenty-two-year-old with freckled cheeks and bright green eyes when he accepted his first assignment with the LAPD, as a patrol officer in Southwest Division, working out of a station near The Coliseum. "The department didn't try to prepare me for what it was to be a white officer in a black neighborhood, because there's no way to do that," he recalled. "But you learn real quick. All of a sudden this shy kid from La Mirada is working ten hours a day in South Central Los Angeles. It's like you've been given a front-row seat on life in the inner city."

At La Mirada High School, situated on the border between Orange and Los Angeles Counties, Poole had been voted most valuable player on a baseball team that won the Suburban League Championship. Pete Rose was his childhood idol, and Poole's teammates tagged him with Rose's nickname, "Charlie Hustle." "I ran everywhere I went, full blast," he explained. "It was the way I was brought up, to give all you had all the time."

His father was a twenty-seven-year veteran of the L.A. County Sheriff's Department who had spent much of his career as a supervising sergeant of the detective bureau at Norwalk Station. "I looked up to my dad," Poole recalled. "He had been in the Marine Corps during the Korean War, and I used to love to look at his medals. We were a very traditional family. My father was the breadwinner, my mom stayed home and took care of us kids. My two sisters shared one bedroom, while my brother, Gary, and I shared another. I thought that was pretty much how everybody lived." His father never encouraged him to become a cop, and Poole kept his dream of playing baseball in the major leagues alive until a torn rotator cuff during his second season at Cerritos College ended his athletic career. Although he graduated with a degree in criminal justice, the young man went to work in a supermarket and was night manager at an Alpha-Beta store when he married his wife, Megan, in 1979. The two had known each other since they were children, and the bride wondered out loud whether her young husband would be satisfied with a comfortable life in La Mirada. Her question was answered less than a year later, in the autumn of 1980, when Russell Poole entered the Los Angeles Police Academy. "I decided that I needed something more stimulating than the grocery business," he explained. Fewer than half of those who entered Poole's Police Academy class would finish with him.

The culture of the LAPD back then was "quasi-military," recalled Poole, who liked it that way. Every day began with a three-mile run that ended with alternating sets of pull-ups and push-ups, followed by wind sprints. "I went into the Academy at a pretty solid 185 pounds and finished at a little over 165," he recalled. "But you learned pretty fast that physical ability wasn't the point—character was. They wanted to see whether you would drop out or keep trying. Would you quit if you got cramps while you were running, or would you grind it out, cry it out, gut it out. A lot of the women in the class impressed me in that way."

Only about a year after Poole graduated, though, a series of lawsuits forced the Academy to make failure all but obsolete. "After that, if you were lousy or wouldn't try hard enough, they'd pat you on the back and say, 'It's okay, we have remedial classes you can take,'" Poole recalled. "They'd get you counseling. They also started lowering the standards on written tests, in order to encourage diversity and avoid controversy."

Poole didn't think the department was doing its new recruits any favors. "When you get out on the streets, nobody's going to baby you there," he explained. "You are going to be caught in situations where all you can do is survive."

The more harrowing the circumstance, the more intense the experience of connection to one's fellow officers, as Poole discovered soon after his assignment to patrol duty in South Central L.A. "What I remember most about those early days was how it felt to stop a car and approach it from the rear," Poole recalled. "The whole key was to stay alert, but not come on aggressive. On patrol, you had to be ready for anything. You might go through a whole day totally bored, then plunge into an experience of complete terror fifteen minutes before the end of your shift."

The most feared part of Southwest Division was an area called the Jungle, a collection of apartment buildings along Martin Luther King Boulevard between Crenshaw and LaBrea that was surrounded by huge, droopy eucalyptus trees. All that low-hanging foliage was what made the Jungle so dangerous, along with an unusual layout of buildings that created a lot of places where a suspect could hide until an officer was almost on top of him. "Anytime we went in there, the only color we saw when we looked at each other was the blue of our uniforms," Poole recalled.

Before crack cocaine, PCP was the street drug of choice in the ghetto, and Poole had never been more frightened than the first time he was attacked by a suspect high on horse tranquilizer. "I had dropped my guard because at first he appeared to be friendly—'Hi, officer, how you doin'?'—but when he got close he grabbed for my throat," Poole recalled. "My first instinct was to throw out my hands to push his face back, but he caught my left forefinger in his mouth and bit it all the way down to the bone. My partner was trying to hit him upside the head to get him to release, and finally he did, but we went to the ground and the guy was spitting and scratching and punching and kicking. He was shredding our shirts and uniforms, scratching our arms and faces. I had deep cuts all over my face and so did my partner. Blood was everywhere and my finger was dangling, barely attached.

"Pretty soon we were surrounded by this big crowd of people, all black, and this was very scary for me, because I was fairly new and had never been in a situation like that. We didn't have handheld radios back then, so I looked up at this one older black man and said, 'Please get on that radio and request help.' I didn't want to draw my gun so I took out my sap and hit the guy across the forehead. It didn't even faze him. So I hit him a second time, as hard as I could, and that split his head open. Right about then I started hearing those faint sirens from far away, gradually getting louder and louder. Nothing ever sounded better to me. And in a couple of minutes there were like twenty LAPD patrol cars on the scene, with cops of all colors, and the crowd was breaking up. I remember thinking, 'This is what they meant by backing each other up and being there when another officer needs you.' It made me feel really good to be part of this organization filled with people I could count on, no matter where they came from."

One of Poole's first mentors was a black training officer named Richard Lett, "a shy, nice man who had about fifteen years on the job." During the entire time they worked together, Poole recalled, the two of them never spoke once about communicating across racial lines. "He saw that I take people as they come, and so he really didn't think it was necessary," Poole recalled. "I was making friends of all races and I felt this was my education in life. My time as a patrol officer taught me how to connect with people from very different backgrounds, and I learned not to make general assumptions about anyone."

Back in those days, the LAPD talked about itself as a family, Poole recalled: "We greeted each other with hugs, brother officer, sister officer, civilian employees." The only discordant note was sounded at roll calls, where black officers invariably sat in a section of the room separate from the white and Hispanic officers, who tended to intermingle. "But nobody ever talked about it," Poole remembered.

Everything changed in 1991, though, when the videotaped beating of Rodney King by four LAPD officers at the end of a vehicle pursuit was broadcast on local television. Poole was at home ironing a shirt the first time he saw it: "I remember thinking, 'Oh, shit, I wonder how many times they're gonna play that?' I never imagined it would be hundreds and hundreds. That wasn't the LAPD I knew, but it became the LAPD to the rest of the world, and that was awful to live with. It created terrible tensions within the department. Getting along with both civilians and your fellow officers along racial lines suddenly became a lot more difficult. Even people you thought were friends weren't saying 'Hi' when you passed them in the hallway."

The riots that followed the acquittal of the four officers accused in the Rodney King beating at their first trial in Simi Valley only increased racial divisions within the LAPD. The department maintained a mobilization plan for such emergencies, but for some reason it wasn't implemented. Chief Daryl Gates had been relieved of duty (by the first black president of the Los Angeles Police Commission), and then reinstated, but his position was weakened. "Everybody wanted to be the new chief," Poole recalled. "All these deputy chiefs were practically begging Gates to retire so they could take over, and the early response to the riots was controlled by some of these same people, who really didn't mind if the LAPD looked bad, because it would make Chief Gates look bad. We had subcommanders pulling units out of the area around Florence and Normandie when they should have been pouring in."

When Gates, who had been attending a function in Mandeville Canyon, finally arrived at the LAPD Command Post in the bus depot at 54th and Van Ness, he was astonished to find captains and lieutenants standing around in groups. When a black captain approached him carrying a coffee cup, Gates slapped the cup out of the man's hands and shouted, "What the fuck is happening? Why aren't my men out there deployed?"

Even before the rioting stopped, word of this incident had spread through the department, "and people of different races were even more uncomfortable with each other," Poole remembered. By the time Gates was replaced by the LAPD's first black chief, Willie Williams, an import from Philadelphia, the department had become an institution seething with thinly veiled resentments. White offi-cers did not doubt that Williams had won the job with the color of his skin, while black officers wondered why the position hadn't gone to the LAPD's highest-ranking African American, Assistant Chief Bernard Parks.

To a lot of people, and for the longest time, it had looked as if Bernie Parks might be the one man who could reconcile the contradictory legacies that he had inherited from his two most notable predecessors, William H. Parker and Homer Broome. During the 1930s and '40s, Parker had occupied the unenviable position of a clean cop in a dirty department. The LAPD of that period was almost astonishingly corrupt; Los Angeles's mayor sold hiring and promotion exams out of his office in City Hall, while vice officers earned the bulk of their income by protecting prostitutes, pimps, and pornographers. At one point, the LAPD's head of intelligence was sent to San Quentin for bombing the car of an investigator who had been hired by civic reformers to ferret out crooked cops. When Parker was appointed Los Angeles Police Chief in 1950, conditions within the department changed dramatically. Parker's insistence on integrity was so adamant that he fired officers for the sort of infractions that wouldn't have resulted in an admonishment a few years earlier. The LAPD's new chief even demanded that his officers pay for their own coffee. Parker, who coined the phrase "thin blue line," also made the LAPD over into an ultra-efficient police force renowned for the discipline, mobility, and aggressiveness that allowed it to cover the enormous geographical area of Los Angeles with fewer than one-fifth the number of officers employed by the New York Police Department. By the early 1960s, LAPD officers believed that they belonged to the best police department in the world, and by most measures they were right.

Racial sensitivity was not a theme that resonated particularly well with Chief Parker, however. Parker was no racist, but the mission he gave LAPD officers to "stop crime before it happens" inevitably led to a concentration of police forces in South Central Los Angeles. Then, as now, black males committed a hugely disproportionate amount of crime in Los Angeles and across the country. For the LAPD of William Parker, that was the essential point, and the chief was not particularly interested in complaints against white cops who beat the black suspects they had charged with "contempt of officer."

The black LAPD officer who most successfully challenged the petty injustices of the period was Commander Homer Broome. He had joined the LAPD in 1954, the same year the U.S. Supreme Court struck down the concept of "separate but equal," and rose steadily through the ranks for the next quarter-century. Broome would be best remembered, however, for his very last appearance in an LAPD uniform. This was at his retirement dinner in the Ambassador Hotel during February of 1979. Los Angeles's mayor and police chief were in attendance, along with dozens of local politicans, all there to take advantage of an occasion when the observation of one man's success could be made into a milestone of community progress. Broome was "living proof," one speaker observed, that color was no obstacle to success in Los Angeles.

The audience naturally was shocked when the guest of honor rode a wave of applause to the microphone and, instead of responding with the thanks that were expected, chose to remind his listeners of some unpleasant facts. Although the LAPD had employed black officers since 1886, Broome began, it was not until 1969, when he was promoted to captain, that one had occupied a command position within the department. Those who knew the LAPD's history did not want to be reminded that during the 1920s Chief Louis Oaks had been a proud member of the Ku Klux Klan, or that in the years before World War II the department had restricted black officers almost entirely to foot-traffic beats along Alameda Avenue, permitting just a few of them to patrol in jitney cars, and then only between the hours of 2 A.M. and 6 A.M., when they were not likely to be noticed.

When the LAPD appointed its first two black watch commanders in 1940, Broome recalled, the move was heralded as a huge leap forward, but the backsliding began almost immediately. To prevent the two new lieutenants from commanding white personnel, an all-black morning watch was established. And department administrators soon decided that two black lieutenants were one too many. After learning of his demotion from an article in the *Evening Herald*, Earl Broady needed another three years just to regain the rank of sergeant. When he failed repeatedly to win a second promotion to lieutenant, Broady resigned from the department and enrolled in law school.

Eventually he became a Superior Court juuge of Los Angeles County. His experience was repeated again and again; the LAPD's refusal to promote black officers to command rank had resulted in the resignations or early retirements of men who had become city councilmen, municipal court judges, Los Angeles Port warden, and the city's first black mayor, Tom Bradley.

It was Bradley who had made the first attempt to integrate the LAPD. In 1960 Bradley, only the third black lieutenant in the department's history, found three white officers who were willing to share a single patrol car with black partners in separate shifts. When word leaked out, however, the white officers began to absorb a barrage of abuse from their cohorts, and each of the three eventually explained to Bradley that he would have to withdraw from the "experiment." William Parker would, to his credit, issue an order to fully integrate the LAPD in 1963, but by then Tom Bradley was gone, having submitted his resignation one year earlier.

The indignities and abuses that had become a fundamental condition of relations between white police officers and black citizens in Los Angeles would explode during the late summer of 1965 into the most destructive display of civil disobedience in modern U.S. history. It began when a black teenager was arrested for drunk driving by a white motorcycle officer on the evening of August 11. By the time it was over, battles between police and more than 10,000 black civilians had raged for six days across an area of 46.5 square miles, leaving 34 persons dead, 1,032 injured, and more than 600 buildings burned and looted.

Homer Broome was promoted to lieutenant one year later, replacing Tom Bradley as the LAPD's single black watch commander. Over the next ten years, twelve more blacks were promoted to lieutenant, with five rising to captain and two to commander. There were mutterings, however, that LAPD administrators had chosen only the most compliant of black officers, and were moving them from job to job, so that they could boast about breaking the race barrier in this position or that one. The sole black commander who achieved exemption from such complaints was Bernard Parks. His ability to win the trust and admiration of white superiors without being labeled a lackey by black peers was what made Parks's advance through the ranks of the LAPD so remarkable.

Parks had been negotiating such difficult passages since his senior year in high school, when he was elected president of a nearly all-white class. As a young LAPD officer, he was singled out for special attention by Chief Ed Davis, who made Parks first his driver then his protégé. Daryl Gates, despite a reputation as a man who was not particularly fond of people with dark complexions, had promoted Parks from lieutenant to captain to commander to deputy chief to assistant chief, making him the number-two man in the department. Parks, though, was devastated when the Los Angeles City Council chose Willie Williams as the LAPD's first black chief.

The job of police chief in Los Angeles was not quite what it had once been, of course. In the aftermath of the 1992 Los Angeles Riots, a commission headed by former U.S. Secretary of State Warren Christopher had created the office of a civilian "Inspector General" to oversee the police department, while LAPD chiefs were limited to five-year terms. It did not help that Willie Williams became, by virtually every account, the worst LAPD chief of the modern era.

Labeled a bungler within a few months of taking the job, Williams destroyed any hope for political survival when he demoted Bernie Parks to deputy chief. Williams's decision to advise the news media of the demotion before personally informing Parks made him look especially despicable. Only through the intervention of the City Council did Parks obtain the plum assignment of Operations Bureau, a job that gave him control over the most politically powerful division of the LAPD, Internal Affairs. Embittered, Parks dug in until he became the immovable object that blocked the eminently resistable force of Willie Williams, who would spend his last three years in Los Angeles as, essentially, the lame duck chief of a police department that many felt was falling apart all around him. Senior police officials soon began to complain openly that departmental standards had virtually collapsed, and that the Los Angeles City Council's cure for the LAPD's racial ills might be worse than the disease itself. The written examinations that long had been the great equalizer for LAPD officers seeking promotion were steadily discounted because black candidates, in general, did far more poorly on them than did white candidates. Background checks became increasingly cursory, while minor crimes or a juvenile record no longer barred applicants from gaining admission to the Los Angeles Police Academy, because liberals had successfully argued that this limited the number of blacks and Hispanics who could join the LAPD. Behavior by a police officer that would have resulted in immediate dismissal only a decade earlier now was either overlooked or met with requests that the offending officer seek counseling.

"I don't think Willie Williams was personally corrupt," Russell Poole said, "but his command staff definitely was, and a lot of the best captains and lieutenants in the LAPD either retired or refused to seek promotions while he was chief. They didn't want to be part of what was going on in Parker Center. And meanwhile, Chief Williams made enemies of people who were in positions where they could hurt him."

Williams's appointment as LAPD chief produced at least some improvement in relations between the department's black and white officers, "but then along came the O.J. Simpson case," Poole recalled, "and suddenly racial tensions were inflamed again. A lot of the black officers said they thought Simpson was innocent, and that was just an outrage to the rest of us, because it was so obvious that he was guilty. So suddenly you not only had black officers angry at white officers, but also white officers angry at black officers. That situation got a lot worse when the Mark Fuhrman tapes came out, and people heard this white detective saying nigger-this and nigger-that. Fuhrman was just an arrogant fool shooting off his mouth to impress a woman, but he did so much damage." So did the subsequent spectacle of black citizens in the streets of Los Angeles cheering the acquittal of a man who had gotten away with murder.

By early 1997, most LAPD officers knew that Willie Williams would not be rehired as chief when his five-year term expired that

August. A huge majority of the department's rank-and-file officers endorsed the appointment of Deputy Chief Mark Kroeker as Williams's replacement, but the powers that be seemed to be leaning toward the man favored by the LAPD's black cops, Bernie Parks.

"So we had this atmosphere where any case involving racial issues was overshadowed by the politicians," Poole explained. "Everybody on the department was afraid to make a mistake, or even to do the right thing if it exposed them to criticism."

Poole could claim more immunity to charges of racial insensitivity than nearly any other white officer in the department. During his sixteen-and-a-half years on the job, he had been partnered with a series of black officers who uniformly praised his ability to deal with the citizens of South Central Los Angeles. At South Bureau Homicide, he regularly sat in on meetings of the black officers' organization, the Oscar Joel Bryant Association. And as a patrol officer in Southwest Division, Poole had been widely admired for insisting that if the LAPD was going to bust black gangbangers for spraying freeway underpasses with graffiti, then it had to do the same when it caught the fraternity boys from USC painting city streets with their insignia. Poole became a minor celebrity within the department when he arrested the white starting quarterback of USC's football team.

As Poole soon would discover, however, neither his sterling reputation nor Frank Lyga's persuasive story of self-defense would be enough to protect them in a maze where corpses collected in cul-de-sacs, and criminals with badges blocked the exits.

From Sharitha Knight's house, Poole and Det. Supervisor Miller drove to the LAPD's North Hollywood Station to interview Frank Lyga. The detectives already knew that Lyga had started his day with a practice session at the LAPD shooting range, scoring 100 percent with both a 12-gauge shotgun and the same Beretta pistol that had killed Kevin Gaines. Lyga then joined seven other undercover officers in a surveillance operation that ended shortly before 4 P.M., when the group was ordered to return to its office. During the drive back to Hollywood, the other members of the team drove both ahead of and behind Lyga in separate vehicles.

Lyga said had no idea what set Gaines off initially, describing his fellow officer as "a full-on gangbanger." For one thing, the guy was driving a green SUV, which had become the vehicle of choice for both Crips and Bloods. And he had recognized those hand gestures Gaines made as West Coast gang signs, Lyga said. Describing his verbal exchange with Gaines and the subsequent car chase, Lyga sounded genuinely frightened. As he saw Gaines pursuing him south on Cahuenga Boulevard, Lyga said, he activated the concealed radio in his car with his left foot and spoke into the microphone hidden behind a visor at the top of his windshield, using Tactical Frequency 2 to advise the other members of his team that he needed assistance with a black guy in a green Jeep who was acting crazy and possibly had a gun.

When he was stopped by the red light at Regal Place and looked in his rearview mirror to see Gaines's vehicle closing fast, Lyga said, he drew his own pistol and placed it on his lap. Gaines was shouting at the top of his lungs when he braked to a stop in the far left lane, Lyga said, screaming, "I'll cap you, motherfucker!" as he raised a pistol and pointed it through his open passenger-side window. He knew "cap" was street slang for kill, and fired his own weapon first because he believed he was about to be shot. He had never seen Kevin Gaines before and did not realize the mess he was in, Lyga said, until his supervisor Dennis Zeuner arrived on the scene and told him, "You're gonna have to suck this one up, Frank. The guy was a policeman."

Poole returned to the shooting scene from the North Hollywood Station and did not get home until almost 3 A.M. He caught four hours sleep, then awoke the next morning to the first of many "Cop Kills Cop" headlines that would be published worldwide. This was followed shortly by the news that as many as a dozen off-duty black police officers had begun to canvas the neighborhood surrounding the shooting scene, looking for witnesses who would "dirty up Lyga." The first to complain was an employee of the coffee importing company whose offices were directly across from the intersection where Gaines had been shot. Five black men wearing civilian clothes showed up at her place of business that day, the woman said, told her they were police officers, and began to question her in a manner she found "intimidating." When the man who did most of the talking began "trying to get me to change my story," the woman said, she demanded proof that he was a police officer. The man showed her his badge, the woman explained, and she wrote down the name and serial number. He was Derwin Henderson, a close friend and former partner of Gaines. Several other witnesses told LAPD investigators that the black officers who visited them had tried to put words in their mouths, and that they had been shaken by the experience.

Lyga's version of events was supported by every bit of available evidence, however. Several members of his undercover team, as well as a clerk assigned to monitor tactical frequency radio calls at the LAPD's West Bureau Narcotics Unit, had heard the detective turn on his radio shortly before the shooting and announce in an excited voice, "I've got a problem. There's a black guy in a green Jeep on my ass. I need you guys." "I think he's got a gun," they heard Lyga call in an even louder voice a few moments after that. "Where are you guys?" Approximately thirty seconds later, the members of Lyga's team heard him shout, "I just shot somebody! I need help!"

Witnesses to the shooting gave statements that agreed with Lyga's account in every detail. On the floor of the Montero next to Kevin Gaines's body, the two CHP officers on the scene had found a Smith and Wesson 9mm semiautomatic pistol with a hollow-point round in the chamber and eleven more bullets like it in the magazine. The gun was registered to Gaines.

Pressure on Frank Lyga, though, continued to mount. Even as media trucks laid siege to the detective's home, rumors spread that Lyga was part of a white supremacist group that had "targeted" Gaines as a warning to uppity black cops, or that Lyga had killed Gaines to cover up his part in a drug deal gone bad, or that Lyga had a history of armed attacks on black people and the LAPD was covering it up.

Detectives involved in the investigation of the shooting, however, already knew that the bad cop in this case was Kevin Gaines. Within forty-eight hours of Gaines's death, Poole and Miller learned that the dead officer had been involved in at least four other off-duty "roadway incidents" in which he had threatened motorists with violence. One of these drivers was retired LAPD Detective Sig Schien, who reported that during the later summer of 1996 Gaines had used a dark green Mitsubishi Montero to cut him off as he turned out of the Valley Credit Union parking lot on Sherman Way. He responded by flipping the Montero's driver off, Schien admitted. Gaines became so enraged that he attempted to run Schien's car off the road, then began motioning to pull over. When he did exactly that, Schien said, Gaines braked to a stop, jumped out of his SUV, and began shouting, "Hey, motherfucker, you going around giving people the finger? I ought to cap you. I ought to blow your motherfucking head off." Only when he told Gaines, "You'd better be a faster shot than me," then began repeating the Montero's license plate number out loud, Schien said, did a "flustered" Gaines climb back into his vehicle and burn rubber as he sped from the scene.

A civilian named Alex Szlay reported that just two weeks before his death, Gaines, accompanied by an attractive black woman, had swerved the green Montero in front of him so sharply that he was forced to change lanes to avoid a collision. When he became infuriated, Szlay said, Gaines shouted at him through his open window, "Do you have a problem? Because we can settle this quick." He asked what that meant, Szlay said, and Gaines replied, "I have this and this," then held up a pistol and an LAPD badge. Gaines and his female passenger were laughing hysterically, Szlay said, as they peeled away.

A Pacific Bell repairman told investigators that he had been on Laurel Canyon Boulevard just north of the Hollywood Freeway when Gaines pulled up alongside his truck in an SUV and began shouting that "he was going to put a cap up my ass." He wasn't sure what he had done to offend the driver of the SUV, the repairman said, and didn't know how seriously to take the threat, since the "nice-looking black female" in the passenger seat was laughing and grinning. Suddenly, though, the driver pulled up right next to the truck's open passenger-side window and pointed a gun at him, the repairman recalled. Fortunately, instead of firing, the driver made an abrupt U-turn and entered a Hollywood Freeway on-ramp.

Gaines's commander in Pacific Division, Captain David Doan, advised Poole that Gaines had been accused repeatedly of "discourtesy" and "unnecessary force" in his dealings with white, Hispanic, and Asian suspects. Doan described Gaines as a "mediocre" officer, and said the man had a history of domestic violence; his wife Georgia twice had called the police to complain that Gaines was beating her, but both times recanted.

Internal Affairs investigators confirmed reports that Gaines had been detained by LAPD officers on three separate occasions while off duty. The first incident had occurred on Sunset Boulevard when Gaines stuck his head through the moonroof of a passing limousine and shouted at some passing cops, "Fuck the police!" When they pulled the limousine over, officers said, Gaines did his best to provoke a physical confrontation before finally identifying himself as an LAPD officer. Gaines also had been investigated by the LAPD for stealing another officer's customized handcuffs and scratching out his initials. Gaines should have been fired for that offense, but Internal Affairs claimed to have misplaced the file.

All these reports of the slain officer's misbehavior had been compiled during the investigation of an even more bizarre incident involving Gaines. On the afternoon of August 16, 1996, two separate patrol cars from the LAPD's North Hollywood Division responded to a report that an assault with a deadly weapon had just taken place at a home on Multiview Avenue belonging to Sharitha Knight. Shots had been fired, an anonymous caller told the 911 operator, and there was a possible victim down by the pool area. When four LAPD officers arrived at the address, they were confronted by Kevin Gaines. Gaines answered the first few questions they asked, the officers agreed, but then became uncooperative, refusing them access to the residence. At one point, Gaines threw his shoulder into Officer Pedy Gonzalez, and was placed in handcuffs. "I'm a Police Officer III just like you, motherfucker," Gaines told him, according to Gonzalez. "I work at Pacific and you motherfuckers are not coming in. Tell these motherfuckin' assholes to take the cuffs off me, motherfucker." Gaines also said he hated "fucking cops," Gonzalez recalled. What made the incident really strange, though, was that when LAPD officers listened to the tape of the 911 call (made from a pay phone near Sharitha Knight's home) reporting that someone had been shot at the Multiview mansion, they unanimously agreed that the voice of the caller belonged to Kevin Gaines. Perhaps oddest of all, Gaines had described himself as the suspect: a black male with a muscular build, 5'10", 200 pounds, thirty years old.

Poole would conclude that Gaines's intention in making the call had been to produce an incident that might provide grounds for a lawsuit. And this Gaines had accomplished, persuading former Rodney King attorney Milton Grimes to file a multimillion dollar court claim against the city of Los Angeles, alleging that the incident had damaged the "emotional and psychological well-being" of a "competent African-American adult."

"Attempting to profit financially is what elevates a fraudulent 911 call from a misdemeanor to a felony," Poole explained, "and I can guarantee that any civilian who did what Gaines did would have faced prison time." Yet Kevin Gaines was never charged with any crime at all. The investigation of his conduct was handed over to Internal Affairs, which proceeded to build its case for Gaines's dismissal from the department with such deliberation that from outside it looked like a stall.

"I was completely shocked when I read the LAPD reports about Gaines's criminal behavior," Poole recalled, "because both Willie Williams and especially Chief Parks had to have known about this stuff for months. Yet they both showed up at Gaines's funeral and stood there nodding as Gaines was praised as this great police officer and fine family man. They knew what he was, but neither of them said a word. And meanwhile Frank Lyga is just hanging out there, getting crucified in the media."

Lyga's media crucifixion was orchestrated mainly by O.J. Simpson's attorney Johnnie Cochran, who had filed a $25 million lawsuit against the city on behalf of Kevin Gaines's family. "As soon as Cochran got involved in this case the race card was being played," Lyga recalled. "Suddenly I saw myself being described in the media as 'a racist, out of control cop with a history.'" A week after the funeral, nearly a dozen television cameras were positioned inside the First African Methodist Church, where nearly forty black police officers, most of them members of the Oscar Joel Bryant Association, joined Gaines's family in venting their outrage over the shooting in North Hollywood. The Inglewood City Council presented the Gaines family with a plaque that recognized the dead man as an "honorable and fine police officer" who was "killed in the line of duty." Spokespersons for the activist group Police Watch said they believed the shooting had been racially motivated. Online postings described Gaines as a target of LAPD harrassment and insisted that "physical evidence points to a cover-up." The *Los Angeles Watts Times* and Louis Farrakhan's *The Final Call* published articles that all but portrayed Frank Lyga as a cold-blooded killer.

After his transfer from the undercover unit to an office assignment, Lyga was not only shunned by many fellow officers, but also subjected to a series of anonymous death threats. Even though it had been reported by the media (and was unchallenged by even a single witness) that Frank Lyga and Kevin Gaines had never met before the day of the shooting, the president of the Oscar Joel Bryant Association, LAPD Sergeant Leonard Ross, told the Los Angeles *Daily News* that a number of white officers had envied Gaines's "lifestyle." "I'll say it," Ross told the newspaper. "There were a number of officers, who weren't black, who were jealous of his ability and resources."

Frank Lyga received almost no support from the LAPD brass until Russell Poole presented them with a piece of evidence that ultimately vindicated the undercover officer. This was a videotape shot from a surveillance camera aimed out the front door of the *am-pm* mini-mart where Kevin Gaines had died. The tape clearly showed Lyga's Buick being chased by Gaines's Montero, then recorded the sound of two gunshots (fired two seconds apart, in a "controlled pattern," just as Lyga had claimed) shortly after the Montero passed out of the camera's range. The Montero reentered the picture thirteen seconds later, as it coasted into the mini-mart's parking lot.

"I'm glad I got that tape when I did," Poole recalled, "because the very next day Johnnie Cochran's people showed up at the market and tried to buy it. The owner called me up and said, 'I need my tape back.' I said, 'Sorry, pal, it's evidence.' He said, 'I'm gonna get my attorney and sue.' I said, 'See you in court.' When I saw what was on the tape, I was awfully happy I kept it."

Cochran's incursion into the case changed everything for the LAPD detectives in charge of the investigation. "As soon as Cochran gets involved, the brass is too," Poole recalled. "They're all putting their heads together and figuring out how to control this thing. And then we had Farrakhan's people following the case. It was almost like the racial aspect of this thing was taking on a life of its own." Two days after the shooting, Captain Doan of Pacific Division reported to Internal Affairs that he sensed a growing "divisiveness among his officers along racial lines."

"Pretty soon after that we're getting reports from all over the city about debates between black police officers and all other police officers about who is at fault here," Poole recalled. "We were told that a group of officers almost came to blows at a gas pump. But nobody really knew the truth about Gaines. If they had, I think most of the black officers would have backed off."

Frank Lyga knew that Det. Poole was his hope for vindication. "I filled him in about Gaines's past bad conduct, and Lyga needed to hear that, because nobody was on his side and the media was pounding him relentlessly," Poole said. "I told him to hang tough, but I also had to tell him that the brass didn't seem to want to make any of this information public. I said, 'Frank, it's out of my control, but I'm getting a funny feeling. They don't want me to investigate Gaines's background.' He said, 'You're kidding.' I said, 'Sorry, that's the orders. But I want you to know that any information I collect I am writing down and passing along. And I'm convinced that the truth will come out eventually.'

"What worried me, though, was that everything seemed to be funneled into Internal Affairs Division. I'm beginning to understand that this is how they control an investigation, and limit what comes out in the media. I see how each report that the IA investigators file is a little more watered down than the one before it. But even then, I was shocked when I saw the final Internal Affairs report, because of how much they left out. It was amazingly incomplete. And Chief Parks was in charge of that."

Deputy Chief Parks and his Internal Affairs investigators also were in charge of investigating the complaints made by witnesses about the bullying tactics of Derwin Henderson and the other off-duty black officers who had questioned them. After interviewing the woman who worked at the coffee company, Poole and Miller reported that they believed Henderson's conduct had crossed the line into felony intimidation of a witness. One day later, an order came down from the upper echelon of Internal Affairs Division that Henderson was to be served with a "stay away" order, then placed under surveillance by a team of IA investigators. That surveillance lasted only one day, however. When the IA investigators reported that they had followed Henderson to "three locations they suspected might be bookmaking locations," they immediately were advised that "surveillance of Henderson is discontinued pending further direction." Even when Henderson showed up at the LAPD's Scientific Investigation Division to take personal possession of the green Montero, no order to resume surveillance was issued. "Henderson already had committed what would have been considered a serious crime if a civilian did it," Poole said, "but it was becoming obvious no charges would be filed."

Internal Affairs also made little effort to identify the other officers who accompanied Henderson when he questioned witnesses to the Gaines-Lyga shooting. The coffee company employee, who by now was so worried about her personal safety that she requested LAPD protection, refused to identify two black Pacific Division officers, Bruce Stallworth and Darrel Mathews, as members of the group that had been with Henderson when he showed up at her office. (On the night of the shooting, Stallworth had been paged by Sharitha Knight in the presence of Captain Doan, and Mathews was Stallworth's closest companion.) The next time the LAPD detectives contacted the woman from the coffee company, she informed them that she had quit her job and was moving to Arizona. "That's how scared she was by the publicity and by Henderson's aggression," Poole recalled. "But when she left the state, IA used this as an excuse to drop the criminal investigation, and make the case an internal investigation." In the end, Henderson would receive a slap-on-the-wrist suspension, while none of the other officers involved were even identified, let alone disciplined.

"I'd been on the department for almost seventeen years and I'd never seen anything like this," Poole recalled. "But I was new to Robbery-Homicide and had never worked out of Parker Center before. So I kept my mouth shut and told myself they did things differently downtown. At the same time, though, I promised myself that I would not let the politics of this case control my investigation. I figured if I did everything by the book, I was covered. That shows you how little I knew."

CHAPTER TWO

Knowing what needed to be done was no guarantee that you
would be permitted to do it, Russell Poole was learning, at
least not for a detective assigned to the LAPD's Robbery-
Homicide Division. Poole had joined RHD only four months earlier, and considered it an honor to be part of "the department's elite
division." Even better, he was assigned to the unit still known as Major
Crimes, but now officially titled Homicide Special, that handled all
of Los Angeles's "high profile" murder investigations. Well before
he arrived at LAPD headquarters in Parker Center, however, Poole
had been warned about Robbery-Homicide's "country club atmosphere." Only a detective who was "sponsored" could win an assignment to RHD and the only detectives who got sponsors, Poole
discovered, were golfers. "It sounds ridiculous, but it's true," he said.
"Most of the senior detectives, and some of the brass, too, would be
out on the golf course while on duty, with their pagers and cell phones
on if anyone needed to get in touch with them."

Poole had spent most of the past eight years at South Bureau
Homicide, a unit that covered just four of the LAPD's eighteen divisions but handled half of the department's murder investigations.
South Bureau Homicide boasted a "solve rate" of nearly 70 percent,
yet maintained a list of 1,500 unsolved gang murders between 1985
and 1998, "which tells you how many gang killings there were in
South Central during those years," Poole said. In 1993 alone Poole

had arrested twenty-three killers involved in seventeen murders. Of the seventy-five suspects he had arrested for murder during his years as a homicide detective, only two were acquitted at trial, and in both cases the victims had been drug dealers. While few killings in South Central Los Angeles made headlines, Poole had received twenty-two commendations for his murder investigations, and was proud of his reputation for success.

South Bureau Homicide detectives put in long hours and "lived our cases," as Poole put it, but the atmosphere in Robbery-Homicide was much different. Cases were given priority on the basis of media interest and political considerations. A lot of RHD detectives, especially among the more senior ones, seemed to feel they needed to be available only for major mobilizations and were free to float the rest of the time. Fred Miller told Poole that the tone had been set by his old partner, the most famous homicide detective in LAPD history, "Jigsaw John" St. John, who had investigated the Black Dahlia case, among others. "Jigsaw John was a media legend, this great detective who had handled all these big cases back in the forties and fifties, and was still working as a homicide investigator at an age when most guys have long since retired," Poole said. "But Fred told me that Jigsaw John had just coasted for the last fifteen or twenty years he was on the department, and that the brass let him. Fred said the two of them would work from seven to eleven in the morning, then go out for a martini lunch that might last until ten or eleven at night. They spent most of their time sitting in restaurants or bars, with their pagers on if something big happened."

When Poole first interviewed for the job at RHD, Miller had been his biggest backer, openly opposing the lieutenant who had preferred another candidate. Despite their differences in age and rank, the two got on well at first, but the more Poole heard about his senior partner, the more leery he became. "People began telling me that whenever Fred identifies a suspect, he moves on to another case," Poole recalled. "Other detectives told me, 'Fred hasn't made a murder arrest in years.' I took the position that I'd have to see for myself."

What Poole saw almost immediately was that Miller regularly put his caseload second to his golf game. That approach to the job first had become a real problem for Poole on the morning of February 28, 1997. "Fred and I and [another senior detective] went out for an early breakfast," Poole recalled, "and afterward they started driving east. I didn't know where we were going until we arrived at this giant golf warehouse out in the City of Industry, which is about twenty-five miles from Parker Center." The detectives were still shopping when all three pagers went off simultaneously. A pair of twenty-something weight lifters wearing ski masks and encased from ankle to neck in body armor had just robbed the Bank of America branch on Laurel Canyon Boulevard in North Hollywood. Now they were using assault rifles modified to fire on full automatic to battle the LAPD officers who had surrounded the building.

"Fred and [the other detective] were shitting when we got the call," Poole recalled. "We had to drive through heavy traffic to get back to Parker Center, where we dropped [the other detective off]. I knew that Fred never carried a homicide kit in the trunk of his car, because he needed the space for his golf clubs, so I ran upstairs and grabbed as many supplies as I could, then brought them back down and threw them into the backseat. We took off to the scene, but it took forever, and by the time we got there the two robbers had been shot dead." Poole volunteered to serve as evidence coordinator at what had become the largest crime scene in LAPD history, and would work onsite until the following morning. "Fred let me know he didn't think that was too bright," Poole remembered. "And I let him know I was not going to stand around and watch other guys work. So we already had a little tension between us by the time of the Gaines-Lyga investigation."

Miller, who had more than twenty-five years on the job and was perpetually planning his retirement, was one of the RHD detectives most affected by the ordeal of the lead investigators on the O.J. Simpson case. "After watching what Tom Lange and Phil Vannatter were put through on the witness stand and in the media, and the way

they went into retirement under this giant cloud of controversy,"
Poole explained, "a lot of the older RHD detectives, but Fred especially, made up their minds that they were not going to get drawn
into something like that at the end of their careers.

"So as soon as Fred finds out that Johnnie Cochran is involved
in Gaines-Lyga, he's scared to death and doesn't want anything more
to do with the investigation. After about the first week, you won't find
my partner's signature on anything connected to the case. Because
he doesn't want to find himself in a courtroom being cross-examined
by Cochran. So I'm pretty much going it alone."

Poole *was* getting plenty of advice from his superiors in the department, but found their instructions more troubling than helpful:
"When I asked what was happening with Henderson, the brass told me
to stay away and keep my mouth shut. When I asked if IA had identified the other officers who were with Henderson when he confronted
[the coffee company employee], they told me it was none of my business. Then my lieutenant tells me that I am not to make any mention
of Sharitha Knight or Gaines's connection to Death Row Records in
my follow-up report, because that document will become a public
record, and that this order is coming down all the way from the chief's
office. Other detectives already had told me I had to leave that information out of my reports, 'because we don't want people to know that
one of our officers is involved with Death Row.' I said, 'Why not? It's
the truth.' What I got back was, 'Do as you're told.' And I did. I'm fairly
new and I don't want to rock the boat. I'm still getting acclimated to
working downtown, but I'm thinking, 'Is this the way it works in RHD?
No wonder they got embarrassed in the O.J. trial.' There's a bad taste
in my mouth, but I'm sure the truth will come out eventually."

Poole's problem was that his pursuit of the truth forced him to
investigate the links between Kevin Gaines and Death Row Records.
The existence of such links was suggested by the clues Poole had
started with, those gathered from Gaines's vehicle, from his locker
at Pacific Division, and from his corpse at the hospital where he was
pronounced dead.

The evidence collected from the green Montero established mainly how intertwined Gaines's life was with Sharitha Knight's. Among the items inventoried were a love note Gaines had written to his girlfriend, an invitation to the fourth birthday party of Suge and Sharitha Knight's daughter Kayla, and, in addition to three of Gaines's LAPD pay stubs, a stub for another check bearing this note: "Sharitha, from Marion Knight, Monthly Allowance, $10,000."

Inside Gaines's locker, investigators found betting stubs from Las Vegas, "various phone numbers of unknown females," a business card for a security company embossed with the name of Officer Bruce Stallworth, a confusing collection of real estate documents, plus 8 x 10 glossies of Suge Knight and Tupac Shakur that were taped to the locker's back wall.

Gaines seemed to have made idols of the slain rapper and his boss at Death Row Records, yet Sharitha Knight insisted that she knew of only a single tense encounter between Kevin and Suge. She and Kevin and several of her relatives were in Las Vegas for a concert that had just ended when they stepped outside and were met by Suge and a man she did not recognize, Sharitha said. Suge and his companion pushed their way into the van the group was traveling in and asked for a ride to their hotel, according to Sharitha. Kevin, who was driving, put his gun in his lap and asked, "Where you guys want to go?"

"I'll tell you. Just keep driving," Suge replied, then began whispering into her ear, "threatening me, basically," Sharitha recalled. Eventually she realized Suge was directing them to "this deserted spot," Sharitha said, and became alarmed.

"That man [Gaines] is a police officer," she told her husband, "and I don't think we're going to play games with you." She told Kevin to turn the van around, Sharitha said, and a few minutes later they dropped Suge off at his hotel. From there, Kevin drove straight to the airport and got on a plane to Los Angeles.

According to Captain Doan of Pacific Division, the first words Gaines's wife Georgia spoke when informed of her husband's death were, "Suge Knight's people killed him."

If Kevin Gaines wanted to avoid Suge Knight and his "people," however, he had gone about it in a strange way. At the time of his death, Gaines's wallet contained a ten-day-old receipt from Monty's Steakhouse in Westwood, a well-known hangout for Death Row executives. A number of LAPD officers acknowledged that Gaines had tried to recruit them to work security at Death Row parties. Frank Lyga reported that an informant had told him Gaines was an active member of the Bloods gang; Suge Knight had long been associated with Compton's Piru Bloods.

There was as well the question of how Gaines had managed to support an exorbitant lifestyle on his police officer's salary. That receipt from Monty's showed Gaines had paid $952 for a single lunch. Also in Gaines's wallet were ten credit cards, each one carrying high limits that "no cop can afford," Poole recalled. Other patrol officers from Pacific Division told Poole that Gaines regularly showed up for work wearing Versace shirts costing $1,000 a piece. His fleet of cars included a BMW, a Ford Explorer, and a Mercedes 420 SEL sporting vanity plates that taunted the LAPD's Internal Affairs Division: ITS OK IA.

Derwin Henderson maintained that Gaines covered some of his costs with thousands of dollars won at the blackjack tables in Las Vegas (Henderson, who drove a Mercedes of his own, claimed that he made $20,000 a year betting on horse races at Hollywood Park). Other LAPD officers, however, said Gaines had bragged about earning $250 an hour working security for Death Row Records.

Among Gaines's other boasts, according to the officers who worked with him, was that he owned so much real estate he no longer needed to work for the LAPD. His locker had been filled with blank rental and lease agreements from a company called "Scott Properties," yet his wife said she knew nothing about any of that, and insisted her husband had owned just the house where she and the children lived in Gardena, plus one other modest property. Internal Affairs investigators asked for a warrant to search for other real estate owned by Gaines, but their request was denied. Poole told his superiors in Robbery-Homicide that he needed a search warrant to check Gaines's financial records for the past ten years, but he too was refused. "All the brass would tell me," Poole recalled, "was, 'Gaines is dead. Leave it alone.'"

Within the rank and file of the LAPD, stories had been circulating for several years that there was a growing cadre of black officers whose involvement with Death Row Records superseded their loyalty to the department. A good deal of this gossip was generated by an incident that had taken place just after midnight on March 14, 1995, at the El Rey Theater in L.A.'s Wilshire District. The occasion was a Soul Train Record Awards "after party." Three uniformed LAPD officers had been called to the El Rey when a fight broke out earlier in the evening. The officers were standing on the sidewalk under a sign that read "Death Row Private Party, Guest List Only," when they heard a commotion inside the theater. One of the three turned just in time to see a young man named Kelly Jamerson get his head split open by a beer bottle, then watched as a crowd of more than a dozen black males surrounded the bleeding Jamerson, and "began kicking and hitting the victim on all areas of his body." By the time the LAPD officers reached Jamerson, the young man was dying of injuries that included a brain hemorrhage. Then, as the report filed by Wilshire Detectives put it, "Approximately four hundred people exited the theater as officers attempted to protect the victim. Many were intoxicated and failed to comply with instructions to remain where they were."

By the time the officers at the scene got around to asking questions, the only available witness was a bartender who said he had seen Jamerson arguing with four black males. The bartender "believed that one of the suspects was a member of Death Row Records Company," according to the Wilshire Detectives report, "whom he described as a male black, 6'4", 390 pounds with short hair cut into an angle. He observed the suspect remove a Miller beer bottle from the counter and strike the victim on the head."

It was almost daybreak when LAPD investigators arrived at the El Rey to find a large bloodstain on the paisley carpet in the lobby and, under an arch of red, white, and silver balloons, a dance floor littered with torn Death Row Records posters, broken glass, and shards of china plates. Kelly Jamerson was pronounced dead shortly after noon, when the case officially became a murder investigation. The victim was so badly beaten—covered with "lacerations, abrasions, swelling and bruising to the head, torso and extremities," the deputy medical examiner who performed the autopsy reported—that it was virtually impossible to pinpoint any single injury as the cause of death.

Much of the evidence detectives collected came from anonymous callers who had been at the El Rey party when the beating took place. Combined with the statements of the bartender, the club manager, the ticket taker, the theater's security guard, and the two guests at the party who were willing to be identified as witnesses, these reports provided a remarkably consistent picture of what had taken place.

The party had been staged as a "classy" affair, detectives kept hearing from the people who had been there. Except for the white strippers who worked the stage area wearing only glitter and G-strings, nearly everyone present was black, and the guests ranged from executives to homeboys. The centerpiece of the event was a giant ice sculpture of the Death Row Records logo, and the record company's CEO had been in an especially exhilarated mood. Suge Knight was roving through the hall with a "wild, excited look in his eyes," as one guest described it, grabbing the strippers by the hips and grinding against them at the same time he carried on conversations with his associates.

The trouble began when the party's guest of honor, rapper Snoop Dogg (at the time facing first-degree murder charges) took the stage to perform his lastest single, "Murder Was the Case." Suge Knight and nearly every one of his associates at Death Row were affiliated with the Blood gangs from Compton, but Snoop Dogg came from Long Beach and claimed Crips membership. In the middle of his number, Snoop had been inspired to throw Crips gang signs to several members of the gang's Rolling 60s set, and to give the crowd a flash of the Crips color, blue. Though the Crips in the audience were badly outnumbered, several emboldened gang members responded to Snoop by throwing gang signs back at him, thereby infuriating the Bloods. Almost immediately, Death Row rapper DJ Quik (David Blake) began to throw Blood signs at one of the Crips. DJ Quik had been attacked two years earlier by Rolling 60s members who broke his jaw, according to the Compton police, and publicly sought revenge. Almost immediately, according to the El Rey's security guard, one of DJ Quik's bodyguards attacked the Crip who was jawing with his boss. DJ Quik himself then picked up a chair and used it to knock the Crip to the ground, where his bodyguards pummeled the man. DJ Quik, dressed in the same black-and-red Pendleton shirt the Death Row bodyguards wore, kicked the man while he was down, then broke away from the melee to step onto the El Rey's stage, where he spoke briefly to Suge Knight, who promptly left the theater.

DJ Quik almost immediately initiated a second attack, this one on Kelly Jamerson, witnesses said. Jamerson, also a member of the Rolling 60s Crips, was chased into the El Rey's lobby, where a crowd of twelve to fifteen Bloods surrounded him. One of them knocked him to the ground by hitting him in the head with a beer bottle, and the rest of the group closed in. "We're going to kill this motherfucker," the El Rey's security guard heard one of the men say, as he joined the others in kicking and stomping Jamerson for at least ten minutes, by which time the man on the ground was covered with blood and clearly unconscious.

The El Rey's ticket taker told police that, immediately after the fight, he was approached by a man who handed over three claim tickets and said, "We need these cars brought up right away. We're with DJ Quik and he's the reason this fight started. We need the cars brought around back."

At least five witnesses, including three who were willing to give their names, said they had seen DJ Quik kicking Jamerson while he lay on the ground. Nearly all of the others who were identified in the attack on Jamerson, however, were not DJ Quik's bodyguards, but members of Suge Knight's personal security detail. These included Alton ("Buntry") McDonald, Crawford ("Hi-C") Wilkerson, Jai Hassan Jamaal ("Jake the Violator") Robles, and Ronald ("Ram") Lamb.

Easily the most knowledgeable and compelling of the witnesses police interviewed was a young man who spoke to them several times by telephone but refused to give his name. The Crips had believed it was safe to attend a Death Row party, this witness said, because Snoop Dogg was one of their own. DJ Quik was the first to physically attack Kelly Jamerson, according to the witness, and struck him with both a chair and a champagne bottle before joining the others in stomping Jamerson after he fell to the ground. The witness confirmed the participation of Jake, Buntry, and Hi-C in the attack, then added two other names, Bernard "Zeek" Thomas and Donell Antwayne "Donzel" Smith, both associates of DJ Quik. He himself was a close friend of DJ Quik's, this witness said, and actually grabbed the rapper by one shoulder during the attack on Jamerson to try to pull him away, but "DJ kept on like he didn't hear a word I said." When police tried to convince the witness to give his name, the man refused, explaining that it wasn't just his own life he was concerned about. "If they knew I was talking to you, they might kill my whole family," he explained, then added this observation: "You police do not realize how powerful Suge Knight is. Going up against Suge or any of his people is like going up against the Mafia. It's a death sentence."

Despite what looked like an overwhelming case against DJ Quik, and strong cases against Jake (who had been seen leaving the El Rey missing one shoe), Buntry, and Hi-C, no criminal charges were ever filed in the murder of Kelly Jamerson. "The most amazing thing was that there was almost no official explanation of why they weren't arresting anybody," recalled Russell Poole, who had been on temporary assignment to Wilshire Detectives at the time, but was not directly involved in the investigation of the El Rey incident. "The D.A.'s office said it was a case of 'insufficient evidence,' but didn't elaborate, and the media barely noticed. It was like the whole thing got swept under the carpet."

Detectives at Wilshire Division whispered among themselves that this was a "political decision." The Rodney King riots and the O.J. Simpson trial had left Los Angeles so traumatized that the threat of racial conflict in any form sent shudders of dread through L.A.'s civic leadership. "At that time Suge Knight was being portrayed as one of the most important black entrepreneurs in the country, and anyone who criticized him could expect to be called a racist," Poole remembered. Knight also had powerful political allies, including the most influential black office holder in Southern California, Congress-woman Maxine Waters, who earlier that year had responded to questions about the Death Row Records CEO's alleged criminal activities by telling reporters, "The only thing Suge is threatening is the status quo."

The most troubling report made by a witness who had been present at the El Rey Theater during the killing of Kelly Jamerson, Russell Poole would learn, never became part of the official case file. The witness in this instance was a Long Beach Police Department officer who had infiltrated Death Row Records as the agent of a federal task force probing allegations that Suge Knight and his record label were heavily involved in drug dealing and illegal gun sales. According to the task force agent, a number of off-duty police officers, including members of the Los Angeles Police Department, had been working without permits as bodyguards at the El Rey Party. These officers not only failed to rescue Kelly Jamerson, the task force agent said, but all left the theater without identifying themselves to uniformed cops on the scene, and never reported later that they had been present when Jamerson was killed.

Poole would not see the task force agent's report until he was nearly finished with his investigation of the Gaines-Lyga shooting, and even then the report was not provided to him by either his supervisors or any other member of the department's brass. "What it told me, when I read it, was that the LAPD had known for at least two years that some of our officers were working for Death Row Records," Poole recalled. "With all the stuff that had come out about Kevin Gaines's connection to Death Row, you'd think the brass would have wanted the detectives investigating Gaines to know about this, but in fact the opposite was true. They wanted to keep it hidden from us. That really started me wondering what the hell was going on."

The task force agent's report related at length the stories he had been told by other Death Row employees about the company's involvement in drug trafficking. Before starting Death Row, Suge Knight had made most of his money by dealing drugs he stole from Hispanic suppliers, according to the task force agent's sources. Suge's record company had been started with drug money, other Death Row employees said, and since its inception it had served as a kind of clearinghouse for the transport of cocaine from the West Coast to the East Coast by members of the Bloods gang. The agent's report went on to state that the gangbangers paid $18,500 for a kilo of coke in L.A. and sold it to rappers in New York for $26,000. "I already had heard from a number of sources that Suge Knight regularly paid some of his performers with drugs that they could deal, instead of checks," Poole said. "So I found the information in [the task force agent]'s report pretty plausible."

On the basis of such stories, Poole and Miller had arranged within forty-eight hours of Kevin Gaines's death for a drug-sniffing dog from the LAPD's narcotics group to check the green Montero. According to official police reports, the dog "showed strong interest for the odor of narcotics" in the rear passenger area of the Montero. "The narco guys told us they were sure that cocaine had been transported in this vehicle," Poole recalled, "but all they could find was dust."

On March 31, Poole received a memo from a black LAPD officer named Stuart Guidry. According to Guidry, an informant who was an inmate at Lancaster State Prison and insisted that he had "loaned Suge Knight the money to start Death Row Records" claimed to know a good deal about Kevin Gaines's involvement with the record company. "The inmate stated Officer Gaines and other LAPD officers provided security for members of Death Row Records during various criminal activities," Guidry's report read. "The officers accompanied the members during drug deals and acted as lookouts and advisors. The officers monitored police frequencies, assisted in choosing locations for drug transactions and gave information on police tactics. The inmate stated he was not surprised at Officer Gaines' death, but he believed it would be from someone else as opposed to a fellow officer. The inmate also stated, 'Just wait until they search his house and see all the expensive things he got from working for Death Row.'"

Poole immediately renewed his request for an expanded investigation of Kevin Gaines's background and activities. "My superiors, though, said there was not enough probable cause for a search warrant," Poole recalled. "It was total bullshit. We got Gaines transporting drugs, we got him stiffing in a 911 call and assaulting cops at the scene, we have four other roadway incidents, we have him linked directly to Death Row Records and Suge Knight. I wrote a twenty-page report detailing all this stuff, but still couldn't get a warrant to search either Gaines's home or his financial records. The average citizen's home would have been raided by a whole squad of cops on the basis of what we had. I knew the decision was coming straight down from Chief Parks. My superiors, though, just kept telling me, 'Gaines is dead. Let's forget about it.'"

Kevin Gaines's name kept popping up, however. One day after reading Officer Guidry's memo, Poole received a phone call from a detective in Wilshire Division advising him that homicide investigators there had information suggesting that Gaines might be involved in the recent assassination of rapper Biggie Smalls. They needed a recent picture of Gaines, the Wilshire detective said, to use in a six-pack photo lineup.

This phone call was one of the main reasons that Poole readily agreed, on the morning of April 9, 1997, to take over as lead investigator in the Biggie Smalls murder investigation.

PART TWO

DEATH ROW
INMATES

Poole is the type of employee who every supervisor wishes he had more of. He is thorough—NOTHING gets past him! He constantly reviews his and his partner's work product for anything that may have been missed.

—From the "Performance Evaluation Report" filed on Detective Trainee Russell Poole for period 3/1/89 to 9/30/89

CHAPTER THREE

Biggie Smalls aka Notorious B.I.G. aka Christopher Wallace had been shot to death fifteen minutes after midnight on March 9, 1997, one month to the day before Poole was assigned to investigate the rapper's murder. The Smalls murder was an eerie replication of Tupac Shakur's killing six months earlier. Shakur had been riding in a BMW on the Las Vegas Strip when a white Cadillac pulled up alongside and a black male with a Glock pistol fired thirteen shots into the BMW's passenger side. Four of those bullets hit Shakur, who lingered for several days after doctors removed a shattered lung, then died on the afternoon of September 13, 1996. Biggie Smalls was riding in a GMC Suburban when the black driver of a dark-colored Chevrolet Impala SS pulled up on the Suburban's passenger side and sprayed the SUV with shots from a 9mm pistol. Smalls was pronounced dead at Cedars-Sinai Medical Center forty-five minutes later.

The Suburban in which Smalls was riding had been the second vehicle in a caravan of three SUVs that had just pulled out of a parking structure at the Petersen Automotive Museum on Wilshire Boulevard's Miracle Mile. The occasion was the same one that had resulted in Kelly Jamerson's death two years earlier, a Soul Train Record Awards "after party," only this event was sponsored not by Death Row Records but by Quincy Jones's *VIBE* magazine. Riding in the front passenger seat of the lead Suburban was Bad Boy Entertainment CEO Sean "Puffy" Combs, whose vehicle had not been fired upon. None of the four other

passengers in Biggie Smalls's Suburban had been hit by any of the bullets fired from the Impala. "I was right behind [Biggie] in the backseat,
but not one bullet hit my door," rapper James "Lil' Caesar" Lloyd told
the *Los Angeles Times*. "Not one bullet hit any other window. Every
single shot fired hit Big's door. They was after him for some reason."

At least seven witnesses had seen the shooter, whom they described as a clean-shaven black male with a medium complexion and
a fade haircut, wearing either a gray or light-blue suit with a bow tie.
In wardrobe and grooming, the killer had looked a lot more like a
member of Louis Farrakhan's security group, the Fruit of Islam,
witnesses agreed, than any kind of gangbanger. He had been alone in
the Impala, firing across his body through the car's open window with
a blue steel pistol held in his right hand.

From the outset, a lot of people let it be known that they suspected
the deaths of Biggie Smalls and Tupac Shakur were connected by more
than just the violent milieu of gangsta rap. Within a few hours of Smalls's
murder, LAPD detectives told reporters that they believed the rapper's
killing might be linked to "bicoastal tensions in the rap world," as a *Los
Angeles Times* article put it. "Everyone knew that was just another way
of saying that the primary suspect was Suge Knight," explained Russell
Poole, who would come to believe that Knight not only was responsible for Biggie Smalls's death, but Tupac Shakur's as well.

Like a lot of the rappers who worked for him, Marion Hugh Knight Jr.
had grown up in Compton, a city of 110,000 surrounded by the black
and brown neighborhoods of southern Los Angeles County. Compton
was still racially mixed and working class when Maxine and Marion
Knight Sr. bought their house in the city. That was in 1969, five years
after the birth of their only son, a boy they called "Sugar Bear," the
parents said, because he had such a sweet disposition. By the time
"Suge," as he became known, reached his tenth birthday, however,
Compton was ravaged by two concurrent developments: first, the loss

of its manufacturing base, and second, domination by the two most murderous gangs in U.S. history, the Bloods and the Crips.

The Crips had come first. The gang was started a year before the Knights settled in Compton by a group of Fremont High School students who at that time called themselves the Baby Avenues. The name was a way of honoring their older friends and relatives who belonged to the Avenue Boys gang. Black gangs had existed in Los Angeles since the 1920s, when groups like the Goodlows and the Boozies controlled prostitution and gambling in the Central Avenue section of town. During the 1950s, civic leaders in Los Angeles persuaded many gang members to join car clubs, but these soon became little more than headquarters for groups like the Businessmen and the Gladiators, whose members fought with knives, chains, or baseball bats and soon were held responsible for dozens of robberies and assaults. Car clubs vanished quickly after the Watts riots in 1965, and in the increasingly militant atmosphere of the late '60s many of L.A.'s gangs claimed at least some measure of association with the Black Panther Party.

Right around this time, the Baby Avenues committed a robbery that would profoundly shape the future of L.A.'s inner-city neighborhoods. The victims were a group of Asian merchants who had been confronted as they left a meeting on store security measures by Baby Avenues members who brandished sticks and demanded their money. One of the merchants, who spoke very little English, tried to explain to police that the robbers, like cripples, had carried walking sticks. A reporter was standing nearby when the frustrated victim shouted at the police officer who was questioning him, "Crip! Crip!" When an article about the "Crips" gang appeared in the newspaper the next day, the Baby Avenues were so flattered by the publicity that they adopted the name and began committing even bolder robberies. Soon the gang spread into divisions—Eastside Crips, Westside Crips, Compton Crips.

By the early seventies, when the Crips adopted the color blue as their badge of honor, they were by far the most feared black gang in

California and had spread across much of southern Los Angeles County. In the summer of 1972, however, the Compton Crips became involved in conflict with another Compton gang called the Original Pirus. The Pirus had been a Crips gang, but they broke away after a much larger Compton Crips set beat them bloody in a brawl along Alondra Boulevard. Embittered but determined, the losers called a meeting on Piru Street in Compton, where they were joined by the Lueders Park Hustlers and several other independent gangs that were tired of the Crips' domination: the Bishops, the Athens Parks Boys, and the Denver Lanes, as well as the L.A. Brims, who had lost one of their leaders earlier that year when he was murdered by the Crips. The new alliance agreed to answer the blue railroad handkerchiefs the Crips wore (initially to conceal their identities during robberies) by adopting the color red, and to call themselves the Bloods.

The lengths the two gangs went to separate themselves from each other were almost comically elaborate. The Crips began using the letter "C" to replace the letter "B" in nearly everything they said or wrote: Instead of, "I rode the two-oh-three bus to the beach," it was ,"I took the two-oh-three *cuss* to the *ceach*." The Bloods answered in kind, then began signing their graffiti "CK," for Crips Killer.

Within a few years the Bloods had become L.A.'s second-largest gang, but still they were outnumbered by Crips three to one. "The only reason the Bloods could hold their own was that they could mobilize members from all over South Central," explained Russell Poole, who had worked as a gang intelligence officer in South Central L.A. for four years during the mid-1980s. "Cliques like the Hoover Crips and the Rolling 60s figured they had enough people to take care of their own business and very rarely turned to one another for assistance. If the Bloods wanted payback, though, they'd have a big conclave of groups like the Van Ness Gangsters, who were the biggest Bloods gang in South Central, and the Black Pee-Stones, who controlled the Jungle. They could bring in Bloods from Compton and Inglewood, and they'd all decide together how to deal with the Crips. That's what made them so dangerous. They were equally if not more vicious than the Crips."

As a young police officer in South Central L.A., what most astounded and appalled him, Poole said, were "the number of shootings, nearly all of them gang-related, that would occur in a single eight-hour shift. I'd never seen even a single gunshot victim before I encountered them in the field, and let me tell you, there is nothing that can prepare you for the real blood and guts of gun violence. Seeing people die in front of you, and the agony of friends and loved ones who are present, the screaming and wailing and incredible chaos of a shooting scene in South Central."

For years Poole carried a photograph that had been taken at the scene of a gun battle between two carloads of Crips and Bloods. "Two Bloods were in this car near Fremont High School when this car full of Crips pulls up on the driver's side, flashing signs and exchanging epithets, and finally their guns come out. The passenger in the Bloods car whips out a sawed-off shotgun and points it past the driver's face in the direction of the Crips. Just at that moment, though, they come to a curve, and as they go around the Bloods driver leans forward and the shotgun goes off. When I arrive, the driver is sprawled out the car's open door and half his head is gone. One eye is blown to bits and the other is just lying in the cavity of his head. There's pieces of brain and bone and blood everywhere. It was the goriest thing I ever saw, and believe me, I saw a lot of gory things. You never get used to it. Anyway, I kept the crime scene photographs to show to some of the young kids I met who were just starting off in the gangster life. They all said they expected to die young, but when I'd show them these photographs, they'd get a lump in their throat, some of them. I always wondered if it made any difference."

Suge Knight's childhood was idyllic compared to that of most youngsters in his Compton neighborhood. He had two gainfully employed parents, Marion Sr., a janitor at UCLA, and Maxine, who worked on the assembly line in an electronics factory, and both doted on him, excessively in his mother's case. Suge also could claim the ghetto's one universally accepted exemption from membership in a street gang—he was an athlete. Six feet, two inches tall, with a strong body that was growing thicker every year, Suge earned letters in both football and track all four years at Lynwood High, then won a football scholarship from El Camino Community College after his graduation in 1983.

In 1985, now listed on the program at 260 pounds, Suge transferred to the University of Nevada at Las Vegas. Wearing number 54 and starting at defensive end, Suge was voted UNLV's rookie of the year, got elected defensive captain, and won first-team all-conference honors. On campus, he was regarded as a big, friendly guy who slapped backs, told jokes, and indulged with remarkable moderation in drugs, sex, and alcohol. Other teammates from the inner city were arrested for armed robberies, carjackings, and sexual assaults, but Suge made his extra spending money by working as a bouncer at the Cotton Club.

During his senior season, though, Suge became a more remote and mysterious character. Overnight, he had enough money to rent an apartment by himself and to purchase a series of late-model sedans. He regularly received visitors from Compton, and developed a reputation as perhaps the biggest drug dealer on campus. When he was drafted by the Los Angeles Rams after his last season at UNLV in 1987, Suge promptly dropped out of school and moved back to L.A. He made the Rams' roster during the strike-shortened 1988–89 season, and crossed picket lines to perform as a "replacement" player, but was cut from the team when the strike ended and the real pros returned to action.

Suge Knight's criminal record began at almost the same time his football career ended. In October of 1987, his future wife, Sharitha Golden, first obtained a restraining order against her possessive boyfriend, then had him arrested for grabbing her by the hair and cutting off her ponytail during an argument in the driveway of her mother's house. Two weeks later, on Halloween night, Suge was arrested in Las Vegas for shooting a man twice—once in the leg and once in the wrist—while stealing his Nissan Maxima. When the Las

Vegas police arrested him, Suge was carrying a .38 caliber Smith and Wesson revolver in the waistband of his pants. Incredibly, though, a well-connected attorney, a contrite courtroom appearance, and his reputation as an athlete helped Suge have the felony charges against him reduced to misdemeanors. He escaped with a $1,000 fine and three years' probation. In 1990, also in Las Vegas, Suge used a loaded pistol to break a man's jaw, and pleaded guilty to felony assault with a deadly weapon, yet managed to walk away with a $9,000 fine and a two-year suspended sentence.

By then, Suge was working in Los Angeles as a bodyguard for Whitney Houston's future husband, singer Bobby Brown. He soon found a new employer, though, in Beverly Hills sports agent Tom Kline, who had become fascinated by the music business and hired Suge as a driver-bodyguard–talent scout. Once he began using the agent's office to audition rap acts, however, Suge was talking about forming his *own* record label. His best listener was a lanky, yellow-complected young rapper named Tracy Curry who performed as the D.O.C. When the D.O.C.'s first album, *No One Can Do It Better*, produced a single ("It's Funky Enough") that hit No. 5 on *Billboard*'s Top Rap Singles chart, he started hanging with a group of young men from Compton who would become the core members of the group N.W.A. (Niggaz With Attitude). These included Eazy-E (who owned N.W.A.'s label, Ruthless Records), Ice Cube, and a young producer-composer named Andre Young, better known as Dr. Dre and widely regarded as the best ear in rap.

With the D.O.C. (as, later, with Tupac Shakur), Suge practiced what would prove his greatest skill as a businessman, exploiting an artist's vulnerability. When the D.O.C. was hospitalized after a serious auto accident, Suge not only visited him daily but became a combination chauffeur/confidant to the rapper's mother. Knight soon began setting up autograph-signing appearances for the D.O.C., and eventually persuaded the rapper that Eazy-E was robbing him blind. More important, Suge used his relationship with the D.O.C. to cap-

ture the attention of Dr. Dre, convincing Dre that he was not receiving anything like a fair share of royalties from N.W.A's hugely
successful 1988 album, *Straight Outta Compton.*

A lot of what Suge offered performers like the D.O.C. and Dre
was protection. All the rappers talked tough, but very few actually
were. With an album on the charts, the D.O.C. was a local celebrity
who suddenly had to contend with lots of hard-core gangbangers who
believed that whipping his ass would give them status on the street.
Having Suge at his side solved that problem. In an early interview,
the D.O.C. described leaving a club one evening and having "some
nigga run up on me like he was fixin' to hit me in the jaw. Suge just
tore his ass up," the D.O.C. recalled. "I mean he broke him down to
his component parts."

Dre was a big man, 6'1" and 230 pounds, who appeared in videos
carrying assault rifles and threatening to kill cops, but in reality his
history of criminal violence involved mostly beating up women and
throwing sucker punches at men half his size. Before joining N.W.A.,
Dre had belonged to a group called The Wreckin' Kru that took the
stage wearing spandex jumpsuits, flowing scarves, knee-high boots, Jheri
curls, and eyeliner and mascara. Growing up in Compton, he lived in
both Blood and Crip neighborhoods but never joined either gang. What
Dre had going for him was a magical ear for how sounds—especially
rhythms—could be combined to complement one another. He'd begun
to develop his talent at age four, when he began to play the role of deejay
at the parties thrown by his young, single mother.

Dre's career in gangsta rap was launched during the late 1980s,
when his Mazda RX7 was impounded for unpaid parking tickets.
When he couldn't find anyone who would put up the $900 he needed
to get the car released, Dre turned to a Compton drug dealer named
Eric Wright, but better known as Eazy-E. He would pay the fines,
Eazy-E said, but only if Dre promised to produce songs for the record
company he wanted to form.

Rap was just beginning to realize the commercial potential of
a form that had been in development for almost thirty years. The

origins of what would become known as "hip-hop" culture went back at least to the year 1966, when New York City's Bronx borough was transformed by a pair of seemingly unrelated events. The first involved the completion of a 15,382-unit co-op apartment complex near an expressway on the northern edge of the Bronx. As thousands of poor families poured into the borough, the Bronx's middle class began an evacuation that resulted in the sale of one apartment building after another to slumlords, many of whom would eventually abandon the structures. That same year, a group of young men who lived on or near Bruckner Boulevard began to bill themselves as the Savage Seven and to prey on the residents of the Bronxdale Project. As the group added members, it became known as the Black Spades, the first and largest of the street gangs that rapidly took control of street corners all across the Bronx. These gangs were the first to use graffiti to create both collective and personal identities. Monikers like TAKI 183, SLY II, and TRACY 168 began to appear on walls in every corner of the borough. The largest group of graffiti writers attended DeWitt Clinton High School, directly across from a New York Transit Authority storage yard that gave them easy access to city buses.

Subway cars soon became an even more popular target. Gangs and graffiti writing groups became increasingly indistinguishable. TRACY 168 was a white street kid so tough that he became a sort of honorary member of the Black Spades, until he formed his own group, The Wanted, which maintained a permanent headquarters in the basement of a building at the corner of 166th Street and Woodycrest Avenue. By the mid-'70s, groups like Bad Artists, Mad Bombers, and Wild Style were covering whole subway cars with murals. When the Transit Authority developed a petroleum hydroxide wash that stripped even enamel paint from its trains, TRACY 168 and the even more famous graffiti artist Lee Quinones began to cover the walls of handball courts with their work. Quinones eventually joined a group formed by fellow graffiti artist Fred Braithwaite that called itself the Fab Five, and began to sell its work in Manhattan art galleries. Braithwaite, soon known as Fab Five Freddy, eventually formed a relationship with the white painter Keith Haring, whose own graffiti art was the basis of his early fame.

The graffiti writer who made the greatest impact on the culture of the Bronx, and ultimately on the rest of the United States, was a young man who signed his work with the moniker Kool Herc. Around 1973, Kool Herc began to work as a deejay at local dance parties. Kool Herc very quickly recognized that his audiences responded most enthusiastically to the "break" sections on the records he played, the half-minute mid-section of a dance tune in which drums, bass, and rhythm guitars stripped the song to a pounding, primal beat. Kool Herc soon began to play only these sections of the songs, using two separate turntables to repeat the same break section again and again. "Break beats," these repeated riffs were called. Those who danced to Kool Herc's sounds soon became known as "break dancers." Break dancing swiftly yielded other styles, such as "electric boogie," which required its practioners to twitch their muscles in time to the music, and the more improvisational "free style," which sent dancers to the floor, spinning on their hips and shoulders. The baggy clothing that eventually became associated with rap music and hip-hop was intially worn to accommodate the break dancers' range of movement. The style of wearing pants low on the hips was said to have originated in New York's state prisons, where inmates were forbidden to have belts.

Kool Herc's practice of shouting out either encouraging or incendiary rhymes during his break beats led other deejays to become more and more vocal, eventually composing what amounted to spoken-word lyrics that accompanied the music they played. A young deejay named Theodor implemented a technique that involved spinning a record back and forth with the needle in the same groove, which became known as "scratching." The Bronx deejay George Saddler, better known as Grandmaster Flash, developed what was called "punch phrasing," a sound that layered one break beat onto another.

A relatively mainstream group called the Sugar Hill Gang produced the first rap records to gain significant radio airplay. Soon after, Run-D.M.C. and Public Enemy became the first rap groups to sell large numbers of records to white teenagers. Both groups (whose members were all raised in middle-class families) were inspired to some degree by the former Black Spades leader Afrika Bambaataa. "Bam," as he had become known, was the closest thing hip-hop culture had to an ambassador, and his organization, Zulu Nation, was a persuasive advocate of the movement to replace gang membership and drug use with a devotion to rap music and break dancing. Just as Run's brother, Russell Simmons, launched the first successful rap label, Def Jam, however, the advent of gangsta rap was about to change everything. At once a derivation and a degradation of hip-hop culture, gangsta rap was inaugurated in 1986. A duo from the South Bronx called Boogie Down Productions put out an album that year called *Criminal Minded* with a featured single titled "My 9mm Goes Bang," all about a drug dealer who shoots his rivals in the head and gets away with it. Soon after, Schoolly D's "PSK" (a song celebrating the grisly exploits of North Philadelphia's Parkside Killers street gang), and Ice-T's album *Rhyme Pays* became gangsta rap's first big hits. Southern California—or, more specifically, Compton—was about to become the epicenter of the gangsta rap universe, however, and Dr. Dre soon would be the genre's most sought-after talent.

Straight Outta Compton was an astonishing hit, despite early reviews that reviled the album. Even black radio stations refused to air songs that celebrated shooting police officers, beating and degrading women, smoking pot, getting drunk on malt liquor, and making money any way you could, but *Straight Outta Compton* was an immediate hit among the Crips and Bloods. The man who did most to boost sales of the album, however, was FBI public relations director Milt Aerlich, who responded to the album's anthem "Fuck Tha Police" with a letter to Ruthless Records that chastised N.W.A. for "encouraging violence and disrespect" toward police officers. Ruthless immediately forwarded the letter to dozens of newspapers and magazines. The resulting articles and editorials that condemned the group almost instantly created a huge new audience of white teenage boys for N.W.A. *Straight Outta Compton* promptly sold 500,000 copies in a single month and more than two million by the end of 1988.

Almost at this moment, Suge Knight, armed with little more than a promise from the D.O.C. that he might consider leaving Ruthless Records, began trying to form a rap label he called Funky Enough Records. Suge quickly signed his friend DJ Quik, a Piru Blood who fronted a group called the Penthouse Players, and a few other local rappers, among them a young man named Mario Johnson who went by the stage name Chocolate. In late 1990, when a white rapper named Vanilla Ice put out the first rap song to top the *Billboard* Pop Chart, "Ice Ice Baby," Chocolate complained to Suge Knight that he had both written and produced the song. Chocolate was even more incensed when Vanilla Ice brought out an album titled *II the Extreme* that sold a staggering 18 million copies; he had written seven of the album's twelve songs, Chocolate said, yet received almost nothing in the way of credit or money.

Suge, who had just finished defending himself against a charge of felony assault with a deadly weapon in Las Vegas, promptly showed up at The Palm restaurant in West Hollywood, where Vanilla Ice was eating with his security team. According to Vanilla Ice, Suge was accompanied by two guys just as big as he was who grabbed the white rapper's bodyguards, lifted them out of their seats, shoved them aside, and sat down in their places. Suge stared at him for a long time, then said, "How you doin'?" Vanilla Ice recalled. Similar incidents were repeated on several occasions before Suge showed up at the white rapper's suite on the fifteenth floor of the Bel Age Hotel, accompanied by Chocolate and a member of the L.A. Raiders football team. For several years, Vanilla Ice claimed that Suge and his companions drew guns to chase away two security guards, then pulled the white rapper out onto a balcony and threatened to throw him off unless he signed over the disputed song rights. Suge Knight denied this story (and so, eventually, did Vanilla Ice), but something happened in the room that convinced the white rapper to sign over the rights to all seven songs, free of charge.

However he accomplished it, Suge's successful "negotiation" with Vanilla Ice swiftly made him a legend in the rap world. He was the first black music executive many rappers had ever met who would not answer to white corporate masters, or even try to appease them. Now Suge wanted to show Dr. Dre and the D.O.C. that he could deal with Ruthless Records. The main object of Dre's animus was Ruthless Records' white business manager, Jerry Heller, whom he claimed had made more money from N.W.A.'s *Straight Outta Compton* tour than had the members of the group. When Dre began to boycott the sessions where he was scheduled to work as a producer for Ruthless's other rappers, the label stopped paying him, and Dre soon was at risk of losing not only his new home in Calabasas but all of the vehicles that filled his four-car garage.

According to Heller, he began receiving threats when a man he had never seen before walked into his office one day, put a finger to his head, and said, "I could have blown you away right now." Suge Knight began to phone in threats to Heller's assistant, Gary Ballen, then arrived at Ballen's office one day with a whole squad of Bloods and forced him to sign a written apology to Dre's girlfriend, the R&B singer Michel'le, for "disrespecting" her. Ballen began carrying a stun gun and taking karate classes but still couldn't sleep at night. Neither could Jerry Heller, who hired a pair of weight lifters (one named Animal) to serve as his bodyguards and put a shotgun in a drawer of the front desk at his office. Suge would claim he came to the office one day when Heller was gone and "made those two motherfuckers get down on they hands and knees and walk around like dogs."

Heller had known for some time that Suge wanted to see Ruthless Records' contracts with its artists, but it was early 1991 before he asked. When Heller refused, Suge showed up at the offices of Ruthless's corporate attorney, forced his way inside, and searched the file cabinets until he found what he wanted. Ruthless was screwing everybody, he told Dre and the D.O.C. after he read their contracts. By now Jerry Heller was driving home (by a different route every day) with an armed bodyguard who searched under the beds and in the closets of his Mountainview Estates mansion before the Ruthless executive would enter it. He had installed a state-of-the-art security system, Heller said, slept with a .38 under his pillow, stocked his cupboards with canisters of pepper spray, armed his girlfriend, and kept more than two dozen guns around his house "in places where I could get caught." Every time a car drove by or he heard a dog bark, Heller said, he grabbed a gun and went outside to check for danger.

Only Eazy-E, however, had the power to release Dr. Dre from his contract with Ruthless.

Suge now was in business with Dick Griffey, chairman of Solar Records and owner of the *Soul Train* TV show. Solar had signed a contract in 1989 with Sony Records calling for the delivery of several albums. Griffey told Sony executives in the spring of 1991 that he could arrange to have those records produced by Dr. Dre. Sony wanted Dre to produce the soundtrack album for a movie called *Deep Cover*. Griffey said he could make that happen, but only if Ruthless Records would surrender its claim on Dre. Sony proposed to buy Dre's music publishing rights from Ruthless for a million dollars if the label would let him go. The two labels were still negotiating in April of 1991 when Eazy-E got a call from Dre inviting him to a meeting at the Solar Records building in North Hollywood to "discuss our differences."

Eazy was so convinced of Dre's sincerity that he showed up for the meeting without his security team. When he reached the third-floor headquarters of the record label (Futureshock, it was called back then) that Suge Knight and Dre were putting together, however, his old friend wasn't there. Instead, Eazy was met by Knight and two of his thugs. Suge began the meeting by explaining that several of his artists—Dre, the D.O.C., Michel'le, Above the Law—wanted to leave Ruthless Records, recalled Eazy, who promptly refused. Suge replied by stating that he was holding Jerry Heller hostage in a van outside and knew where Eazy's mother lived. At that moment, Suge's thugs walked into the room carrying lead pipes and stood on both sides of him, said Eazy, a former Crip.

Suge again denied the story, but something the big man said or did that day must have made a powerful impression on Eazy E, who signed away five of his top acts—including the leading talent in rap—for no compensation whatsoever.

* * *

With Dre on board, all Suge needed was financial backing for his record label. His first major investor was the legendary drug lord and "Ghetto Godfather," Michael "Harry-O" Harris. A Blood member, Harry-O during the mid-1980s had achieved a level of notoriety that exceeded that of any black gangster in the city's history. Six feet, five inches tall and draped in Versace suits, Harris could go straight from a meeting of gangbangers who worked the streets for him in South Central to a movie premiere in Westwood or a party in Bel Air. He not only maintained three expensive homes in the San Fernando Valley and a fleet of luxury automobiles, but he also invested his cocaine profits in at least a half-dozen legitimate businesses, several of them based in Beverly Hills. When he was arrested for the attempted murder of a criminal associate in 1987, Mayor Tom Bradley personally announced the seizure of Harris's property. Sentenced to a minimum of twenty years in state prison, Harris continued to run an assortment of businesses, aided mainly by his wife, Lydia, an R&B singer. Even with Harry-O behind bars, the couple's production company, Y-Not, financed a Broadway play, *Checkmates,* in which Harris personally cast an unknown actor named Denzel Washington as the male lead. Then during late 1991, Michael and Lydia Harris began to make plans to form a new music label, Death Row Records.

The link between Harris and Knight was David Kenner, a short, thickset Jewish criminal attorney with a slicked-back ponytail, unblinking black eyes, and a ferocious attitude. Born in Brooklyn but educated at USC, Kenner, then in his mid-fifties, lived in an Encino mansion hidden behind high walls and surrounded by surveillance cameras. The attorney enjoyed the story that he kept a loaded Uzi on the desk in his home office and liked to tell people he was best friends with Tony Brooklier, whose father, Dominic, once had been among the biggest Mafia bosses in the country.

Kenner, who was handling Harry-O's criminal appeal at the time, set up the first meeting between Harris and Suge Knight in the fall of 1991 at the Metropolitan Detention Center in downtown Los Angeles. The deal negotiated among the three was an agreement that

the new record company would be a joint venture in which Knight
and the Harrises each owned fifty percent. Kenner would form the
Death Row Records corporation and help run its parent company,
Godfather Entertainment. The contract Kenner eventually drew up
gave Suge control of Death Row's day-to-day operations, while Harris (who was to invest $1.5 million as start-up capital) provided the
company's "overall philosophy and direction." Almost two years
would pass before Harris realized that Knight and Kenner had walled
him off with a barrier of corporate shells from any actual involvement in Death Row Records, including profit sharing.

The money Harris put up helped get Death Row Records rolling,
but Knight and Kenner soon were enmeshed in a complex and costly
legal dispute involving both Ruthless Records and the Sony Corporation. The two needed major backing to make records with Dr. Dre and
the other artists Suge had taken from Eazy-E. In late 1992 the unlikely
partners got what they needed, $10 million dollars from Jimmy Iovine
and Ted Field of Interscope, an independent company that was financed
by and distributed through Time Warner's corporate network. Field was
a department-store heir best known as a playboy until he started a film
company that produced a string of critically panned but commercially
successful movies like *The Hand That Rocks the Cradle* and *Three Men and
a Baby*. Iovine, the son of a Brooklyn longshoreman who had produced
records for the likes of Bruce Springsteen, John Lennon, and U-2, was
the brains of the operation, and he believed Dr. Dre to be a genius.

Death Row Records soon moved out of the Solar Records building (with David Kenner on board, Suge no longer felt he needed Dick
Griffey) and set up shop alongside Interscope's offices on Wilshire
Boulevard near Westwood. The first album released by Death Row
Records, Dr. Dre's keyboard-heavy homage to marijuana, *The Chronic*,
became the biggest-selling gangsta rap album of all time, holding a
place in *Billboard*'s Top 10 for eight months. The same day *The Chronic*
was released, David Kenner filed articles of incorporation for Death
Row Records that listed Suge Knight and Dr. Dre as the company's
sole directors. All Michael Harris received was an acknowledgment
in the liner notes: "Special thanks to Harry-O."

The debut album of Death Row's newest rap artist, Snoop Doggy Dogg's *Doggystyle*, also went multiplatinum, and by the end of 1993, the label's first full year in business, the company had grossed more than $60 million. The label already was becoming known as the first gangsta rap label owned by real gangstas. The release party for *The Chronic* was held at the Strip Club in Century City, where porno "stars" sashayed through throngs of drooling Bloods, and guests were served slices of a cake complete with iced marijuana leaves. The atmosphere, many of those in attendance would remark, was notably more ominous and volatile than at the functions Death Row had sponsored during its start up. Suge Knight now was traveling with an entourage of hard-core gangbangers—"penitentiary niggas," the label's more dignified employ-ees called them—that numbered as many as three or four dozen on some occasions. Suddenly he seemed to think he was Al Capone, other record executives whispered among themselves. At an L.A. club called Prince's Glam Slam, Suge—surrounded by an audience of his homeboys—got into a fight with a security guard named Roderick Lockett and beat the man so badly that several surgeries were required to repair his spleen. When Knight's violent former L.A. Rams team-mate Daryl Henley was suspended from the team for his implication in the operation of a large drug ring, Suge put the football player to work as his general manager and personal enforcer at Death Row's Wilshire Boulevard office. Many of his fellow employees were relieved when Henley's state prison sentence cost him that position.

Death Row's bad reputation became national news when Suge, Dre, and the D.O.C. were arrested following a melee in a hotel lobby at the Black Radio Exclusive convention in New Orleans. After a fifteen-year-old fan was stabbed, the New Orleans cops rode horses into the hotel lobby to break up the brawl. What appeared to be nega-tive publicity, however, only increased sales for Death Row Records.

In a business where bad was good, Suge Knight had positioned himself as the baddest gangsta around. Suge publicly proclaimed his membership in the Bloods gang, and in his office at Death Row's new Tarzana studios the sofa, chairs, and cabinets all were deep red. The carpet was red, too, except for the white outline of Death Row's logo—

a man strapped to an electric chair with a sack over his head. A guard with a metal detector greeted guests at the studio's front door, and kept a list of "security personnel"—many of them Bloods members—who were permitted to bring guns inside. White executives and black journalists were kept waiting for hours; when they finally were admitted to Knight's office, Suge stood up to give them a good view of the 315-pound physique he maintained by lifting weights for two hours every morning, then blew cigar smoke in their faces and told them his German shepherd guard dog Damu (Swahili for "Blood") was trained to kill on command. After one reporter asked him a question that Death Row's CEO found offensive, Knight dragged the man to a fish tank filled with piranha and threatened to let them eat the man's face.

For Suge, the consequences of such behavior were all for the good. Knight not only was embraced by ghetto musicians and lionized as an authentic gangster in the emerging hip-hop press, but found that he could use his menacing image to cut corners as well as deals; Death Row Records was becoming notorious for stiffing music and video producers, none of whom had the nerve to sue.

At the same time, though, Suge was adept at pandering to the fatuous platitudes of white liberals who wanted to believe that Knight's "act" was some useful form of performance art, the self-serving pantomime of a man who was just doing business, like everybody else in town. Most of his legal problems had been created by "police out looking for trouble," Suge told one reporter. "It don't bother me none, though. That's the way it's been as long as I can remember. I'm used to it." Knight's commitment to violence was genuine, however, and his rap sheet showed it. In 1992 alone, Suge was charged with assault with a deadly weapon and convicted of misdemeanor battery in Beverly Hills, convicted of carrying a concealed weapon in West Covina, and convicted of disturbing the peace in Van Nuys. The most serious charge filed against Knight that year, however, and the one that would haunt him the longest, involved an incident that had taken place at Solar Records shortly before Suge made his deal with Interscope.

Dre, the D.O.C., and the newly signed Snoop Dogg were among the performers working in various studios on the building's third floor that evening when Suge noticed an aspiring producer named Lynwood Stanley using his company line. "Say, Blood," Suge told the man, "don't be on the phone." Lynwood replied, "Don't be coming at me with that gangbang shit. I'm not from L.A." Lynwood's brother George intervened and hustled his brother into the lunchroom to use the pay phone there, but Suge came in after the two a moment later, pushed the receiver on the pay phone down, pointed a loaded pistol at Lynwood Stanley's head, and asked, "Whassup?" Suge then proceeded to beat both brothers senseless as they retreated down a hallway to a recording studio. Suge stopped at the door to tell Dre, Snoop, the D.O.C., and others in the crowd that followed him, "Get out. Close the door. Go upstairs," then followed the Stanleys into the studio, where he continued to beat the two, finally ordering them to their knees. When Lynwood Stanley refused, Suge fired off a round, smacked the producer across the temple with the barrel of his gun, threatened to shoot both brothers in the head, then forced them to take off their pants and lay naked from the waist down on the floor in front of him. After removing Lynwood's wallet from his pants pocket, Suge said he would keep the producer's ID, so that if the brothers went to the cops he could have them and their family members killed.

The Stanleys called Suge's bluff, though, and less than an hour later a team of LAPD officers stormed into the building. Performers and producers scrambled to escape, screaming at one another to get rid of their drugs and guns. Some locked themselves in closets, others dashed to the stairway. The Stanley brothers stepped onto the third floor surrounded by cops and pointed at Suge, who immediately denied everything. Only when the brothers showed the cops the bullet embedded in the wall of the studio where they had been beaten did the police arrest Knight.

The prosecution's case would be tough to beat, but David Kenner (aided by Suge's newest defense counsel, Johnnie Cochran) was able to delay Knight's trial date for almost three years, and in the meantime Suge still was living large. He had homes in Westwood, Encino, and Anaheim Hills, as well as his parents' old place in Compton, which he had completely remodeled, adding a four-car garage. Nearly every morning, Suge stopped at Death Row's auto customizing business, Let Me Ride, where he kept a fleet of luxury vehicles for his personal use. He also began to branch out into a variety of new and socially accepted directions, hosting an annual Mother's Day celebration for fifty single moms at the Beverly Wilshire Hotel, sponsoring Christmastime toy giveaways at Compton churches and hospitals, establishing (most amusingly) an anti-gang foundation in Compton, and volunteering to underwrite Maxine Waters's new youth program.

Suge was becoming a sort of living urban myth, especially after gangbangers threw shots at him outside the Roxbury and Glam Slam nightclubs. A minor scuffle outside the Beverly Hills restaurant, Larry Parker's, soon was inflated into the story that Suge had survived unscathed a shoot-out in which four of his attackers were wounded. And Suge really had escaped death one afternoon at nearby Lawry's, where he was lunching with the former Black Entertainment Television anchorwoman Madeline Woods when a Crip at a nearby table spotted him and used his cell phone to set up an ambush. Just as Suge stepped outside and the Crips prepared to open fire, however, an LAPD patrol car pulled into the parking lot, and the Crips sped away. The guy even had dumb luck going for him, the gangbangers said.

Suge's business, meanwhile, was booming. At the very first Source Awards ceremony at the Paramount Theater in Manhattan, Death Row artists Dr. Dre and Snoop Dogg swept nearly every major award: Album of the Year, Solo Artist of the Year, Producer of the Year for Dre, New Solo Artist of the Year and Lyricist of the Year for Snoop.

The second annual Source Awards ceremony, though, was dominated not by Death Row Records' artists but by its CEO. Suge stunned the crowd in the hall—not to mention the television viewers at home—by storming to the stage trailed by his effeminate new R&B singer Danny Boy, who brought the Death Row contingent to its feet by flashing both Blood and Crip signs. Knight stood by himself at the microphone for several moments, staring balefully into the audience, then announced, "If you don't want the owner of your label on your album or in your video or on your tour, come to Death Row." The crowd gasped, understanding that Suge had just made a very public attack on Sean "Puffy" Combs, the New York–based CEO of Bad Boy Entertainment, who during the past year had made cameos in most of the records and albums his label produced.

The melodrama that enveloped Knight and his outlaw label had been taken up one very big notch. Suge had now not only named a legitimate rival, but acquired an archenemy whose defeat would become his overriding ambition.

Perhaps the ultimate commentary on the perverse ethos of gangsta rap was that, by 1994, Puffy Combs had taken to telling the people he worked with that he grew up in Harlem as the son of a drug dealer. That *was* the true story of Puffy's first two and a half years. His father, Melvin, was a street hustler who died in Central Park when he was shot in the head during a drug deal. Puffy's mother told the children their father had died in a car accident, however, and enrolled her only son in an all-white Catholic school where he became an altar boy. The family moved to Westchester County when Puffy was eleven, and by the time he turned twelve the boy was working two paper routes in the suburbs. He attended an all-boys' prep school in Manhattan, then matriculated to Howard University, where he majored in business administration. Puffy didn't discover until he was seventeen how his father really had died.

During his sophomore year in college, Puffy convinced Uptown Records president Andre Harrell to take him on as an unpaid intern. Within a few months, Combs was on salary as Uptown's director of A&R. Then in December of 1992, Harrell made twenty-two-year-old Puffy the youngest vice president for A&R in the history of the music business. The success of his performers Mary J. Blige and Jodeci made Puffy a celebrity and convinced Andre Harrell that his protégé had become a competitor. Harrell fired Combs from Uptown in 1993, but only a few months later Puffy's new enterprise, Bad Boy Entertainment, signed a $15 million distribution deal with Arista Records.

Suge Knight made his first incursion into the New York rap scene when he began courting not only Mary J. Blige, who had followed Puffy Combs to Bad Boy Entertainment, but also Jodeci, a group that was increasingly disenchanted with Uptown Records. Suge demanded a meeting with Harrell, who was terrified of the big man. When Suge showed up at Harrell's office, though, he said he believed the place was bugged and insisted on adjourning to the bathroom. Afterward, three stories circulated about what had happened in there. One was that Suge pulled Harrell's pants down and threatened to rape him. Another was that Suge held Harrell's head over the toilet bowl and threatened to drown him. The third was that Suge held a gun to Harrell's head, handed him a contract, and said, "Sign this or else." Whatever actually happened during the bathroom meeting, Harrell almost immediately upgraded Jodeci's contracts, doubling their royalty rate to 18 percent and giving them an unusual degree of creative control over their records. And not only Jodeci but Mary J. Blige as well were freed from their management contracts with Harrell.

Suge also arranged a meeting with Bad Boy Entertainment's lawyers and executives in a suite at the Four Seasons Hotel to discuss the company's contract with Mary J. Blige. In an interview, Suge described the meeting succinctly: "I told them they was lettin' Mary out of that fucked-up deal. And they did."

Shortly thereafter, *Newsweek* reported that Jodeci, their leader Devante Swing, and Mary J. Blige had all signed contracts with Suge Knight's West Coast Management. The magazine also made reference to Knight's "unfriendly visit" with Andre Harrell. Both men denied the story, but Harrell, *Newsweek* noted, had since retained the security services of Louis Farrakhan's Nation of Islam security team, the Fruit of Islam: "These days, they go where he goes."

Suge celebrated by presenting Devante Swing with a $250,000 Lamborghini. "That's how I treat *my* people," he told anyone who asked and many who did not.

Puffy Combs continued to flourish, however. He became a recording star in his own right, opened successful restaurants, and developed a line of designer clothing. In 1995 Bad Boy Entertainment would sign a reported $70 million five-year joint venture deal with Arista. The label's brightest star was an immensely obese former Brooklyn crack dealer who recorded as Notorious B.I.G. but was perhaps better known as Biggie Smalls.

Biggie's was the most melodious voice in the history of rap. "It was almost like he was singing," Puffy Combs would say of the first time he heard Biggie rap. "And he was such a clever poet, the way he put words together, the way he saw things." Puffy, who like Dr. Dre tended toward perfectionism, spent eighteen months producing Biggie's first album, the fatefully titled *Ready to Die*, which would become the first platinum recording by a New York rapper in almost two years.

Even as he became rich and famous in his own right, Puffy professed to admire Suge Knight. "Bad Boy was kinda modeled on Death Row," he told *Rolling Stone*, "because Death Row had become a movement." Puffy claimed that whenever Suge came to New York he stopped by Bad Boy's office, and that whenever he flew to L.A., Suge would visit his hotel to hang out. They had driven together to Snoop Dogg's house at least a couple of times, Puffy told *Rolling Stone*. "It was all cool."

Suge already despised Puffy, though, first as an overweening imitator who was putting out weak versions of Death Row's product, and second as puny little peacock who lacked either the body or the heart to fight his own battles. By early 1995 Death Row's CEO was openly mocking Puffy as a weak and cowardly "little nigga."

Puffy, though, continued to attempt appeasement. Even as Suge dissed him publicly at that summer's Source Awards, Puffy made it a point to congratulate Snoop Dogg with an onstage embrace when

Death Row's rapper won the Artist of the Year award. Immediately afterward, Bad Boy's boss stepped to the microphone and pleaded for unity between rappers from both the East and West coasts. Suge's boy Daz of Tha Dogg Pound broke the short-lived peace, however, by following Puffy to the microphone, where he told the New York audience, "Yo, from the bottom of my heart, y'all can eat this dick."

Tensions between east and west turned even nastier one month later, when Suge and Puffy both flew to Atlanta to attend a birthday party for Kris Kross producer Jermaine Dupri. The crowd adjourned to the nearby Platinum Club for an after party that Combs attended in the company of several young men he would insist later were not his bodyguards. Knight was accompanied only by his favorite thug, "Jake the Violator" Robles. At six feet tall and 245 pounds, Jake was a powerfully built man who wasn't inclined to waste words and really didn't need to. After Daryl Henley went to prison, Suge had replaced him at Death Row's Wilshire Boulevard offices with big Jake, who kept people in line just by glancing in their direction.

The most reliable witness to what happened at the Platinum Club that night was a Fulton County Sheriff's deputy who was working off duty at the door as a bouncer. Shortly after 4 A.M., the deputy recalled, he was alerted to an argument inside that was about to become a brawl. When he ran toward the raised voices, the deputy said, he saw Suge Knight and Jake Robles faced off against Puffy Combs's cousin "Wolf" and four other men he believed to be members of the Crips. He broke up the argument, the deputy said, ordered Wolf and his friends to leave, then insisted that Knight and Robles remain inside the club for at least fifteen minutes, so as to avoid a resumption of hostilities in the parking lot. Wolf and his friends agreed to go, and were followed shortly by Puffy Combs, while Suge Knight agreed, "reluctantly," to stay, the deputy said. After only about five minutes, however, Knight and Robles became anxious to leave, and walked out the club's front door to their waiting limousine. The two big men had just taken their seats in the limo when they climbed out again to confront Wolf and his friends, who were approaching from the passenger side, the deputy said. When he saw that Wolf had a gun, the deputy drew his own sidearm and chased Puffy's cousin toward the back of the club but then lost him among the parked cars. Just as he turned around and headed back toward the front of the club, the deputy said, he heard three gunshots. By the time he made it back to the area where Suge Knight's limo was parked, he found Jake Robles on the ground, mortally wounded by bullets that had ripped through his torso. As the screaming crowd fled the building, Puffy Combs stepped up to Suge and asked what had happened. Knight gestured toward the prone figure of his friend and told Combs, "You had something to do with this!"

Back in Los Angeles, word spread swiftly among the Bloods that Jake had died to protect Suge, who was the target of a hit. Shortly after, a black newspaper in Atlanta identified the killer as Combs's cousin. Puffy denied any involvement. "Why would I set a nigga up to get shot?" he asked a writer from *VIBE* magazine. "If I'm'a set a nigga up, which I would never do, I'm'a be in Bolivia somewhere." He was told that Death Row had put out a contract on his life. "Why do they have so much hatred for me?" he asked. "I ask myself that question every day. I'm ready for them to leave me alone, man."

When Knight was asked if he would speak to Combs if Puffy called, Suge replied, "He done that shit a hundred times. What the muthafucka need to do is stop lyin' in magazines! Sayin' shit didn't happen!" Jake Robles had died to protect him from a murder attempt planned by Combs, insisted Knight, who sneered at Puffy for arriving at that year's Soul Train Awards in Los Angeles (the event that had ended with Kelly Jamerson's death) with a squad of Fruit of Islam security guards. Puffy was paying "Muslims money for protection," Suge said, buying "niggas to hang wit' him."

"That type of support don't last," Suge warned, and Puffy would be gotten to, eventually.

CHAPTER FOUR

Russell Poole found many more questions than answers in one of the first LAPD crime reports he read that involved Suge Knight's vendetta against Puffy Combs and Bad Boy Entertainment. The "victim" named in the report was an independent record promoter from New York named Mark Anthony Bell, who worked occasionally for his old high school classmate Puffy Combs. According to Bell, he had been contacted back in September, shortly after Jake Robles's death, by a man who refused to give his name but promised that if Bell "cooperated" he could get a record deal. When he asked what cooperation meant, Bell recalled, the man said he wanted home addresses for both Puffy Combs and Combs's mother. Write those on a piece of paper, step outside, and drop the paper on the ground, he was told, and no one would ever know he had snitched. Bell insisted that he didn't know where Puffy lived, said he didn't want to get involved, then hung up. The caller never identified himself as an employee of Death Row Records, but Bell felt certain that he was.

Bell was in Los Angeles on business three months later when he learned that his friend Roderick Nixon had been hired to photograph the guests at Death Row Records' Christmas party in the Chateau Le Blanc mansion on Astral Drive in the Hollywood Hills. He and Nixon stopped by Death Row's office on Wilshire Boulevard, Bell explained, to ask if he could get an invitation. The manager they spoke to made a phone call, then said there would be no problem. "I should have known they were setting me up," Bell told the police later.

He and Roderick arrived at the party about 10:30 that evening, Bell said. Suge Knight and his entourage didn't show up until almost 2 A.M. Suge was making his rounds when he noticed Bell standing near the dance floor, then approached him and asked, "Why didn't you cooperate when you had the chance?" He insisted he didn't have Puffy's home address and told Knight that Puffy's business number was listed in the phone book, Bell explained. Suge then asked him to come upstairs to the "VIP room" for a little chat. Before he could decline the invitation, Bell said, he was surrounded by six other men. Two of them he recognized immediately as Dr. Dre and Tupac Shakur.

All seven men escorted him upstairs to a room where a reporter from MTV and a photographer from *The New York Times* were being entertained. Suge's brother-in-law Norris Anderson asked the media to leave, held the door for them as they exited, Bell said, then stationed himself as a lookout. Suge pulled a chair into the middle of the room and told him to take a seat, Bell recalled, then sat in another chair directly in front of him, while the others formed a semicircle to his right and left. Suge again demanded to know why Bell wouldn't cooperate and began to ask him a series of questions about Puffy Combs. Tupac Shakur was whispering in Suge's ear the whole time. Meanwhile, an especially scary-looking Blood whose teeth were covered with gold crowns, began to pace back and forth, then whirled and hit him several times in the face, Bell said. "This is for Jake," Gold Teeth told him, according to Bell. "We're going to kill you." Finally, Suge Knight stood up and walked into the bathroom, Bell said. Moments later, Suge came back with a champagne flute he had filled with urine and told Bell to drink it. When he refused, Bell said, Gold Teeth hit him in the face again.

Figuring he was a dead man, anyway, Bell explained, he dropped the champagne glass and dashed across the room, hoping to escape off a balcony that was suspended above the mansion's lobby entrance. The whole group caught him at the guardrail before he could get over it, Bell said. Suge had him by the left shoulder and leg while the others tried to pull him back, all except Tupac, who was using his fists to pound on the promoter's fingers where they clung to the rail. When they finally pried him loose, Bell said, the whole group fell on him, punching, kicking, swinging bottles and throwing champagne glasses. "Body blows only!" Suge roared. Gold Teeth got him in a chokehold, Bell said, and squeezed until he nearly passed out. The beating and choking stopped, Bell said, only when he played dead on the floor. Someone stripped him of his wallet, his Rolex watch, and a gold necklace studded with diamonds that was worth almost $20,000. Then Suge told him to stand up.

When he finally got to his feet, Bell said, Suge began acting as if they were old friends. "You can be part of this team," Knight told him. "I can make you rich. Do you want to make half a million dollars? Do you have friends that could deliver?" Suge then walked him to the bathroom and told him to clean up. From the corner of his eye, Bell said, he saw a couple of the Bloods talking on what appeared to be police radios, and getting excited.

As Suge opened the bathroom door, he said, "If you want your jewelry back, call me tomorrow and we'll talk about it," Bell recalled. Gold Teeth immediately walked up and asked Suge, "Should I do him?" "He's good," Suge replied. "You're lucky he said that," Gold Teeth told Bell, then turned and headed toward the door. "Don't let him leave till he's cleaned up," Suge told Norris Anderson, then walked out of the room trailed by Tupac and Gold Teeth.

Anderson let him leave a few minutes later, but by then a pair of LAPD officers already were at the mansion. Roderick Nixon, who said he knew "something wasn't right" when he saw Bell being led upstairs by Suge and the others, had spotted his friend about fifteen minutes later hanging from the rail of the balcony as Tupac Shakur threw punches at him. Nixon promptly called the police on a pay phone and fled the scene.

The female LAPD officer who met him at the bottom of the stairs asked, "Are you Mark?" Bell remembered, then said he had a friend who was worried that his life might be in danger. The men who had assaulted him were all within ten feet, eavesdropping on the conversation. Suge Knight chose that moment to straighten a Christmas tree nearby, then turned to look at him over the female officer's shoulder, Bell said. The expression on Suge's face convinced him he would never get out of L.A. alive if he talked, Bell explained, and he told the officer, "Everything's okay." "Did you fall?" the officer asked. "Yes," Bell answered, then asked if she would call him a cab. The officer stayed until the taxi arrived to take him to a friend's house in West Covina.

The next day, his friends took Bell to the hospital, where he was treated for a hemorrhaging left eye, a laceration on his left elbow, an abrasion on his right arm, a large swelling behind his left ear, and bruises that covered most of his body. Bell did show up at the LAPD's Hollywood Station to tell the police what had really happened to him at the party, but not until until four days later, when he filed a complaint of assault and robbery against each of the seven men who had been in the VIP room with him.

Russell Poole was astounded to discover that the district attorney's office had refused to file charges. Numerous witnesses had seen Bell being forced up the stairs to the VIP room, and his friend Nixon had observed part of the assault while Bell was attempting to escape off the balcony. Even five days after the beating, officers who interviewed Bell noted that both his eyeballs were reddened by ruptured blood vessels and that he had cuts, scrapes, contusions, and swellings over most of his body. The D.A.'s office, however, insisted that its case had been compromised by Bell's failure to report his beating at the time of the incident while police officers were present. "You see enough police reports, though, and you learn to read between the lines," Poole said. "They didn't want to prosecute because they knew if they charged Suge Knight he would accuse them of racism. They figured this was all some kind of black shit that they didn't want to get involved with."

Mark Anthony Bell eventually filed a civil suit against Suge Knight and Death Row Records, and received a reported settlement of $600,000. He moved to Jamaica after collecting the money, and had been lying low ever since.

To Poole, the only thing more amazing than the D.A.'s refusal to file charges was the fact that Suge Knight would expose himself to criminal prosecution in such a public way, especially given his legal situation at the time. Ten months earlier, in February of 1995, Suge finally had been forced to plead guilty to the felony assault of George and Lynwood Stanley at Solar Records in July of 1992. Given his criminal history, it looked as if prison time was inevitable. If Suge Knight had learned anything, however, it was that almost any problem went away when you threw enough money at it. Person after person praised Knight to Judge John Ouderkirk and pleaded with the jurist to keep him out of prison. Among those offering testimonials were the Stanley brothers, who recently had signed a $1 million contract with Death Row Records (a deal negotiated, of course, by David Kenner). Also speaking on Suge's behalf was the deputy district attorney assigned to prosecute him, Lawrence Longo, who observed that Mr. Knight had become head of one of the largest record companies in the country and employed numerous residents of Los Angeles County, then recommended a nine-year suspended sentence, with five years of probation. Judge Ouderkirk, who did not know that a few months later Longo's eighteen-year-old daughter, Gina, was going to become the first white singer signed to a recording contract with Death Row Records, or that a few months after this Suge Knight would move into Longo's Malibu Colony home, or that David Kenner would pay the prosecutor's family $19,000 in rent each month for the use of that property, went along with the deal. Any violation of his probation (including association with convicted felons) would send him to prison, but in the meantime all Suge owed the state was one month in a halfway house.

Thirty days later, Knight was back in his Encino mansion, ready to begin the pursuit of his biggest coup to date, a Death Row Records contract with rap's brightest star, Tupac Shakur. Tupac was in New York State's Dannemora prison during the summer of 1995, serving a sentence of fifty-two months for a sexual-assault conviction. During the past four years he'd been arrested eight times, narrowly avoiding conviction in the 1993 shooting of two off-duty Atlanta police officers, and barely escaping death when he was shot five times in the lobby of the Quad Studios just off New York's Times Square. Despite recording three hugely successful albums during this period, Shakur was broke and desperate. Suge Knight recognized an opportunity. Immediately after his release from the halfway house in Los Angeles, Suge began making a series of trips to Dannemora that lasted all through that spring and into summer. Eventually he persuaded Shakur that if the rapper agreed to join Death Row's roster he would be out of custody in short order. One week after Tupac signed a three-page agreement handwritten by David Kenner, the New York Court of Appeals announced that it was releasing Shakur from prison on $1.4 million bail. Interscope put up the money, and when Shakur walked out of Dannemora, Knight and Kenner were waiting outside in a white stretch limousine.

Suge and Tupac appeared to be flying high and in tandem during the next twelve months. Attacks on gangsta rap by William Bennett and C. DeLores Tucker rattled Interscope's corporate masters at Time Warner, but executive anxiety was considerably eased when Shakur's first album for Death Row, *All Eyez on Me,* released in February 1996, sold 3 million copies. Knight draped his stars in luscious groupies and ruby-studded jewelry, achieving an acme of in-house excess when Death Row celebrated Snoop Dogg's acquittal on murder charges with the purchase of four Rolls-Royces. Both Death Row and Suge Knight were about to experience a rapid reversal of fortune, however. And Tupac Shakur, all of twenty-five, had only a few months left to live.

During her 1971 pregnancy, Afeni Shakur was standing trial as a member of the Panther 21, a group accused of conspiring to blow up several New York department stores. She named her son Tupac, Afeni Shakur liked to tell people, for the last Inca chief to be murdered by the Spanish conquistadores.

Tupac's mother had been born Alice Faye Williams. She was a farm girl from North Carolina who took her new name after moving to Brooklyn and starting an affair with one of Malcolm X's bodyguards. Chants of "Black Power" were "like a lullaby when I was a kid," Tupac himself once said. Her acquittal in the Panther 21 trial gave Afeni Shakur a short-lived celebrity in the early '70s. While living in a subsidized apartment in Manhattan near Columbia University, she lectured at Harvard and Yale. Her only son was called the "Black Prince" and forecast as the future leader of "the revolution." By the late '70s, though, as the epoch of radical chic passed, Afeni and her son were reduced to living on welfare in the South Bronx, while many adult members of Tupac's Black Panther "family" were either behind bars or on the run. Tupac's godfather, Elmer (Geronimo) Pratt, was convicted in 1968 of murdering a schoolteacher during a robbery in Santa Monica and sentenced to life in prison. The boy's "aunt," Assata Shakur (Joanne Chesimard) was found guilty in 1977 of murdering a New Jersey state trooper, though she did manage to break out of prison two years later and flee to Cuba. Tupac's stepfather, Mutulu Shakur, was found guilty of conspiring in that prison escape, as well as in the attempted robbery of a Brinks armored car in which two police officers and a guard were killed.

Tupac was never certain about his father's identity. Afeni had been married to Black Panther activist Lumumba Shakur when she became pregnant, but told him that her son's father was either a Harlem drug dealer who answered to "Legs" or another Panther party member, Billy Garland. Garland claimed paternity, but Tupac reaped little benefit from this; he rarely saw the man, who never amounted to much anyway. Garland was a far better choice than Legs, however, who reentered Tupac's life when the boy was about twelve and stayed around just long enough to turn Afeni into a crack addict. Afeni and her two children (Tupac had a younger sister named Sekiwa) moved to Baltimore in 1984 when Legs was arrested for credit card fraud. The man died of a drug-induced heart attack a short time later. Legs's death "fucked Tupac up," Afeni once told an interviewer. "It was three months before he cried. After he did, he told me, 'I miss my daddy.'"

"I remember crying all the time," Tupac told an interviewer about his early childhood. "My major thing growing up was that I just couldn't fit in." Baltimore would be good to the boy, though. His mother enrolled him in the city's School for the Arts, where he studied ballet, poetry, jazz, and acting. He performed in Shakespearean plays and played the mouse king in *The Nutcracker*. The teenager who had been teased about his slight build and effeminate features in New York would say that he finally felt "in touch" with himself during his time at the School for the Arts. "I was starting to feel like I really wanted to be an artist," Tupac explained. "I was fucking white girls."

The idyll ended when Tupac moved to California in 1988 to escape the squalor and poverty of a home where his mother smoked a crack pipe all during her third pregnancy. His new residence was in Marin City, an isolated ghetto in a geographic depression surrounded by rolling hills where white people with money had created a quasi-rustic suburbia. He didn't fit in with the black kids he met in California, Tupac said: "I dressed like a hippie. I couldn't play basketball . . . I was the target for [street gangs]. They used to jump me . . . I thought I was weird because I was writing poetry and I hated myself. I used to keep it a secret . . . I was really a nerd."

Tupac's self-esteem was considerably enhanced in 1990, however, when he got a job as a dancer with the rap group Digital Underground. Only one year later, executives at Interscope heard a demo tape Tupac had made and signed him to a recording contract of his own. The young rapper's 1991 album *2pacalypse Now* sold 500,000 copies, thanks in part to Vice President Dan Quayle, who declared that Tupac's tales of young black men in pitched battle with the pigs who invaded their neighborhoods had "no place in our society."

Tupac had started a film career that same year, landing a part in *Juice*, even before his first album was recorded. When he moved to Los Angeles in 1992, however, Shakur immediately became absorbed in the gang culture of Crips and Bloods. In part he was doing what artists

and writers always do—sponging up stories, characters, and attitudes
he could use in his songs. The young men who controlled the streets
of Compton and South Central L.A., however, placed an unusually high
premium on authenticity. The only options they gave anyone, even
visiting rap stars, were hard or soft, gangsta or punk. Either have the
heart of a killer or expect to be treated like any other sucker, fair game
for anyone who was bad enough to take the watch off your wrist or the
money from your pocket. At 5'8" and 150 pounds, with fine, soft features and eyes that just wouldn't go dead, Tupac scared absolutely
nobody, at least not until he bought his first pistol and began practicing with it at local firing ranges. He started lifting weights, too, and
began to cover his torso with tattoos—the most famous being the huge
letters that spelled out "Thug Life" across his solar plexus, with the
image of an assault rifle etched into his flesh above it.

Tupac's first major brush with the law made headlines that summer, when he went home to attend the celebration of Marin City's
fiftieth anniversary and got into a shouting match with some young
men from the neighborhood that did not end until shots were fired
and a six-year-old boy was killed by a bullet to the head. Tupac's
half brother was arrested for murder, only to be released because of
insufficient evidence, but all that most people remembered were
headlines with the name Shakur in them.

Back in L.A., Tupac kept even the gangbangers guessing. When
he wore red on the cover of his second album, 1993's *Strictly 4 My
N.I.G.G.A.Z.*, word spread that he had joined the Bloods, but soon after
he posed for pictures with a blue bandanna on his head. During a drive
to the Fox lot in Hollywood, where he was to tape a segment for *In
Living Color*, Tupac pulled a gun on a limo driver who had asked him
not to smoke pot in the vehicle, then looked on as the members of his
entourage beat the man senseless. He played opposite Janet Jackson in
his second movie, *Poetic Justice*, that summer, then on Halloween got
into a shoot-out with two off-duty white police officers in Atlanta,
wounding one man in his abdomen and the other in his buttocks.
Charges of aggravated assault were dropped only when it came out

that the cops Tupac had shot were a pair of drunken yahoos who had started things by brandishing a pistol stolen from a precinct evidence room, and that on the day of Tupac's first court hearing one of them had been charged with aggravated assault, while both were accused of using the word "niggers" in a police report.

The attendant publicity made Tupac simultaneously a media villain and a ghetto champion. By November of 1993, when he moved to New York for the filming of *Above the Rim*, Tupac's legal expenses had mounted to the point that he began telling people he had to change his life and clean up his act or declare bankruptcy. Smelling blood in the water, Suge Knight made his first overture to Tupac, paying $200,000 for a single song, "Pour Out a Little Liquor." When Knight offered a long-term recording contract, however, Tupac turned Suge down, choosing to align himself instead with the Haitian-born music promoter Jacques Agnant.

The rapper's bad press, meanwhile, continued to mount. He was the target of civil suits that blamed his lyrics for the shooting of a Texas state trooper and the paralysis of a young woman who was hit by a stray bullet during a near-riot at one of his concerts in Arkansas. The headlines were louder still when, shortly before Thanksgiving, Tupac was arrested for the sexual assault that would send him to Dannemora.

What had happened would never be clear, largely because the victim was a young woman whose own behavior inspired neither trust nor sympathy. Tupac claimed he first encountered Ayanna Jackson when she approached him on the dance floor of the downtown Manhattan nightclub Nell's, unzipped his pants, and led him by the penis to a dark corner of the club where she performed oral sex on him. Jackson insisted that Tupac had chased her all over the club before a brief and furtive encounter in which he "pushed my head down on his penis in a brief three-second encounter." Whatever, the young woman not only slept with Shakur that night but showed up four days later at Tupac's suite in the Parker-Meridian wearing a tight dress and within minutes was giving him a massage in the bedroom. The two soon were joined by Jacques Agnant and a friend of the promoter's. Tupac and the other two men claimed Jackson was a willing participant in group sex; the young woman said she was the victim of a gang rape. One year later, a New York jury would essentially split the difference, but in the meantime Tupac was attending to other troubles.

On February 1, 1994, Tupac was in Los Angeles municipal court to answer assault charges filed against him by film director Allen Hughes, who, along with his partner-brother, Albert, had tried to cast Tupac in the film *Menace II Society*. When he read the script, however, Tupac decided the Hughes brothers had cast him as a sucker, and showed up on the set of a video they were filming with an entourage of gangbangers. Allen Hughes was beaten, while his brother fled the scene. After pleading guilty in court, Tupac was to face sentencing on March 10. Less than twelve hours before his scheduled court appearance, however, Tupac was confronted by five Crips at a convenience store on Sunset Boulevard. When one of the five smashed him in the face, Tupac grabbed a pair of scissors from a display case and chased the group into the street while dozens of witnesses looked on. The news was in the morning papers, and national TV crews were on hand at the courthouse the next day as the prosecution argued that Mr. Shakur was a young man who could not control his temper. Tupac, sentenced to fifteen days in jail, flew back to New York as soon as he finished his time.

On the evening of November 28, 1994, shortly after a Manhattan jury began to deliberate charges of sodomy, sexual abuse, and weapons possession against him, Tupac was smoking pot as he made his way to the Quad Recording Studios off Times Square. He had been promised seven thousand badly needed dollars for a guest appearance on a song by an obscure Uptown Records rapper named Little Shawn, a deal set up through Tupac's new friend Biggie Smalls. Biggie's friend L'il Caesar shouted greetings to them through an open window as Tupac and two companions entered the building. At the elevator, however, Tupac and his friends were confronted by a pair of black men who wore army fatigues and held identical 9mm handguns. Neither of Shakur's friends was hit, but Tupac was shot five times; one bullet creased his head, while another shattered a testicle. The men in fatigues stripped him of a $30,000 diamond ring and $10,000 in gold chains, yet left the diamond-studded Rolex watch Jacques Agnant had given Tupac as a present. Though wounded as well in the thigh and abdomen, Tupac managed to make it into an elevator and ride eight floors up to the studio where he was scheduled to perform. Andre Harrell, Puffy Combs, and Biggie Smalls were among those in the room. All were dripping with jewelry, and none would look him in the eye, said Tupac, who would become convinced the three men viewed him as a rival they wished to eliminate.

A team of twelve doctors at Bellevue Hospital operated on Tupac during the early morning hours of November 29, then were shocked when he checked himself out that evening. His life was in danger if he stayed, explained Tupac, who chose to spend the night of the twenty-ninth at the home of his friend actress Jasmine Guy A team of bow tied Fruit of Islam security guards surrounded Tupac's wheelchair as he arrived in court to hear the jury's verdict. Relief at his acquittal on the more serious sodomy and weapons charges was almost instantly overwhelmed by the knowledge that being found guilty of sexual abuse would mean prison time. He was given two and a half months to convalesce, first at Metropolitan Hospital then at Jasmine Guy's apartment, but on Valentine's Day 1995 he received a sentence of four and a half years in state prison.

He began doing his time at Riker's Island, where he read Machiavelli's *The Prince* until he had memorized it, then announced in an interview with *VIBE* that he was done with gangsta rap. "That shit is dead," he told the magazine's reporter. "If Thug Life is real, then let somebody else represent it, because I'm tired of it. I represented it too much." As his single "Dear Mama" rose on the charts, a rumor spread on the streets that he had been raped in Riker's by members of a Latin gang. Tupac then was transferred to Clinton Correctional in Dannemora, where he was initiated into prison life by a strip search and rectal examination.

From the beginning of his career, Tupac had come across as a young man torn between his demons and his angels. The hit single on *2pacalypse Now* was "Brenda's Got a Baby," a song Tupac said was inspired by the newspaper account of a twelve-year-old girl who got pregnant by a cousin, then threw her baby down an incinerator shaft. "No male rappers at all anywhere were talking about problems females were having," he explained when asked why he had written the song. Yet on the same album Tupac boasted in another song, "This is the life, new bitch every night, never tripped off a wife." He showed up for his first film audition wearing the tattooed words OUTLAW on one arm and HEARTLESS on the other, then recited the lyrics of the Robert Frost poem "Nothing Gold Can Stay."

At Dannemorra, Tupac became engaged to a recent graduate of John Jay College who planned to go to law school, didn't smoke marijuana, and refused to sleep with him on their first date. "She's my first and only girlfriend ever," he told an interviewer, shortly before marrying the young woman. *VIBE* printed a prison interview in which Tupac seemed to take full responsibility for what had happened to Ayanna Jackson at the Parker-Meridian Hotel: "Even though I'm innocent of the charge, I'm not innocent in terms of the way I was acting . . . I'm just as guilty for doing nothing as I am for doing things." He was "ashamed," Tupac said, about not intervening to defend the young woman from the two men who actually did rape her.

At the same time he made these pronouncements, however, Tupac was plotting revenge against those he believed were responsible for the shooting at Quad Studios: Puffy Combs, Andre Harrell, and Biggie Smalls (whose single "One More Chance" had just hit No. 1 on *Billboard*'s chart). Biggie's involvement was what cut him deepest, said Tupac, who had been convinced by letters he received at Dannemora that the Brooklyn rapper helped set him up. When Tupac made his accusations public in an interview with *VIBE*, Biggie, Puffy, and Andre Harrell replied with a brief letter to the editor in which the three denied they had anything to do with the shooting, then expressed the hope that the feud between the East and West coasts could be brought to an end. Puffy Combs claimed that he had written personally to Tupac asking for a meeting to clear the air, and assured the imprisoned rap star that he and Biggie "got nothing but love for you."

Next to his prison sentence, Tupac's biggest problems were financial. The attorneys he hired to defend him against lawsuits and criminal charges all across the country had exhausted his bank accounts. During the past several years, he had become the sole supporter of his mother, his sister, her baby, his aunt, her children, as well as assorted cousins and hangers-on. Even as he renounced gangsta rap and made plans to move to Arizona with his new bride and raise children in the sunshine, Suge Knight was beckoning from the shadows, promising not only to solve all his money problems but to secure his release from prison as well. Tupac's childhood friend Watani Tyehimba visited him in prison during the late summer of 1995 and begged the rapper not to sign a contract with Death Row Records. Sobbing, Tyehimba recalled, Tupac hugged him tight and said, "I know I'm selling my soul to the devil."

Tupac signed the three-page handwritten agreement drafted by David Kenner during the early autumn, and on October 12, the day he was released from Dannemora, he flew back to Los Angeles with Knight and Kenner aboard a private jet. He was in a Death Row recording studio that same night. Overwhelmed with gratitude for his release from prison, Tupac parroted Suge Knight in an interview with *Source* magazine: "Whether the odds are in your favor or appear to be stacked against you, the Death Row family sticks with you."

Tupac Shakur's mother, sister, aunt, and assorted other relatives who depended upon him for support now were part of the Death Row family, also. Shortly after he signed Tupac to a recording contract, Suge Knight bought Afeni Shakur a new home, and when she and her relations visited Los Angeles, Suge lodged them in a luxury hotel, the Westwood Marquis, where they ran up huge room service bills. Tupac was spending his days, and most of his nights as well, at Death Row's studios in Tarzana, where producers were amazed by the facility with which he wrote and recorded rap lyrics, despite being high on marijuana and drinking heavily most of the time.

What Suge received in exchange for his largesse was the reflected glow of his new rapper's starlight. Tupac was by far the biggest celebrity in the history of the genre, aided considerably by his film appearances. During late 1995 and early 1996, dozens of stories appeared in the hip-hop press suggesting that only the fearsome Suge Knight, with his gangbanger thugs and audacious street tactics, could protect Shakur from those who wanted him dead. Tupac bristled at stories that described him as a frightened and demoralized figure who had lost a testicle in a shoot-out, then been raped in prison, yet continued to sing the praises of Suge Knight and Death Row Records. "There's nobody in the business strong enough to scare me," he boasted in one interview. "I'm with Death Row 'cause they not scared either. When I was in jail, Suge was the only one who used to see me. Nigga used to fly a private plane all the way to New York to spend time with me."

Suge, meanwhile, was going ever more public with his thuggery, and Death Row's partners at Interscope seemed not to mind much. Jimmy Iovine would tell federal investigators he was unaware that Michael Harris had bankrolled Death Row's inception until December of 1995, when Harry-O threatened Interscope and Time Warner with a lawsuit that demanded his share of the company's profits. Most people in the record business had been hearing rumors for years that the "Ghetto Godfather" had financed Death Row's startup, however. And Harry-O himself had sent Iovine a threatening letter in the summer of 1995 that prompted the head of Time Warner's music division, Michael Fuchs, to attempt a prison meeting with Harris. Few employees of Death Row doubted that Iovine was informed when Jake Robles and a group of other Bloods showed up at the offices the record label shared with Interscope and literally seized the office of Fade Duvernay, the head of Interscope's rap promotion department. And Iovine, they said, had to know that when Duvernay objected Suge and his henchmen responded by dragging the Interscope executive out of a meeting and choking him nearly unconscious in an adjacent office.

Suge seemed to believe he could get away with just about any-thing, more than a few observers said, especially since the appear-ance of David Kenner at his side. Those who did business with Death Row felt increasing dread. Happy Walters, who managed rap acts like Cypress Hill and House of Pain, was said to have engaged in a shout-ing match with Suge over who would appear on a soundtrack album. A few days later, while withdrawing money from an ATM machine, Happy disappeared, and terror spread like a virus through the music industry in Los Angeles. Loud Records owner Steve Rifkind, who was said to have engaged in a public dispute with Suge over the group Wu-Tang Clan, reportedly hired Knight's former UNLV football teammate Bigga B as his personal bodyguard, insisting that Bigga escort him between his home and office each morning and evening. Rifkind denied the story, but Bigga B told a reporter that the Loud owner was so scared "he wouldn't even go take a piss by himself."

Happy Walters turned up several days after his disappearance, wandering the streets "incoherent, shaved, and naked," as one report put it, and covered with cigarette burns, according to another. When he was taken to a hospital, Walters claimed he had amnesia and re-fused to speak Suge Knight's name.

The rapper and producer Warren G., angry that he was being robbed of credit by Knight and Dr. Dre, rashly advised an interviewer from the *Source* that he had "made" Death Row Records, only to phone the magazine a few days later and plead that the editors not publish his remarks. The quote appeared in print anyway, and soon after a story spread among Death Row's staff that Warren G. had been visited in the middle of the night by several Bloods who stuck guns in his face and warned him to watch what he said. All anyone knew for certain was that Warren G., obviously shaken, began carrying a pair of 9mm pistols.

Suge Knight demonstrated an ability to control his employees with more subtle but equally ruthless methods. He brought dozens of rappers and musicians, both aspiring and established, into Death Row's studios to collaborate on songs he might or might not use, on this record or that one. Very rarely did the unknowns among them ask for or receive contracts, and when the songs did appear on CDs, very few of them asked for money. Advancing their careers in any way they could, most felt, was payment enough. Even stars were kept on short leashes, often working for future considerations that might be some time in arriving. Months after his album *Doggystyle* rose to the top of the charts, Snoop Dogg still was living in an unfurnished apartment. Suge frequently rented apartments for songwriters, musicians, or singers who showed him talent, and even after their work began to appear on hit records some continued to exist hand-to-mouth, dependent upon Suge not only for a place to live but even for food money.

For Tupac Shakur, however, Suge spared no expense. Tupac's inclusion in the Death Row roster not only fueled the gaudy opulence that for many young Bloods had become the signal fact of affiliation with the label, but also resulted in an increased definition of the organization's hierarchy. Shortly after signing Tupac, Suge purchased a dozen gold rings that spelled out M.O.B. (for "Member of the Bloods"), one with the letters outlined in diamonds and rubies for himself, five more with just diamonds for his most trusted thugs, and six others in plain gold for executives of lesser status. Suge's gifts of heavy gold medallions, in which the hooded figure in the electric chair—still Death Row's symbol—had been encrusted with rubies and diamonds, marked recipients as members of his inner circle.

The red leather chair behind the desk in Knight's office had become the throne of a tyrant who liked to impress visitors by feeding his piranhas live rats, or bringing his guard dog Damu to a full bristle with a whispered command. Obsessed with the Cuban drug dealer Tony Montana, played by Al Pacino in the film *Scarface*, Suge began to mimic the character's paranoia, filling a cabinet behind his desk with six television sets that permitted him to surveil virtually every square inch of Death Row's studios.

The killing of Kelly Jamerson at the El Rey Theater in March of 1995, followed by Mark Anthony Bell's beating nine months later, along with persistent rumors that Death Row Records was dealing in drugs and guns, increased scrutiny of Knight and his record label both in the media and among law enforcement, but Suge shrugged off accusations that he was more criminal than businessman, as the gossip of those motivated by either envy or prejudice. "There are still individuals in this society who can't stand the thought of a young black person with a gang of money in the bank," he told one interviewer. When the *Los Angeles Times* reported that Death Row was the subject of a federal investigation into alleged ties with organized crime figures in New York and Chicago, Suge told the paper's reporter, "A black brother from Compton creates a company that helps people in the ghetto, so what does the government do? They try to bring him down. Sometimes people get sacrificed when they stand up. Martin Luther King, Malcolm X." And now, apparently, Suge Knight. "Sometimes they take away your life," Suge told the *Times.* "Sometimes they take away your freedom. It's sad."

Unlike Martin and Malcolm, Suge was lucky in his enemies. Attacks on gangsta rap had begun in the early 1990s, when a Harlem minister named Calvin Butts organized a protest march outside Sony's headquarters in midtown Manhattan. After the reverend changed his mind, however (deciding that rappers were only reflecting the problems of life in the inner city), the cultural right made a gigantic mistake by replacing him with Dr. C. DeLores Tucker. For the ten or twelve months after Tucker formed the National Political Congress of Black Women in 1993, demanding that corporate America assist in the suppression of this hateful music, the woman enjoyed enormous success. Allied with William Bennett and his Empower America movement, she made appearances on virtually every major television news program, saw her letters printed on *The New York Times* op-ed page, obtained a position on the NAACP's Board of Trustees, and then used it to prevent the organization from giving Tupac Shakur its 1994 Image Award. After Tucker delivered a seventeen-minute speech at Time Warner's annual shareholders meeting, the company's executives were so cowed that they decided to sell their 50 percent interest in Interscope back to Ted Field, who promptly sold the same shares to Edgar Bronfman Jr.'s MCA.

An enraged Suge Knight mounted a highly effective counterat-
tack, aided in considerable part by the questionable character of
C. DeLores Tucker. At first Suge's claim that Tucker had asked him
to leave Death Row and work for her at a new Time Warner label,
promising $80 million and two state-of-the-art recording studios,
sounded ludicrous. But as the media learned more about Tucker's
background, what Suge said sounded increasingly plausible. Though
she called herself "Doctor," it turned out that Tucker had no college
degree. And while she had indeed been the highest-ranking black
woman in the state government while serving as Pennsylvania's com-
monwealth secretary during the 1970s, Tucker also was the subject of
a three-month investigation at the end of her term in which it was discovered that she had used state employees to write speeches for which
she was paid more than $66,000. When Tucker claimed that the FBI,
at her instigation, was investigating the sale of gangsta rap records to
minors, the agency quickly issued a denial and her credibility was further undermined. An embarrassed Bill Bennett was already backing
away by the time Suge purchased a two-page ad in *The Source* that
printed a long list of "Freedom Fighters," including Martin Luther King
Jr., Harriet Tubman, Nelson Mandela, Marcus Garvey, and others.
The name "C. DeLores Tucker" also appeared on the list, but it had
been crossed out by a red line, which among members of the Bloods
was a way of marking someone for death. That same month, Suge
delivered Snoop Dogg's new album *Dogg Food* to stores on Halloween.
"Suge thought, 'They're all so scared of it, I'll release it on the scariest
night of the year,'" a reporter explained.

The album quickly went platinum, and by early 1996 just about
everyone in the music industry agreed with what David Geffen told
Rolling Stone: "The decision to dump Interscope was a gigantic error
for Time Warner and a great opportunity for Edgar Bronfman."

By February of 1996, as Snoop Dogg sat in a downtown Los Angeles
courtroom listening to final arguments at his first-degree murder trial,

many of Death Row Records' biggest names had begun to ask them-selves where exactly Suge Knight was leading them. "This is some serious shit," said an obviously daunted Snoop outside the courtroom, where he stood wearing a suit and tie that had replaced the flannel shirts he'd worn early in the trial.

The charges against the rapper arose from a killing almost three years earlier in which a twenty-year-old Ethiopian named Philip Woldemariam was shot in the back by Snoop's bodyguard McKinley Lee. Apart from Snoop's celebrity, the scenarios of Woldemariam's death offered by both prosecution and defense were depressingly fa-miliar. The incident began outside Snoop's apartment in Palms, each side agreed, when Snoop's friend Sean Abrams flashed a gang sign at Woldemariam as the young Ethiopian and two of his friends drove past. The car stopped, epithets were exchanged, and Snoop's body-guard Lee ran downstairs to intervene. Woldemariam and friends drove away, but less than an hour later Snoop was behind the wheel of his Jeep, with Lee in the passenger seat and Abrams in the back, as they prowled the neighborhood. The three found Woldemariam and his friends at nearby Woodbine Park, where the group was dining on takeout Mexican food. What happened next was a matter of dis-pute. According to the defense attorneys (David Kenner for Snoop, Johnnie Cochran for Abrams and Donald Re for Lee), Woldemariam reached for the .38 he wore in his waistband, forcing McKinley Lee to draw his own gun and shoot the Ethiopian in self-defense. The prosecution countered that Snoop and his friends had pursued Woldemariam to the park and that the shots fired by Lee had hit the Ethiopian in his buttocks and back. How could that be self-defense?

Apart from Snoop's celebrity status (among those who made an appearance in court to show their support were Suge Knight, M.C. Hammer, and Tupac Shakur), the defense had three major advan-tages. The first was Kenner, who hammered at several key prosecu-tion witnesses so relentlessly that jurors sat shaking their heads and suppressing smiles. Secondly, one of Philip Woldemariam's compan-ions astounded the prosecution by changing his story, explaining in court that the Ethiopian *had* reached for his gun, and that, after the shooting, he and Woldemariam's other companion removed the gun from their friend's hand to ensure Snoop's conviction. Thirdly, key evidence in the case that included bloody clothing and shell casings had been destroyed or removed from the property room at the LAPD's Pacific Division.

The jury returned not guilty verdicts on all counts. Snoop was collected outside the Criminal Courts building by a chauffeur-driven Rolls-Royce dispatched by Suge Knight. That evening, Snoop joined Suge and his entourage for a party at Monty's Steakhouse, where guests, who included not only Tupac and Hammer but also several members of the jury, dined on crab legs and lobster tails.

Though all smiles that evening, Snoop was badly shaken by his ordeal. Within a matter of months he would begin talking about the "change of direction" that resulted eventually in his parting of the ways with Suge Knight and Death Row Records. Others, though, would leave first. The only performer to meet Suge head-on was RBX, who also happened to be the single Death Row rapper who was a match for him physically. The beef between the two had started in a dressing room at the New Regal Theater on Chicago's south side, over something so stupid that those who heard the story could barely believe it: Suge had become infuriated when RBX ate some fried chicken Knight had ordered for his homeboys. An incredulous RBX stayed right in Suge's face until Knight pulled out a pistol and handed it to one of his homies. "If I whup your ass, this nigga's likely to shoot me," RBX observed. Violence was averted when Snoop Dogg reminded Suge that RBX was his cousin and said to please let it pass, but the incident raised serious doubts about Knight's leadership. It had been obvious for some time that Suge was more concerned with how he looked to the Piru Bloods who made up his entourage than about maintaining good relations with his performers and musicians. To end his relationship with a rapper who had performed on records that sold millions of copies over nothing more than a few pieces of fried chicken, though, was flat-out insanity. And more than a few people listened when RBX began to say that Suge was not only a bully but a coward who couldn't fight a man his own size without thugs on hand to make sure he finished on top.

The D.O.C. was the next to pull away, explaining that he had relocated to Atlanta because "there was too much drama out there in L.A." Soon after, RBX made a final break with Death Row by refusing to perform as the voice of Satan on Snoop's "Murder Was the Case," a song about a murdered young man who returns to earth by making a deal with the devil. RBX signed shortly thereafter with Giant Records, where he promptly recorded an album that attacked Death Row in general and Dr. Dre in particular.

Several interviewers would force Dre to acknowledge that the departure of RBX from Death Row was similar to the way he had left Ruthless Records. Snoop Dogg, caught in the middle, broke with RBX and told an interviewer, "This is a family thang on Death Row, and Dre is the godfather."

The godfather, however, was no longer happy in the Death Row family, either. Dre's life was a debacle, and he had mostly himself to blame. During the past four years he had pleaded guilty to battery of a police officer in New Orleans, escaped criminal assault charges by settling out of court with former *Pump It Up* hostess Deniece Barnes, and pleaded no contest to breaking the jaw of rap producer Damon Thomas. After leading several LAPD squad cars on a high-speed chase that ended when he drove off a cliff, Dre was under house arrest for the third time since October of 1992. He owned a beautiful home in which to serve his confinement, but the place had burned nearly to the ground a few months earlier during a crapulous barbecue at which many of the guests were hard-core gang members. Suge's Bloods had been turning Dre's "swim parties" into melees for months, deafening neighbors with the thumping bass lines of their music, having public sex with groupies, weaving drunkenly through a neighborhood where most of the homes were surrounded by gates, and turning the living room of Dre's own French Colonial into a boxing ring. Jerry Heller, who lived only a few doors down, described driving past when the house caught fire and seeing a drunken Dre in the street laughing with his friends. Dre moved temporarily into an apartment on Venice Boulevard, but was promptly evicted. Now the twenty-nine-year-old Grammy winner, who had just been dubbed by *Newsweek* "the Phil Spector of rap" was living with his mother.

Throughout the music industry, Dre was regarded as a talented producer and a dangerous fool. He never had been a real gangbanger, though, and a lot of people who knew Dre well said his personality was softer than that of almost anyone else at Death Row. When a judge threatened to put Dre in L.A. County Jail, Suge Knight told David Kenner, "He can't go in there. Them motherfuckers will kill him. He ain't from the street."

Dre finally was ready to agree. In March of 1996 he put in a call to Jimmy Iovine at Interscope, said he wanted out of Death Row, and suggested starting a new label. "I don't like it [at Death Row] no more," Dre explained to an interviewer. "The mentality there is that you have to be mad at somebody in order for yourself to feel good or make a record." Observers were astonished that Suge accepted Dre's departure, though most understood this better when they learned that Dre had agreed to forfeit an enormous financial stake in the company in order to obtain his freedom.

At Death Row, however, Dre became almost as hated an enemy as Puffy Combs during the next few months. Everyone who wanted to stay with the label was required to revile him. All during that spring and into early summer, Tupac Shakur went out of his way to prove his loyalty to Suge by dissing Dre, accusing him in one interview of regularly robbing credit from other producers. "He was owning the company and chillin' in his house," Tupac said, "while I'm out here in the streets stompin' nigga's asses, startin' wars and shit, droppin' albums, doin' my thang, and this nigga takin' three years to do one song!" Tupac then accused Dre in not one but two new songs of being a closet homosexual—"gay ass Dre," he called his former producer on "To Live and Die in L.A."

Shakur also joined in a brutal attack on one of Dre's closest friends,

producer Sam "Sneed" Anderson. The incident took place at Death
Row's offices in Westwood. Sneed had been summoned to the meeting supposedly to discuss working on a new album by Snoop Dogg.
Things turned nasty very quickly, however, and after Suge accused
him of being "slick," Sneed was certainly beaten and possibly subjected
to a sexual assault. "I don't wanna go into that," Sneed later told an
interviewer. "A few people put their hands on me and I lost respect for
all of them." What Suge really wanted from Sneed, reportedly, was the
name of Dr. Dre's homosexual lover. When Sneed said he had never
even heard that Dre was gay, an entire gang of rappers, Tupac included,
fell on him, punching him to the ground, then kicking and stomping at
him where he lay rolled up in a ball. He thought he was about to die,
Sneed said, but Suge stopped the others short, and let him stagger out
of the office with his face bathed in blood.

Suge continued to harrass Dre, phoning his house to demand
that he surrender Death Row's master tapes. Finally, "I sent somebody over to Dre's house to get the masters," Suge told *The Source*.
When Dre wouldn't open the door, he went over himself, Suge explained: "I come through the gate, see motherfucker's runnin' and
hidin'." Eventually a dozen LAPD squad cars were summoned to the
scene. "But it wasn't no thang," Suge said. "I played a couple games
of pool, got my shit, and left."

Dre's version of the incident was that someone rang his bell,
claiming to be Jimmy Iovine. When he opened the door, Dre said,
"In comes Suge with eight or nine niggas . . . Suge said, 'We tryin' to
get the tapes.'" When he told Suge the tapes were being copied right
now, Dre recalled, Suge said he would wait, then suggested that he
put the Death Row logo on his next album. Several days later the
two met at Gladstone's restaurant in Malibu and reportedly worked
out their differences. But when Suge was asked about their parting
of the ways, he answered, "The nigga just kind of hid. Stopped callin'."

All Dre cared about was that Death Row at last seemed ready
to leave him be. Suge couldn't afford to let Tupac Shakur simply walk
away, however.

CHAPTER FIVE

Tupac tipped his hand more by what he did than by anything he said. During early 1996, he insisted upon negotiating his movie deals without Suge Knight's agency. And in February of 1996, Death Row's biggest star formed his own and entirely separate production company, Euphanasia, then brought his old friend Yaasmyn Fula to L.A. to run the business. From the first, Fula found it difficult to obtain any financial accounting from Death Row Records. Whenever she sent Suge Knight's office a request for documents, Fula said, what she received instead were cars and jewelry. She began to feel "there was this dark cloud over us," Fula told *The New Yorker*'s Connie Bruck. "I knew so much was wrong." While Tupac would not let Fula prod Suge Knight with legal threats, he did refuse to let any of his younger cousins sign contracts with Death Row. Tupac also began to rely increasingly on his East Coast attorney, Harvard Law School professor Charles Ogletree, who was frustrated by his dealings with the rapper's Los Angeles lawyer, David Kenner. Since Tupac's finances were entirely controlled by Death Row, he had no choice but to rely on the record company's assistance in settling Tupac's numerous civil lawsuits, Ogletree complained. David Kenner would tell him the check was in the mail, then that it was being sent by FedEx, then that it was being wired. The money never seemed to arrive, however.

By that summer, Tupac had become increasingly overt about his plan to escape Death Row. "He had a strategy," Ogletree told

Connie Bruck. "The idea was to maintain a friendly relationship with Suge, but to separate his business." That was not a difficult thing to accomplish legally, Ogletree said, "but you have to live after that . . . It was a question of how to walk away with your limbs attached and your bodily functions operating."

Tupac and Suge at least were still united in hostility toward their rivals at Bad Boy Entertainment. Tupac's first album released by Death Row Records, 1996's *All Eyez on Me*, sold more than half a million copies during its first week in the stores, earning $10 million, second only to *The Beatles Anthology* as the best commercial opening in the history of the music industry. Executives at other labels were duly impressed, but even more astonished by the vehemence of Tupac's attack on Puffy Combs and East Coast rappers in the song "Hit 'Em Up." Especially startling was Tupac's vicious assault on Biggie Smalls, whom he continued to blame for his shooting at Quad Studios. For several months before the album's release, Tupac had been seen at parties in L.A. with Biggie's wife, singer Faith Evans. Evans, who knew that her husband had been carrying on with his former flame L'il Kim, called Tupac "mad cool" in one interview, and agreed to perform with him on a number for Shakur's new album. Biggie's wife was startled and embarrassed, however, when the song came out with the title "Wonda Why They Call U Bitch." Even more humiliating was Tupac's claim to an interviewer from the *Source* that he had been sleeping with Faith. Tupac repeated this claim, only much more crudely, on "Hit 'Em Up:" "I fucked your bitch, you fat motherfucker."

Biggie handled the attendant publicity with an impressive aplomb. "If honey was to give you the pussy," he told an interviewer, "why would you disrespect her like that? If you had a beef with me, and you're like, 'Boom, I'm a fuck his wife,' why would you be so harsh on her? Like you got a beef with her. That shit doesn't make sense."

Little more than a month after the release of *All Eyez on Me*, Biggie came to Los Angeles to accept an award at the 1996 Soul Train Awards and in his speech thanked Brooklyn. Loud jeers erupted from the Death Row section of the audience. Afterward, Biggie and Tupac came face to face for the first time in almost two years. When he looked in Tupac's eyes, Biggie said, "I thought, 'Yo, this nigga is really buggin' the fuck out.'" Suge Knight was at Tupac's side, and both were surrounded by a security squad of bad-looking Bloods as they began to shout, "We gonna settle this right now!" Bad Boy rapper L'il Caesar shouted from behind the Southside Crips who were working security for Biggie, "Fuck you! Fuck you, nigga! East Coast, motherfucker!" Tupac yelled back, "We on the West Side now! We gonna handle this shit!" As the two sides faced off, one of the Crips drew a gun and the crowd scattered from the clutch of scuffling, shouting gangbangers.

After the incident, both Biggie and Puffy Combs admitted that the East Coast–West Coast feud was real. Tupac "ain't mad at the niggas that shot him," Puffy told an interviewer. "He knows where they're at. He knows who shot him. If you ask him, he knows, and everybody in the street knows, and he's not stepping to them, because he knows he can't get away with that shit. To me, that's some real sucker shit."

Suge replied that the feud wasn't between the East and West Coasts, but between "ghetto niggas and phony niggas." Puffy, he said, was "a phony nigga. He's frontin', tryin to be somethin' he ain't. Here's the whole thang with Puffy: They say shit to make themselves bigger. I ain't never did no interview sayin' shit about people. By sayin' shit about Death Row in magazines, they tryin' to put themselves on our level, and it ain't no motherfuckin' comparison." Suge's proposed solution to the conflict was to put Puffy and Tupac in a boxing ring together. "Look at [Puffy's] body," Knight said. "Who can he whup? How you gon' talk shit and be in a girl's body? And I'll beat Biggie's ass all over the ring! We can do it in Vegas and give the money to the ghetto."

In April of 1996, Suge upped the ante by announcing that Death Row Records intended to open an East Coast division in Manhattan. Tupac advised a radio station in Oakland that Suge meant to sign New York–based acts like Big Daddy Kane and Wu-Tang Clan.

Observing from the sidelines, Dr. Dre commented, "If it keeps up this way, pretty soon niggas from the East Coast ain't gonna be able to come out here, and vice versa."

Suge Knight, however, brought a huge entourage with him to New York for the MTV Awards show on September 7. The group made an aggressively grand entrance, stalking past the music industry executives—some of them presidents of other labels, who waited in line with tickets in hand—to take seats without delay. After the show, the Death Row group had to be separated from Bad Boy's contingent by more than twenty NYPD officers.

Only a few weeks earlier, Puffy Combs had made his most ominous comments on the "East vs. West" feud in an interview with *VIBE:* "Bad boys move in silence. If somebody wants to get your ass, they're gonna wake up in heaven. There ain't no record gonna be made about it. It ain't gonna be no interviews; it's gonna be straight up. 'Oh, shit, where am I? What are these, wings on my back?'" Puffy had ended the interview by telling *VIBE,* "I'm ready for [this beef] to come to a head, however it got to go down. I'm ready for it to be out of my life and be over with."

Tupac Shakur seemed finally to feel the same way. His decision to leave Death Row had changed him, according to his fiancée Kidada Jones, whose father Quincy Jones owned *VIBE.* Tupac was tired of the lifestyle he had been sharing with Suge Knight, Kidada said. Instead of hanging out at strip clubs, she told an interviewer, Tupac had taken up cooking. After finishing his next album, the last he owed Death Row Records under the contract he had signed in the prison at Dannemora, Kidada said, Tupac might sign with Warner Bros. Her boyfriend also intended to move out of the house Death Row had leased for him and settle with her in another part of town, perhaps father a child.

Any doubt about Tupac's intention to break with Death Row had been removed on August 27, when the rapper made the move that a lot of people predicted would get him killed—firing David Kenner as his attorney. Outside the MTV Awards show one week later, Tupac seemed intent upon defusing rather than escalating the East vs. West feud. "We are businessmen. We are not animals," he told the interviewer for a film crew who asked what would happen if Death Row met Bad Boy inside. "It's not like we're going to see them and rush them and jump on them."

As word that Tupac Shakur had discharged David Kenner spread through the music industry, Suge Knight insisted the problem was between the two of them and that he had no hard feelings toward Tupac. At the MTV Awards in New York, Suge invited Tupac to join him in Las Vegas for the Mike Tyson–Bruce Seldon heavyweight title fight three days later, on September 7. Tupac seemed to sense that his attendance would put him at risk, and on the morning of the seventh he told Yaasmyn Fula that instead he would go to Atlanta to deal with some problems among his relatives. During the next several hours, Suge Knight convinced Shakur to change his mind and go to Las Vegas after all, but Tupac confided to Kidada Jones that he still felt uneasy about the trip. She advised him to wear his bullet-proof vest, but Tupac said the weather was too hot for that. Late that afternoon, he boarded a flight to Vegas and said good-bye to Los Angeles for the last time.

Suge Knight had spent much of the past year establishing himself as a presence in Las Vegas. The most visible indication of how Suge hoped to be viewed in Sin City was the house he purchased on Monte Rosa Avenue in the Paradise Valley Township, home to both the toniest estates and most influential citizens in the Las Vegas Valley. Suge's new house was right across the street from Wayne Newton's Shenandoah Ranch, and just two doors down from the home of fighter Mike Tyson, who had persuaded Knight to buy the place. Built of red brick, the house was a sprawling 5,215 feet set on 1.33 acres, with a backyard that bordered a golf course. Suge first had seen it in the Martin Scorsese film *Casino,* where it served as the home of the organized crime character played by Robert De Niro, Frank "Lefty"

Rosenthal. Suge wore a seven-carat diamond in his ear when he made the deal to buy the place, then proceeded to redecorate in a style not seen previously even in garish Las Vegas, painting the bottom of his swimming pool blood red, then covering the interior of his home with same color carpet. Much of the furniture was red, too, as was the Rolls-Royce Corniche that Suge drove around town.

Even before he purchased his house in Paradise Valley, Suge had endeavored to form associations with those connected to the organized crime families of New York and Chicago. Among the first Las Vegas attorneys he hired was John Spilotro, whose father, "Tony the Ant" Spilotro, had been headman for the Chicago mob during most of the 1970s (before being brutally beaten, then buried alive in an Indiana cornfield). Suge would step up a class when he retained the services of the notorious Oscar Goodman, an attorney who billed himself as "Mouthpiece for the Mob" and represented most of the important Mafiosi charged with crimes in Nevada, as well as Goodman's partner, the former U.S. Attorney David Chesoff.

To open his new nightclub just off The Strip, Suge had relied upon the only two Caucasians who were significant figures at Death Row Records. The first, of course, was David Kenner, whose connections to the Genovese Family had long fascinated Suge. Perhaps even more helpful, though, was the accountant Suge had hired as Death Row's new business manager, Steve Cantrock. It was Cantrock who introduced Suge to Robert Amira, the Las Vegas "businessman" who several years earlier had been indicted along with Joseph Colombo Jr. and Alphonse "the Whale" Merolla in a scheme to defraud the Dunes Hotel with an airline ticket scam. (The case against Amira had been dismissed—in inimitable Las Vegas fashion—when the judge claimed he had seen the prosecutor and the jury foreman communicating improperly.) With Amira's assistance, Suge was able to take possession of a club that had been known as Botany's back during his days at UNLV, when the patrons were mostly wealthy white people. Botany's previous owner had been convicted a few years earlier for helping the Chicago mob skim money from the Stardust Hotel, however, and the nightclub had languished ever since. Suge reopened the venue as the 662 Club, and catered to a predominantly black clientele. The name "662" had multiple meanings. On a phone pad, those numbers spelled out MOB, for Member of the Bloods. Tupac Shakur liked to say the letters stood for Money Over Bitches. The numbers 662 also appeared in the California Penal Code, however, where they were used to refer to Death Row inmates.

Tupac's first performance after his release from the New York state prison system had been at the 662 Club in November of 1995. The club was packed to nearly twice its capacity that evening, and a crowd that included the entourages of athletes Mike Tyson and Deion Sanders got completely out of hand. The Las Vegas police were not happy about being forced to deal with this many drunk and dangerously violent characters, and threatened to close the place down.

The scene was only slightly less rowdy when Suge brought Tupac and Snoop Dogg back to Las Vegas with him for the Mike Tyson–Frank Bruno fight in the spring of 1996, and again when Suge and his Death Row entourage opened the club after Tyson's fight with Peter McNealy that August. Suge did post himself at the door of the club that night, and personally tossed several troublemakers out into the parking lot, but the cops were furious anyway about the trouble the 662 Club was causing them, and followed through on their promise to close the place. Knight was able to open the club for the evening of the Tyson-Seldon fight on September 7 only by arranging to have his after party sponsored by Las Vegas PD Officer Patrick Barry, a retired professional boxer who was ostensibly using the event to raise money for Barry's Boxing Gym. A big sign on the club's marquee advertised the event as "Barry's Boxing Benefit," while smaller letters identified the organizer as "SKP" (Suge Knight Productions). A line started forming outside the club at 5:30 that afternoon, hours before the fight's scheduled start, and hundreds of people were trying to buy $75 tickets for the 662 Club's party.

Tupac Shakur was staying with Kidada Jones at the Luxor Hotel in one of the rooms Suge had booked for the weekend. Although his backup singers the Outlaw Immortalz served as both an entourage and a security detail, Tupac's two main bodyguards were a pair of black ex–police officers, Kevin Hackie and Frank Alexander. Hackie wasn't in Las Vegas, however, having fallen out with Death Row's head of security, Reggie Wright Jr., over $10,000 he had been paid to work on the set of Tupac's most recent film, *Gang Related*. That money should have been paid to Wrightway Protective Services, insisted Wright, who retaliated by firing the bodyguard. Frank Alexander was alone when he arrived for a meeting with Suge's Las Vegas attorneys, who explained that neither Alexander nor any of Tupac's other security personnel could carry firearms, because Death Row had failed to secure the proper clearances from the police.

While Alexander fretted about Tupac's vulnerability, the rapper himself was losing big at a blackjack table in the Luxor. The other members of the Death Row contingent noticed right off that Tupac wasn't wearing the medallion of the hooded figure in an electric chair that had been around his neck since Suge presented him with it months earlier. The new figure on Tupac's gold chain was a $30,000 diamond-studded replication of the emblem he had chosen for his own company, Euphanasia: a black angel of death, on its knees, head tilted down, backed by enormous wings and a golden halo. Tupac finally broke his losing streak and was ahead of the game when he left the casino and made his way across a footbridge to the MGM Grand, where the Tyson-Bruno fight would take place.

Since his release from prison following a rape conviction, Tyson had become a heroic figure for many ghetto gangbangers and an honorary member of the Death Row family. Suge attended every one of his fights, and so did Tupac. Included with Knight and Shakur in the crowd that evening would be the Reverend Jesse Jackson, basketball stars Charles Barkley and Magic Johnson, as well as the hip-hop acts Run-DMC and Too Short.

At the entrance to the big room where the MGM Grand staged its fights, Tupac was forced to stop and wait for Suge, who had the tickets. It had become commonplace in recent months for Suge to keep even his biggest stars waiting two, three, four, even five hours so that he could make an entrance that established his dominance over them. As he watched other celebrities slip inside and take their seats, Tupac was surrounded by fans who pressed forward, ducking under the arms of security guards to take his photograph or demand an autograph. Finally he lost his temper. "Fuck this shit!" he told Alexander. "Every time we go somewhere, he always has to be fuckin' late! I didn't want to come to Vegas, no fuckin' way. We gonna miss the fuckin' fight." Just as Shakur began to threaten to find his own tickets, Knight showed up. Tupac immediately wiped the angry expression from his face, recalled Alexander, who understood that the rapper still hoped for a more amicable parting with Suge than Dre had managed.

Suge and Tupac sat together, but weren't in their seats long. The fight was over in less than two minutes, as Tyson came out of his corner throwing punches at a furious rate and Seldon dropped to the canvas for good 109 seconds into the first round. While many at courtside were disappointed, and a few even shouted that the fight had been fixed, Tupac was thrilled by what he'd witnessed. He danced around with a wild look in his eyes, pumping his arms and throwing punches at the air as he shouted, "Fifty blows! Fifty blows! I counted them!" Tupac led the Death Row group backstage to mingle with Tyson, but after only a couple of minutes Suge announced that they had to leave. A startled Tupac complained that it would be the first time he had not congratulated Mike personally after a fight, but big Suge grabbed the little rapper's arm and led him toward the exit.

As they approached the auditorium's main entrance, Suge threw his arm around Tupac's shoulders, embracing him like the "little brother" that he often called his biggest star. Just as the two men passed through the doors, however, trailed by Alexander and Suge's entourage of Mob Piru homeboys, a Blood named Travon "Tray" Lane approached Tupac and whispered something in his ear. Alexander could see trouble coming, especially after he watched Tupac turn his head to stare at a young black man who stood on the other side of the hallway, "like he was anticipating the arrival of someone," as the bodyguard would put it later. The young man who stood alone was Orlando "Baby Lane" Anderson, a Southside Crip who, along with seven or eight of his homies, had jumped him, Tray said, outside a Foot Locker store in the Lakewood Mall. Anderson and the other Crips had snatched the Death Row medallion off the chain on his neck as they pummeled him, Tray said.

Anxious to impress Suge and the other Bloods with his continuing loyalty, Tupac immediately charged across the hallway toward Anderson, trailed by Knight and his entourage. "You from the South?" Tupac asked, but before Baby Lane could answer Tupac had thrown a punch at him. The Crip went to the ground immediately, recalled Alexander, who found it difficult to believe the skinny rapper could hit that hard. And Baby Lane offered almost no resistance, Alexander said, as Suge and the other Bloods surrounded him, punching, kicking, and stomping.

When Tupac's Euphanasia medallion tore loose and fell to the ground, the rapper stooped to pick it up. Alexander, a bodybuilder who once had finished second in the Mr. World Championship, seized the opportunity to pull Tupac away and half-drag, half-carry him toward the nearest exit. Suge and the others were still on Anderson, kicking him while he was down, recalled Alexander, until the hotel's security force arrived on the scene. Suge shouted, "Let's go!" and the others immediately scattered in different directions.

Alexander led Tupac outside without waiting around to watch what would happen next, but they were at once spotted by a huge crowd of groupies and hangers-on who chased them back to the Luxor. Kidada (whom Alexander considered a surly, snobbish brat) was waiting in their room at the Luxor, where Tupac regaled her with a description of the beating. She was giggling in excitement, recalled Alexander; the girl seemed to love this stuff, though she never got any closer than hearing about it from her boyfriend. Tupac didn't invite her to the party at the 662 Club, either, largely ignoring the young woman as he changed from a tan silk shirt and blue jeans into a black-and-white basketball tank top and teal-colored sweat pants, then led Alexander back downstairs.

As they stepped outside the main entrance to the Luxor, Suge and the rest of the Death Row entourage were loading into a caravan of vehicles for the drive to the 662 Club. They would go to his house first, announced Suge, who intended to delay their arrival so the group could make a grand entrance. Tupac wanted to drive his Hummer with Alexander in the passenger seat and two buddies from the Outlaws in back, but Suge told him that they had private business to discuss, and persuaded the rapper to ride with him in the big new BMW sedan he had purchased one week earlier. Tupac told Alexander to drive his friend Yafu Fula and another member of the Outlaws to Suge's place in Kidada's Lexus.

The group stayed only briefly at Knight's house, where everyone took a look at the new Death Row emblem painted on the bottom of the pool. The caravan that headed toward The Strip about fifteen minutes later was composed entirely of luxury vehicles—Mercedes, BMWs, Cadillacs, Lexuses. Suge's homies cranked up the Pioneer sound system in the Caddy they drove, so loud that "the ground was trembling," recalled Alexander, who followed right behind Suge's black BMW. Knight and Shakur were listening to Tupac's newest album, *Makaveli,* at an obliterating volume until a police officer riding a bicycle waved them over and forced Suge to turn the sound down. When the cop let them go, Suge continued toward The Strip. Alexander hoped that Suge would turn right on Tropicana, so that they could enter the club from the rear, but instead the BMW blew through a light and turned on Flamingo Road, where Tupac's approach to the club became a public spectacle. Cars filled with groupies whose breasts spilled out of low-cut dresses pulled up alongside to show Tupac their assets and angle for inclusion in his entourage.

By the time the caravan approached the Maxim Hotel, dozens of cars filled mostly with young women had joined it and the unarmed

Alexander was becoming increasingly nervous. Scores of people on the street and sidewalk angled for a glimpse of Tupac when Suge stopped for a red light at Korval Lane, right behind the black Cadillac his homeboy K-Dove drove. A Chrysler sedan immediately pulled up on the BMW's left, filled with four young women who smiled to catch Tupac's attention. Moments later, a white Cadillac screeched to a stop slightly in front and to the right of the BMW. Four young black men were inside, but only the one in the left rear seat opened his window, extending the .40 caliber Glock he used to spray the BMW's passenger side with between ten and fifteen bullets.

At least a hundred witnesses watched as Tupac tried to climb into the backseat of the BMW and was hit four times in the process. Two bullets tore open the "Thug Life" tattoo on his torso, while two others wounded him in the hand and leg. The Cadillac peeled away and made a right turn on Korval, heading away from The Strip.

Instead of calling 911 on his flip phone, Suge made a U-turn against the oncoming traffic as vehicles scattered to avoid a collision. The rest of the Death Row caravan did the same, jumping medians as they headed toward The Strip. Two bicycle cops who had heard the shots gave chase, and were able to catch the BMW only because two of the car's tires had been shot out. The shooting scene itself was abandoned, as witnesses scattered and the white Cadillac sped away.

When Suge stopped the BMW, the two bicycle cops approached with guns drawn and ordered him out of the car. Suge stepped outside with one side of his head dripping in blood and told the officers he had been shot in the head. They made him get down on his knees anyway, as ambulances and cars sped to the scene, which within moments had become a maelstrom of flashing lights and shrieking sirens. Many in the huge crowd rushed forward and tried to retrieve mementos from the BMW, tearing off side-view mirrors, wire-rimmed hubcaps, and door handles. The cops screamed at them to get back and threatened to arrest everyone in sight.

By the time paramedics delivered Tupac to Las Vegas's University Medical Center, he had lost a lot of blood. A team of surgeons removed his shattered left lung that night, then operated again the next morning. Doctors gave him a fifty-fifty chance of survival, then when Tupac regained consciousness said the odds might be better than that.

Outside the hospital, the Outlaw Immortalz held prayer vigils with the rapper's fans, who drove media photographers away whenever they tried to snap pictures. In the hospital lobby, a teenage girl chanted lyrics from Tupac's *All Eyez on Me* album: "Five shots and they still couldn't kill me." Outside Tupac's room, Jesse Jackson and Minister Tony Muhammed, head of the Nation of Islam's L.A. chapter, comforted the rapper's family. Jackson was said to be a close friend of Afeni Shakur's, but didn't sound much like it when he delivered a sermon the next day at a black church in Las Vegas. "Before you condemn Tupac for calling women bitches and ho's in his music, you need to understand and know about the background of this man," Jackson told both parishioners and the media in attendance. "He was raised by a mama who was on crack. He didn't have a real mama. Don't condemn him for talking about his mama and for talking about women."

The man the Las Vegas police were looking for was Suge Knight, who had left town despite being asked not to. When Suge was spotted at Death Row's offices in Beverly Hills on September 9, David Kenner promised the Vegas police that Mr. Knight would appear for questioning the next day, but Suge never showed. He did arrive at the Las Vegas PD's Homicide Headquarters on the evening of the eleventh, however, accompanied by Kenner, David Chesoff, and a third attorney. It was the only interview the Las Vegas police would ever conduct with Suge, and afterward the disgruntled detectives let reporters know that Knight had not been helpful in solving the case.

Less than forty-eight hours later, at 4:04 P.M. on Friday the thirteenth, twenty-five-year-old Tupac Shakur was pronounced dead from respiratory failure and cardiopulmonary arrest. Suge arrived at the hospital in a black Lexus moments after the announcement was made. When he stepped out of the car, the crowd went quiet. Reporters noted that the supposed gunshot wound on his head was barely visible. Upstairs, Suge spoke briefly with Tupac's family, then walked out the front entrance with a cigar between his teeth not ten minutes after his arrival.

Suge would discover his own vulnerability only four days later, when the Los Angeles County District Attorney's office announced that it was removing Larry Longo as the prosecutor on the case involving Suge's assault of the Stanley brothers at the Solar Records studios back in 1992. Word that Longo's daughter had signed a recording contract with Death Row was leaked to the media, and almost every statement that issued from the Longo family during the next few days would be met with derision. The most quoted comment was one Longo had made a month after Suge cut his deal for a suspended sentence: "I have never seen a guy transform as much as this guy has since he was first booked," the prosecutor had told reporters. "It's remarkable."

More remarkable to most of the media was the insistence of Longo's son Frank that he and David Kenner had "independently" negotiated the deal that made his eighteen-year-old sister Gina the first and only white performer signed by Death Row Records. Gina Longo defended herself by saying, "I'm no Milli Vanilli. The reason I'm on Death Row has nothing to do with my dad." Suge, meanwhile, managed to keep a straight face when he said that Gina had the voice of Billie Holiday, only in a white girl's body.

If anyone out there believed that, he was hard to find, especially in the district attorney's office. When Longo reported to work on the morning of October 25, his superiors told him to go home. Reporters who now knew that Suge Knight was living in the Longos' Malibu Colony home peppered the D.A.'s office with phone calls and questions. Lawrence Longo would be fired from his job before the end of the year.

The even worse news for Suge was that the attack on Orlando Anderson at the MGM Grand had been captured on videotape, and the D.A.'s office had decided to argue that Knight's participation in the beating was a violation of his probation. At almost the same moment, the judge who had agreed to Suge's "rather unusual" grant of probation, John Ouderkirk, was replaced by the much tougher Stephen Czuleger. Suge already had been sent to L.A. County Jail after failing a court-ordered drug test three days earlier. A hearing on a motion by the district attorney's office to revoke his probation was scheduled for February of 1997.

Suge's image only darkened during the next few weeks. On November 6, 1996, Knight was the subject of a report by ABC's *Primetime Live* that began, "Some say he's the most dangerous man in music . . ." Though the ABC report later would be discredited because of its reliance upon the exaggerated claims of Vanilla Ice, plenty of damage was done in the short term, as investigations of Suge by both news organizations and law enforcement agencies seemed to crop up on an almost weekly basis.

The most compelling media reports involved claims that start-up money for Death Row Records had been supplied not only by Michael Harris but also by another notorious drug kingpin, Ricardo Crockett. Suge had been stopped by police in Beverly Hills with a gun in his glove compartment that had been purchased illegally by an associate of Crockett's. Though convicted of transporting the gun across state lines, Suge won a grant of probation in federal court. At the same time, however, it was reported that the U.S. Justice Department had organized a multiagency task force to investigate claims that Suge and Death Row were trafficking in both guns and drugs.

The really bad news was that Steve Cantrock had become a federal witness. Cantrock worked for the conservative New York–based firm Coopers & Lybrand, but was known as one of the accounting trade's most colorful figures, a hippie turned hustler who enjoyed socializing with clients like the members of heavy metal rock bands Slaughter and White Zombie. He and Knight had seemed to hit it off at first, but they began to bicker during the summer of 1996 over Suge's suspicion that Cantrock was skimming money. And when American Express filed a lawsuit claiming that Suge Knight, David Kenner, and Kenner's wife had run up more than $1.5 million in unpaid bills, Suge and Kenner said that the expenses had been incurred by their "rogue accountant," Steve Cantrock.

Things came to a head at a meeting in the backyard of a San Fernando Valley home owned by singer Michel'le. From County Jail, Suge told reporters the meeting was Cantrock's idea and described what happened this way: "After I caught him stealing millions of dollars and confronted him, he started crying. I said, 'Okay, Steve, don't get so bent out of shape.'"

Cantrock's account was considerably different. Suge showed up for the meeting accompanied by not only David Kenner but also several of his Blood henchmen, Cantrock said, then began the meeting by stating, "All right, cut the bullshit. Steve, how much did you steal from me?" Before he could respond, Cantrock said, Suge doubled him over with a punch to the solar plexus. As he sank to the ground sobbing, Cantrock said, he heard Suge tell someone that he wanted a confession. David Kenner produced a handwritten document moments later and passed it to Suge, who handed it to him, Cantrock said, and told him he better sign it. Convinced he would die if he didn't, Cantrock said, he wrote his signature.

The accountant promptly disappeared. A security guard was posted in the lobby at the Los Angeles office of Coopers & Lybrand, where receptionists told callers that Cantrock was "away on stress leave." Word swiftly spread that Cantrock and his family had fled the country, but by late December of 1996 the *Los Angeles Times* was reporting that Cantrock had become a federal witness and would supply the U.S. Justice Department "with reams of documents detailing Death Row's financial dealings over the last three years."

Even as Suge hired Milton Grimes to represent him in the criminal racketeering investigation being conducted by the feds, he was forced to defend himself against a civil racketeering lawsuit filed by

Afeni Shakur that accused Knight, Kenner, and Death Row of "a pattern of fraud and deception" in their dealings with her late son. Suge
answered by claiming that in fact the Shakur estate owed *him* millions for monies advanced to Tupac and his family. Afeni asked reporters how it was possible that Tupac's albums could generate more
than $60 million in revenues for Death Row while the artist himself
received less than $1 million in royalties.

After American Express filed its lawsuit against Death Row,
creditors came out of the woodwork. One lawsuit asked for $75 mil-
lion and sought to have the record company put into receivership.
Suge's mentor Dick Griffey and his ex-rapper the D.O.C., meanwhile,
filed a $125 million breach of promise lawsuit against Death Row.

More ominous for Suge was the claim by Los Angeles Deputy
District Attorney Bill Hodgeman that Suge should be forced to serve
his nine-year prison sentence for the assault on the Stanley brothers.
The MGM Grand's videotape of the Orlando Anderson beating was
the strongest evidence against Suge, Hodgeman told the court. At
Knight's bail hearing, David Kenner argued that the tape showed Suge
had not been part of the assault, and in fact had tried to prevent others from attacking Anderson. When Judge Czuleger looked at the
tape, he agreed with Hodgeman: "It looks like he's trying to get a last
lick in, that's what it looks like to me." Ruling on Kenner's request
for bail, Czuleger said, "He's had every reason to believe things would
work out ... No one's said, 'Enough's enough. That's it.'" This judge
would; bail was denied.

While Suge sat in his cell at County Jail, word spread on the
street that Knight had bought out the jail commissary in order to
distribute gifts to the other Bloods and buy protection.

Death Row was still a force in the music business, but for how
long no one knew. The label would put out two of the three biggest-
selling rap albums of 1996 while Suge awaited his court hearing. First
came Tupac's posthumous *Makaveli,* followed shortly by Snoop Dogg's
The Doggfather. Unfortunately for Suge, however, Snoop was the only
real star still signed to Death Row, and he wanted to leave the label

in order to save his life. Snoop "presently owns and oftentimes travels in an armored van equipped with gun ports," Sharitha Knight would claim in a lawsuit that accused Snoop of failing to pay agent's commissions of $1.6 million during the time her Death Row subsidiary Knightlife served as his manager. "Death threats have been reported against the defendant. The defendant's life appears in jeopardy." In other words, an *LA Weekly* writer observed, "Sharitha Knight wants her money before Snoop gets shot."

Snoop, meanwhile, was already making plans for a life after Death Row, and during the next few months he would record cameos with nearly a dozen singers and rappers from other labels. He also began talking about a "reunion project" with Dr. Dre. "Snoop can't talk on it—nobody can, really—but everybody's trying to get away from Death Row," his father, Vernall Varnado, would advise another Los Angeles reporter.

When Suge showed up in court for his hearing in February of 1997, he was not wearing one of his famous red suits, but rather the blue jumpsuit of a Los Angeles County jail inmate. His most important witness, Southside Crip Orlando Anderson, also wore blue. Anderson, who had cursed Suge bitterly after the beating, now said that Knight played the peacemaker when Tupac Shakur and seven others attacked him at the MGM Grand. "I seen him pulling people off me," said Anderson, who described Suge as the only one yelling, "Stop this stuff!"

A pair of Compton police officers, however, told the court that Anderson's story had been quite different when they interviewed him in October of 1996. "He basically said he had been jumped by some Bloods. Also Suge and Tupac," one of them explained. A Las Vegas police detective said Anderson had told him that "Tupac and Suge beat him up pretty good." And the MGM Grand's security manager told Judge Czuleger that she had seen Suge kick Anderson three times.

Kenner's answer was a man who said he choreographed fight scenes for action movies and was good friends with Steven Seagal. He had watched the videotape a hundred times, said the man, who testified that a frame-by-frame breakdown had convinced him Suge's hands were in a defensive posture: "He's trying to stop the activity from [going] any further."

Judge Czuleger clearly wasn't buying it, and ruled that Suge was an "active participant" in the attack on Orlando Anderson. Before the judge could issue a final ruling, however, David Kenner produced a psychiatrist who was being paid $250 an hour to tell the court that he strongly disagreed with a probation report that claimed Mr. Knight was "criminally oriented." Mr. Knight was a socially active and concerned citizen of the black community who displayed neither a propensity for violence nor what he would describe as antisocial behavior, the doctor said: "He's not a dangerous person."

Kenner also called witnesses who testified that Suge was an advocate of black citizens who had distributed Thanksgiving turkeys and Christmas toys to the poor people of Compton while an inmate at County Jail. Suge was "a compassionate man," declared Danny J. Blakewell of the Brotherhood Crusade. Another witness noted the presence in court of C. DeLores Tucker, who believed that Suge could use his prominence to steer young black men away from gangs. This was a distinctly ironic moment, given that Suge had almost single-handedly destroyed Tucker's reputation, calling her, among other things, "a hoax" who claimed the title "Doctor" on the basis of honorary degrees from obscure colleges. Tucker was presently the target of a Death Row lawsuit that accused her of having an economic motive for her public criticism of gangsta rap. Still, the woman sat nodding in court as one Rahiem Jenkins told the court that if Dr. Tucker could forgive Suge Knight, then the judge too should "embrace him."

Suge himself took the stand to tell Judge Czuleger, "I definitely don't want to do my life behind bars, but if it's more positive for the community by me being incarcerated, I'm willing to sacrifice myself." He thanked C. DeLores Tucker, and said she had helped him come to a decision that he would never allow the word "nigger" to be used on another Death Row Records release.

Bill Hodgeman replied with a recitation of highlights from Suge's criminal history: A plea of guilty to battery with a deadly weapon in Las Vegas during 1987; pleas of guilty to separate charges of battery in Beverly Hills and Hollywood in 1990, and a plea of guilty to disturbing the peace in Van Nuys that same year; a conviction in 1991 when he gave a false name after being arrested in possession of a concealed weapon; another conviction, this one for assault with a deadly weapon, in Las Vegas in 1992; plus 1995 convictions for conspiracy to illegally possess a firearm and for assault with a firearm.

Judge Czuleger ordered that Suge should be detained by the California Department of Corrections for a ninety-day "diagnostic examination," then return to his courtroom in May to be sentenced to state prison.

Two weeks later, Biggie Smalls was shot dead in Los Angeles, and from the first day investigators let it be known that they considered Suge Knight the prime suspect.

PART THREE

NATURAL LEADS

Detective Poole is a self-motivator who is enthusiastic and consistently gets the job done. He has the quality of knowing what has to be done and does the job without being told. Detective Poole plans and organizes his caseload in a most efficient manner.

—From the "Performance Evalulation Report" filed on Detective Russell Poole for the period 10/1/94 to 3/18/95

CHAPTER SIX

For Russell Poole, his assignment to find the shooter in the Biggie Smalls slaying was an opportunity to escape the stricture of the Gaines-Lyga case. A murder investigation, Poole believed, would not be subject to the sort of bureaucratic intrigue that had frustrated his attempt to probe the links between the LAPD and Death Row Records. "I guess you could say ignorance was bliss," Poole recalled, "at least at the beginning."

By the time Poole joined them, homicide detectives from the LAPD's Wilshire Division had spent nearly one month building a case that appeared to be headed nowhere in particular. Not that the Wilshire detectives hadn't kept busy. The murder book on the Smalls investigation already was thick with witness interviews, clue notes and evidence analysis. The curious quality of it all, though, was that the picture that emerged could be at once so detailed and so sketchy.

Most of what the LAPD knew about Biggie's murder came from the ten young men who had been riding with him in the caravan of three vehicles that had just left the *VIBE* magazine party at the Petersen Automotive Museum. Puffy Combs, who had been sitting in the passenger seat of the Suburban just ahead of Biggie's, understood that coming to Los Angeles for that year's Soul Train Awards entailed a certain amount of risk. But Paul Offord, Bad Boy Entertainment's director of security (who had been riding in the "trail car" right behind Biggie's Suburban), explained to detectives that, with

Suge Knight in jail, there was a general feeling that the East vs. West feud was cooling off.

Prior to the shooting, Biggie and Puffy had spent almost a month in Los Angeles without incident. They were in town to promote Biggie's upcoming album, Puffy had explained to the Wilshire detectives, and to take advantage of L.A.'s superior production facilities to shoot and edit several videos that would be released with the album. Also, Biggie saw the trip as a chance to tell California radio listeners that he loved their state and wanted no trouble with anyone out here.

At the Soul Trains Awards on the evening of Friday, March 7, 1997, Biggie, who had been injured in an auto accident a month earlier, walked onstage to present an award with the aid of the cane he needed to help support his 6'3", 390-pound body. Before he could announce that the winner was R&B singer Toni Braxton, however, Biggie's voice was drowned out by boos from a contingent of Bloods who sat in the balcony throwing West Coast signs at him. "What's up Cali?" Biggie yelled back, his tone light yet defiant. The big rapper left the event almost immediately, however, and watched the rest of it on the television set in his suite in the Westwood Marquis. Puffy remained in his seat until the end of the awards ceremony, and afterward was able to depart without the sort of ugly confrontation that had spoiled the previous year's Soul Train Awards show.

Biggie and Puffy did not decide until the next afternoon that they would attend the *VIBE* after party on Saturday evening. The party was to be a closed event for music industry executives only, Puffy had been told, so security would not be a problem. The Bad Boy group assembled at the Hollywood Hills home of Andre Harrell, who now was CEO of Motown Records. Puffy had been staying with his former boss for the past week. He and Biggie and their entourage traveled to the Petersen Museum in three separate vehicles. In front was the white Suburban in which Combs rode with his man Kenneth Story at the wheel and three bodyguards in the backseat. Next came the gangbanger-green Suburban in which Biggie sat up front with his driver Gregory "G-Money" Young, while Junior Mafia rapper James Lloyd ("Li'l Caesar"), who had grown up with Biggie in Brooklyn, and Biggie's best friend, Damien ("D-Rock") Butler, sat in the backseat. The "trail car" was a black Chevy Blazer in which Bad Boy handyman Lewis ("Groovy Luv") Jones rode with Offord and an off-duty police officer who was working security for Biggie that night.

The scene at the Petersen Museum had been surpisingly mellow, everyone agreed, especially given the complications suggested by the guest list. Among the women in attendance, for example, were Biggie's estranged wife Faith Evans, Tupac Shakur's former fiancée Kidada Jones, and Suge Knight's estranged wife Sharitha. DJ Quik had shown up with ten Tree Top Pirus in tow, while the dozen or so Crips who wangled invitations included Orlando Anderson. Upon arrival, Biggie headed straight for a table in a dark corner, where he remained seated for the entire evening. When the deejay played Biggie's new rap homage to the West Coast, "Going Back to Cali," the crowd erupted in cheers, and there was a general feeling that, with Suge Knight removed from the scene, peace might be at hand.

By midnight, however, the museum was crammed with many more people than it was permitted to contain, and an overwhelming majority were smoking marijuana. At 12:30 A.M. the air was so thick with smoke that an announcer was sent to the microphone to tell the crowd, "Please stop smoking blunts. The fire marshal's gonna turn the party out!"

Biggie, Puffy, and the rest of the Bad Boy contingent headed immediately for the nearest exit, as did many other partygoers who believed they had heard the announcer say the fire department was shutting the party down. Gulping at the cool, fresh air ouside, Biggie and Puffy waited for valets to deliver their vehicles to the curb of the museum's parking structure, debating whether to hit another party or head back to the Westwood Marquis. Puffy decided they should just go back to the hotel, then climbed into the white Suburban next to Kenneth Story, with his three bodyguards in the back of the vehicle. Biggie lifted himself into the passenger seat of the green Suburban next to G-Money, with Li'l Caesar and D-Rock in the next row of seats. Just as the vehicle pulled away from the curb, Groovy Luv slid into the third row of seats. Paul Offord again rode with the off-duty police officer in the black Chevy Blazer.

Biggie's Suburban bore a sticker on one wheel that read "Think B.I.G." It was a promotion for his new double album, *Life After Death*, which was playing at deafening volume on the green Suburban's sound system as the vehicle turned left out of the parking structure and headed north on Fairfax Avenue. Puffy's Suburban, still in the lead, blew through the amber light at Wilshire Boulevard and was preparing to make a left turn as the light turned red and stopped Biggie's vehicle on the south side of the intersection. A white Toyota Landcruiser promptly made a U-turn on Fairfax and tried to cut between the green Suburban and the black Blazer that was approaching from the rear. At that moment, a dark-colored sedan pulled up on the green Suburban's right side. The driver, a black male with with a fade haircut who wore either a light gray or pale blue suit and a bow tie, looked Biggie in the eye for a moment, then reached across his body with a chrome-plated automatic pistol held in his right hand, braced it against his left forearm, and emptied the gun into the front passenger seat of the Sububan.

Clearly the target of the attack, Biggie Smalls had been the only passenger in the green Suburban who was hit by the bullets, which riddled his immense torso.

The dark sedan then sped away eastbound on Wilshire, made a left turn on Ogden Drive, and disappeared into the night. The white Landcruiser made another U-turn and sped away also.

The Suburban in which Puffy Combs rode slowed nearly to a stop when the driver heard gunshots. Everyone inside ducked their heads, then someone shouted that Biggie was under attack. Combs jumped out of the vehicle a few moments later and ran across Wilshire to the green Suburban. When he opened the passenger-side door, Puffy saw Biggie hunched over the dashboard with his tongue hanging out of his mouth, bleeding through his jacket. When he spoke to Biggie, Puffy told police, his friend just stared back, eyes wide open and scarily blank. The terrified Combs jumped into the Suburban behind Biggie as Kenneth Story pushed G-Money aside and drove the vehicle to the emergency dock of the Cedars-Sinai Medical Center, less than five minutes away.

At the hospital, it took six people to lift Biggie onto a gurney. Doctors rushed him into surgery as Combs, Lloyd, Butler, and the others dropped to their knees and prayed, but Biggie was pronounced dead at 1:15 A.M.

Gregory Young and James Lloyd were the only two passengers in the green Suburban who said they had gotten a good look at the killer's face, and at the hospital that night they assisted police in making a composite drawing of the suspect. Both Young and Lloyd had described the assassin's vehicle as a dark green sedan, but police realized that the four vapor lights that illuminated the shooting scene could have given a greenish cast to a black car if it was clean and shiny. Kenneth Story told police that three separate witnesses had approached him at the hospital to say that the killer had been driving "a clean, black Chevrolet Impala Super Sport." He had seen exactly such a vehicle parked on Fairfax Avenue as he and the rest of the Bad Boy group waited for their vehicles in the Petersen Museum's parking structure, Story said.

A Metropolitan Transit Authority driver whose bus had been westbound on Wilshire when the shooting occurred confirmed to police that the shooter's sedan was black, and said he had watched a white SUV speed from the scene after the sedan and make the same left turn on Ogden Drive that it did.

Kenneth Story also gave police four shell casings that had been given to him by two separate witnesses who said they were collected from the shooting scene. LAPD officers already had collected three other matching shell casings, all of them from German-made "Gecko" brand bullets that were rarely seen on the West Coast.

The biggest obstacle the police faced in investigating the murder of Biggie Smalls was that almost no one who had been present at the scene wanted to talk to the cops. As the first LAPD "Progress

Report" filed on the case would note, "Despite the hundreds of people who attended the party, detectives have located few admitted witnesses to the shooting."

Part of the problem was that Suge Knight had been identified as a suspect in the first story that appeared in the *Los Angeles Times* on the morning of March 9. Knight's brother-in-law, Norris Anderson, who had taken over as general manager of Death Row while Suge was "away," told the *Times,* "It's ludicrous for anyone out there to blame Death Row. We do not condone this type of activity, and Death Row certainly had nothing to do with it . . . Death Row knows how bad something like this can feel. It happened in our backyard with Tupac just a few months ago."

Most observers felt that Anderson's last point was the important one: Revenge for Tupac's killing would be the main motive offered by both police and media to explain Biggie's assassination during the next few days. The rumor that Suge Knight was responsible for Biggie's death spread through the worlds of both hip-hop musicians and black gangbangers all during that day, followed soon by a story that Suge had been attacked in prison by an inmate who stabbed him eleven times with a chicken bone. Death Row replied the next afternoon with a prepared statement: "Death Row Records would like to dispel all rumors and speculations of a prison stabbing incident involving Marion Knight, CEO, Death Row Records. Mr. Knight has not been part of any type of attack and is doing fine."

That same day, however, an LAPD lieutenant was quoted in the *Times* as saying that police believed Biggie Smalls's death had been "a hit, a directed target coming out of New York, Los Angeles, or Atlanta." The head of the New York Police Department's Anti-gang Enforcement Section was even more explicit: "All indications are that Biggie Smalls' murder was retaliation for Tupac Shakur's murder."

The first question Russell Poole asked was why the LAPD's Major Crimes unit hadn't taken over the Smalls murder investigation until

four weeks after Biggie's death. "I couldn't recall a single other murder case with that kind of high profile where Major Crimes wasn't
called in right from the start," Poole explained. "The brass gave an
explanation that they needed the resources for the Ennis Cosby case,
but that was bullshit. We had another fifteen or sixteen detectives
available. Somebody high up in the Department didn't want Major
Crimes involved. They only asked us to take over when Wilshire
Homicide said they couldn't handle such a complicated investigation. This was a month after the murder, and I think by that time
they had realized they better move control of the investigation
downtown." Poole was even more troubled when he looked at the
logs of the first twenty-four hours after Biggie's murder and discovered that four Robbery-Homicide detectives and an RHD lieutenant had been at the hospital and the murder scene during the early
morning hours of March 9. "I never could get an explanation of why
they didn't take the case right then," Poole recalled. "It was perplexing, to say the least."

The case clearly had overwhelmed the Wilshire detectives.
"During my investigation of Kevin Gaines, I was constantly over there
trying to probe around," Poole recalled. "But they were going in
circles. They'd start on one thing, go with it for a while, then jump
on another clue that came along and drop the first thing. That's how
confused they were. These were good detectives, but they didn't have
experience in handling a high-profile case, and they still had to handle
their normal workload of murders in Wilshire."

Poole believed the phone call that Wilshire Detective Paul Inabu
had made to him on April 1, asking for a photograph of Kevin Gaines,
was what caused the transfer of the case to Robbery-Homicide. "Word
got around quickly," he recalled. "The lieutenant went to the captain,
the captain went to the commander, and the commander went to
Deputy Chief Parks. Immediately, Fred Miller was called to a meeting with the lieutenant, but no one spoke to me. Your partner is supposed to keep you informed, but all Fred would tell me was that we
had been offered the case and he was in charge." When Poole asked if

detectives had followed up on the report that Kevin Gaines had been
involved in drug deals and gun sales involving Suge Knight and Death
Row Records, he was told to "leave it alone."

"My superiors made it clear they didn't want to probe that clue,"
Poole recalled. "They didn't want cops going around with that photograph showing it to people." Poole decided not to make waves. "I
understood that the brass had political considerations. My approach
was to keep my mouth shut and my eyes open, to be the same detective I'd always been, but keep quiet about it." What most rankled
Poole was his exclusion from Miller's meetings with their lieutenant
and captain. "They already understood that I was an aggressive investigator, and they were concerned about keeping me contained,"
Poole said. "The best way to do that was to withhold information.
But in my entire career I'd never been part of any investigation where
I was expected to work in the dark."

At least he and Miller agreed on one point, Poole recalled: The
Wilshire detectives had wasted a lot of time and energy chasing the
theory that the Crips killed Biggie Smalls. The story had been started
by a pair of anonymous tipsters who phoned Wilshire Division and
told detectives there that Biggie had been killed because he owed the
South Side Compton Crips money for security work, and that Keffy-
D was the shooter. Keffy-D's real name was Duane Keith Davis, and
he was the uncle of Orlando Anderson.

When this story leaked out, Puffy Combs denied ever employ-
ing gangbangers at Bad Boy Entertainment. "We've never hired Crips
or any other gang members to do security for us," he told MTV's Kurt
Loder. "But the misconception is that because we're young and black,
we're not handling business like anybody else." Dozens of witnesses
recalled that Puffy and Biggie had been accompanied by Crips at the
1996 Soul Train Award show, however, and a number of intriguing
clues linking the Crips to Biggie Smalls surfaced almost immediately.
Compton Police Department Detective Tim Brennan told the LAPD
that the South Side Crips had definitely provided security for Biggie
Smalls in the past, and that Biggie had attended a celebrity basket-

ball game at Cal State Dominguez Hills, right next to Compton, the day before the murder. An anonymous informant added that Biggie was at the Crips main hangout in Compton, South Side Park, that same day with members of his entourage.

Yet another anonymous informant, this one offering a more detailed story than any of the others, said the East vs. West feud had turned deadly during the summer of 1996, when Puffy Combs placed a contract on Suge Knight, and offered a reward to anyone who could bring him a Death Row medallion. This was why Tupac Shakur got shot, the caller said. This informant also said the killer of Biggie Smalls was not Keffy-D but one Ozine Bridgeford. What made this interesting was that, according to the Compton cops, Bridgeford was a former Mob Piru Blood who had left the gang when he had a falling out with Suge Knight's scariest thug, Alton ("Buntry") McDonald. Bridgeford had become so convinced Buntry was going to kill him that he went over to the Crips. It was soon after this, according to the informant, that he accepted the contract on Biggie.

The story made no sense to anyone who understood the way Compton's gangs operated. The Bloods were the ones who wanted Tupac Shakur's murder avenged, and who had been threatening Biggie Smalls for the past three years. Why would someone who had abandoned that gang to join the Crips take a contract on Biggie? The *Los Angeles Times* jumped aboard the Crips theory, however, and was riding it into the ground. The *Times* also was reporting that the killer hadn't fired from inside that dark sedan, either, but rather walked up to Biggie's Suburban and struck up a friendly conversation. Biggie was rolling down his window "to give him five," according to the *Times* report, when the man pulled a gun and opened fire. The LAPD could have blown this nonsense out of the water quite easily, but all the department's spokesman, Lt. Ross Moen, would offer in response was, "There are a lot of people saying different things."

The theory that the Crips were behind Biggie's death was given a further infusion of life when LAPD detectives learned that Keffy-D had been issued two traffic citations in 1996 while driving a new, black Impala Super Sport. The LAPD Air Support Division did a flyover of Keffy-D's home on California Avenue in Compton, and spotted a partially covered black vehicle behind the residence. When the police seized Keffy-D's Super Sport, the Crip hired attorney Edi M.O. Faal (who earlier had represented Orlando Anderson) to tell reporters, "Mr. Davis intends to make it absolutely clear that he had nothing to do with the death of Notorious B.I.G." But by then the news had leaked out that Keffy-D was at the Petersen Museum party on the night Biggie Smalls had been killed. On March 20, in an interview at One Police Plaza in New York, James Lloyd told the police that Keffy-D approached him at the party with ten other Crips and said, "Whassup? You need some security, someone by your side?" When Lloyd told him, "We're all right," Keffy-D walked over to Biggie and spoke briefly to him, Lloyd said. There was no hostility, though, Li'l Caesar added; when security hurried over to head off trouble, Biggie waved them off, saying, "He's cool, I know him." And both Lloyd and Greg Young agreed that the shooter had not been Keffy-D or any of the other Crips whose photographs they were asked to view.

Finally, after Keffy-D proved he had an iron-clad alibi, Fred Miller told the *Times*, "We haven't named him as a suspect. We don't think he had anything to do with it."

Russell Poole had considered the Crips theory dubious from the outset. "To me it was obvious this wasn't a gang shooting. Biggie's murder was much more sophisticated than anything I've ever seen any gangbanger pull off. This was professionally executed. We all knew that—it was obvious." Also, the fact that a reward of $25,000 for information leading to the arrest and conviction of Biggie's killer had been offered by the City of Los Angeles mitigated overwhelmingly against the theory that the Crips had been behind the murder. "In my experience, a reward offer of twenty-five-*hundred* dollars would have solved any crime that was committed by a Crip," Poole said. "Somebody would have snitched, I can guarantee you. And for twenty-five thousand, you would have had people lining up to collect the money. There was a big announcement in the media and posters were distributed all over Compton and South Central. Yet no one came forward, not even when Biggie's mother doubled the reward to fifty thousand three weeks later.

"I was convinced pretty quickly that the implication of the Crips was a smoke screen. The only question was who had been blowing the smoke."

On April 14, Poole became the first LAPD officer to speak at length with Biggie Smalls's mother, Voletta Wallace. The woman was blunt in stating her belief that, as she put it to the *Los Angeles Times*, "the police don't care about solving the murders of young black men." She was especially skeptical about a white detective who sounded to her like a character out of a cowboy movie, Wallace admitted. Russell Poole, however, was a police officer who had been praised again and again for an unusual ability to win the confidence of people who had lost loved ones to gang violence. "Empathetic" was an adjective that appeared repeatedly in his personnel package. "In dealing with the friends and family members of homicide victims, Detective Poole is compassionate, sympathetic and, most of all, never too busy to make himself available to discuss the status of the case," his supervisor at South Bureau Homicide had written in 1995. "He consistently leaves them with the confidence that he 'sincerely cares.'" That was true, agreed Voletta Wallace, who eventually would describe Poole as the single officer of the Los Angeles Police Department whom she felt could be trusted. For her, the reason was quite simple: "Detective Poole wanted to know who my son was. None of the others ever asked."

For most of her adult life, Voletta Wallace had worked two jobs to raise her only child in the third-floor walk-up apartment of a row-house tenement on St. James Street in Brooklyn's Clinton Hill neighborhood. Though a young girl when she moved to New York City from Trelawny, Jamaica, in 1959, Voletta still spoke in the lilting accent of her native island. Biggie's father was Jamaican also, a small-time politician and businessman named George Latore who abandoned the family before his son was two years old. Biggie saw

Latore once more at the age of six but grew up without any memory
of the man.

Christopher Wallace was the largest five-year-old in his neighborhood and at the age of ten already was known by the other children as "Big." Voletta, who worked days as a preschool teacher,
enrolled her son at St. Peter's Claver Elementary and Queen of All
Saints Middle School, where he was on the honor roll and won awards
as the best English and math student in his class. Biggie also began
well at Brooklyn's best public high school, Westinghouse, but rapidly lost interest in all his classes except art and, to his mother's
immense displeasure, dropped out during his junior year, at age seventeen. He could make money on the streets, Biggie knew, as a dope
peddler. Soon he was venturing north up Fulton Street into Bedford-
Stuyvesant, selling weed and nickel bags of crack cocaine on street
corners.

He talked a lot tougher than he was, according to the officers of
the 88th Precinct, who remembered Wallace as a soft, scared kid who
would cry whenever they brought him in for questioning. When
Biggie was busted for selling crack during a visit to North Carolina
in 1991, he phoned his mother in tears, pleading with her to send the
$25,000 he needed to make bail.

Soon after his return to Brooklyn, Biggie went back to selling
$3 vials of crack in front of a Chinese restaurant on Flatbush Avenue,
but he also began spending a lot more time at the home of a childhood friend named Chico Delvico. In a small back room, the two used
a pair of Technics turntables to begin mixing the sounds that Biggie
gradually flavored with lyrics about life on the street in Clinton Hill.
Almost everyone who heard the pair remarked that Biggie seemed
to have a natural gift. His mother believed it was hereditary.

Rap has roots in what Jamaicans called "toasting," a musical form
that originated with island disc jockeys like Duke Reid and Prince
Buster who spoke aloud over the American R&B records they played
at "blues dances" in Kingston's ghettos. Early on, the deejays shouted
simple phrases like "Work it" and "Move it up" that evolved into

longer and longer "toasts." Eventually toasting stars like U Roy began to create lengthy singsong rhymes backed by steel drums and a heavy bass line. Bronx deejay Kool Herc, who had been born in Kingston under the name Clive Campbell, was heavily influenced by Jamaica's toasting tradition when he began to pioneer the music form that became known in America as rap during the early 1970s.

Almost twenty years later Christopher Wallace and Chico Delvico formed a deejay group they called 50 Grand, and began working street corners and small clubs with a crew from Bedford Avenue that called itself the Old Gold Brothers. Eventually Biggie began to perform solo as Quest, and produced a crude set of homemade demo tapes. Eventually one of those tapes made it into the hands of the Brooklyn rapper Mister Cee, who passed it along to the new national director of A&R at Uptown Records, Puffy Combs.

Puffy was transfixed. "As soon as I put it on, it just bugged me out," he later told MTV. "I listened for days and days, hours and hours. And his voice just hypnotized me." Biggie's voice was unique in rap, husky and harsh, yet melodic and musical in a way that made speech sound almost like singing. And Puffy, like a lot of people who heard those early tapes, loved Biggie's lyrics. (His mother thought Christopher had developed his ear by listening to the nursery rhymes she read to him every night as a preschooler.) His tales of small-time gangsters, street scuffles, sexual intrigues, and bloody climaxes were, to Combs's ear, the first really authentic gangsta rap produced on the East Coast.

The success in the late '80s of N.W.A.'s *Straight Outta Compton* and the rapid rise of Death Row Records had transformed rap almost overnight. East Coast groups like Def Jam's LL Cool J and Public Enemy were eclipsed by what Dr. Dre, Ice-T, and Snoop Dogg were doing on the West Coast, but Biggie played bad better than anybody who had come before him. He would never have Tupac Shakur's sex appeal, but Biggie's look was unlike anyone else's. A hulking fat boy whose favorite meal was waffles with ice cream and bacon, Biggie's wide, round, pouchy eyes and pudgy, hairless face gave him the look of an immense child, while his deadpan scowl and wandering left eye suggested just enough menace to make him interesting. Even as a drug dealer he'd paid attention to his wardrobe, working the streets in a fashionable ensemble of Timberland boots, Karl Kani jeans, and hockey jerseys, topped by a terry-cloth headband. When he became "Biggie Smalls" (a name borrowed from a character in the Sidney Poitier–Bill Cosby film *Uptown Saturday Night*), the combination of his dark skin and pale pink lips with the pinstriped suits and derby hats he wore suggested a fellow who'd been recruited out of a minstrel show into Al Capone's mob. "I may be a big, black, ugly dude," he once told an interviewer, "but I got style."

Style for gangsta rappers was the product of an outlandish cross-cultural fertilization that combined ghetto gangbanger attitudes and Rastaman spirituality with the patois of Hollywood mafiosi, and Biggie had a natural affinity for all the form's origins. Puffy Combs told the nineteen-year-old he was poised to become a major star, but then one night in 1993 Biggie learned that his mentor was out of a job. Puffy immediately began organizing a plan to launch his own record label, one that would be built around Biggie Smalls. Puffy's greatest challenge was making Biggie believe it could still happen. Despondent over Puffy's ouster from Uptown Records, Biggie had a pregnant girlfriend, a best friend (Damien Butler) who was behind bars, and a mother who had just been diagnosed with breast cancer. Drunk most of every day on the Hennessy cognac he imbibed, Biggie was tempted to return to the streets with his vials of crack, but Puffy hustled to distract him with small jobs performing on remixes with other rappers. Finally, after working on it in the studio for months, Puffy was ready to release Biggie's first solo album under a title that was even more sadly ironic than his posthumous *Life After Death*.

Ready to Die, Biggie's debut on the Bad Boy label, produced two singles that hit No. 1 on *Billboard*'s chart, "Big Poppa" and "One More Chance." Both went double platinum, and "One More Chance" was named *Billboard*'s Rap Single of the Year. Biggie, who was not quite twenty-one, had become rich and famous overnight. Performing now as Notorious B.I.G. (because another rapper out in California had called himself Biggie Smalls first), he was voted *Billboard*'s Best Rap Artist in 1995. By then, though, the lethal idiocies of life as a gangsta rapper already were beginning to threaten not only his success but his very existence. For a lot of it, Biggie had only himself to blame.

Biggie and his entourage were arrested for the 1994 beating of a music promoter named Nathaniel Banks in Camden, New Jersey, a charge that put the rapper in jail for four days. Then in March of 1995, Biggie and a friend became annoyed by autograph seekers as they were leaving the Palladium near Manhattan's Union Square, and exchanged shouted threats with several men in the crowd. When the fans jumped into a taxi to get away, Biggie and his companion gave chase, caught the cab a block away, then proceeded to smash the vehicle's windows with baseball bats. After his arrest, Biggie was forced to plead guilty to criminal mischief and harrassment. Three months later, he was arrested in New Jersey for robbery and aggravated assault. Though the robbery count was dismissed, the charge of assault still hung over Biggie at the time of his death. In July of 1996, police in Teaneck, New Jersey, raided the Courts of Glenpointe town house that Biggie had purchased for $310,000 eight months earlier, and confiscated an infrared rifle, a submachine gun, several automatic handguns, a revolver, a huge cache of hollow-point bullets, and the rapper's marijuana stash. Assorted weapons and narcotics charges that resulted from the raid were pending at the time of his death. Biggie was arrested again in September of 1996, two days after Tupac Shakur's death, when he and several other rappers were caught smoking pot in Biggie's limousine while it was parked in Brooklyn. That same month, Biggie's left leg was fractured in three places when Li'l Caesar lost control of Biggie's SUV on the New Jersey Turnpike; he spent two months at the Kessler Institute for Rehabilitation and was still in a wheelchair when the clinic released him just before Thanksgiving.

Biggie's deepest fears, however, arose out of the hatred Tupac Shakur had harbored against him ever since the shooting at Quad

Studios. Biggie insisted he had nothing to do with that attempt on Tupac's life, but the release of his record "Who Shot Ya?" while Shakur was in prison at Dannemora was widely perceived as a taunt. Biggie at first seemed to view the "East vs. West" feud as grand theater, a terrific publicity stunt that would help both sides sell records. When Snoop Dogg and Tha Dogg Pound began shooting their mocking "New York, New York" video in Times Square, Biggie went on local radio to tell one station's listeners, "This is our city, and you know the beef we have with these muthafuckas." Biggie laughed off the fool from his neighborhood who emptied a pistol into one of the Death Row crew's trailers, but began to realize how serious the war between Bad Boy and the Los Angeles label had become in July of 1996 when he went to Atlanta on behalf of Puffy Combs to perform at a huge outdoor concert where Suge Knight was represented by Tupac Shakur. During Biggie's set, Shakur's crew began to chant, "Tupac! Tupac! Tupac!" Then on the way to their hotel after the concert, Biggie and his bodyguards became convinced that they were being followed by a van filled with paid killers. Biggie's bodyguards had their Glocks locked and loaded as the vehicle they rode in made a series of reckless lane changes before speeding onto an interstate highway. The van stayed with them, though, and soon was joined by a pickup. The three vehicles shadowed one another for nearly an hour before Biggie ordered his driver to stop and his bodyguards prepared for a shoot-out. Only then did the van and truck speed away.

After Tupac released his "I fucked your bitch" record, Biggie shot back with "Dumb rappers need teachin'/ Lesson A, don't fuck with B.I.G./ That's that." And he seemed almost to be boasting when he spoke about the feud with Tupac for the documentary *Rhyme or Reason*: "One man against one man made a whole West Coast hate a whole East Coast, and vice versa."

Biggie's attitude became much more sober after Tupac's death, however. "I had nothin' to do with any of that Tupac shit," he told *Spin* magazine. "That's a complete and a total misconception. I definitely don't wish death on anyone. I'm sorry he's gone—that dude was nice on the mike." Biggie even admitted how afraid for his life he had become. "I think about it every day," he told MTV. "Every day it's real, that's how real it is. I think somebody's tryin' to kill me. I be wakin' up paranoid. I be really scared."

Biggie wrestled publicly with his fear on *Life After Death*. The album opened with the thump of a beating heart; over that, Biggie began talking on the phone to Puffy Combs, telling his producer that he had been thinking about suicide. Gunshots cut the conversation short and Biggie fell to the floor. Then Puffy was at Biggie's bedside in the hospital, telling him they were an "unstoppable" pair, destined to rule the world, and that they had a lot of living left to do. His voice was gradually drowned out by the flat-line tone of Biggie's heart monitor. On "Miss U," a rap dedicated to a friend who had been shot dead on the street in Brooklyn, Biggie admitted that he cried for three days afterward, even though the deceased was a "thug." *Life After Death* ended with a song that featured Faith Evans. "You're Nobody (Til Somebody Kills You)" was his favorite cut on the album, Biggie told *Billboard*, because it "brings to mind the expression, 'You'll miss me when I'm gone.'"

When Biggie arrived in Los Angeles during early February of 1997, though, he tried once again to sound unflinching. If he had to pick, his choice for a home would be the East Coast, because that was where he grew up, Biggie rapped in a song for his new album called "Going back to Cali." But that didn't mean a "nigga" couldn't "rest in the West." California had "the weed, the women and the weather," Biggie told the *Source*. He confided to an interviewer from *VIBE* that he was going to buy a house in L.A., and insisted, "I get love out here. And if they don't love me, they are going to learn to love me. If I'm scared, I'll get a dog."

Biggie sounded more worried about flying to London than about whatever risks he faced in L.A. when he phoned his mother from his suite at the Westwood Marquis on the afternoon of March 8. Biggie had been scheduled to leave that morning for a promotional tour in Europe, but Puffy canceled the trip. Just as well, Biggie said, since he didn't feel that enough bodyguards had been hired for the week he was to spend in London. He had off-duty cops guarding him in L.A., Biggie told his mother, and felt safe with them around. Her son told her he was going to a party that night, Voletta Wallace recalled, but only because Puffy wanted him there.

The night before, Biggie had told a *VIBE* reporter that he was no longer ready to die: "I think there are a lot more lessons that I need to learn. There are a lot more things I need to experience, a lot more places I need to go before I can finally say, 'Okay, I had my days.'"

When he lumbered out of his hotel suite that night, though, Biggie wasn't wearing the Bad Boy medallion Combs had given him, that diapered baby wearing work boots and a baseball cap. Instead, the rapper wore a golden Jesus hanging on His cross.

CHAPTER SEVEN

On April 16, Russell Poole learned that he would not be one of the four RHD detectives sent to New York to interview Puffy Combs and the others who had been part of the Bad Boy entourage on the night of Biggie Smalls's murder. Fred Miller had made the decision that Poole was to prepare witness interview "packages" for the other four detectives, but stay behind to sort through the detritus of the Wilshire Division's investigation. "Follow up," it was called. Poole was not happy. "I was used to watching Fred divvy out most of the hard work to other detectives," he explained, "but when you're a lead investigator on a case, you don't want other detectives doing the witness interviews."

Poole already felt apprehensive about how the "murder book" on the Smalls case was being assembled. "These reports are not just the official record of a case, they're also where any new detective who joins an investigation is supposed to begin. But they also eventually become public record, and it was made clear to me that this was a very important consideration in Robbery-Homicide. I'd already seen how careful they were downtown about what went into the record on the Gaines-Lyga investigation, and they were being even more selective about what they put into the Biggie Smalls murder book. So much was purged or added to change the appearance of the book on the Smalls case that to me it bordered on fraud. And in both investigations, nearly everything that was changed involved clues that linked the LAPD to Death Row Records."

The first political hot potato to land in the lap of the investigators assigned to the Smalls case was the news media's discovery that
at least six off-duty police officers had been working for Puffy Combs
and Biggie Smalls on the night of the murder, and that the only one
of them who witnessed the shooting had left the scene without making a statement to the LAPD's detectives. Inglewood police officer
Reggie Blaylock had been the driver of the black Blazer that served
as the "trail car" in the Bad Boy entourage as it left the Petersen
Museum. Blaylock eventually would provide a detailed account of
his observations, but that was more than a month after the murder
and by then the media was having a field day with the story. OFFI-
CERS MAY HAVE SEEN RAP KILLING; OFF-DUTY OFFICER WAS BEHIND VE-
HICLE WHEN RAP STAR NOTORIOUS B.I.G. WAS SLAIN, AND UNDERCOVER
NEW YORK AGENTS WERE TRAILING THE SINGER THAT NIGHT, SOURCES
SAY, read the headline on the *Los Angeles Times* story.

Damien Butler, James Lloyd, and Greg Young all told the *Times*
that LAPD investigators had shown them surveillance photos of
Biggie and Puffy that were taken in Los Angeles around the time of
the Soul Train Awards. One picture had been snapped "as late as ten
minutes before the killing," according to the *Times* story. "If they were
there all that time before, it just seems impossible to me that they
didn't see the incident," D-Rock told the *Times*. "Where did they go?
They had to see it." In fact, the two "undercover New York agents"
were a detective from the NYPD's Major Crimes Squad and an officer from the federal Bureau of Alcohol, Tobacco and Firearms. The
NYPD detective was looking for a man who had shot an undercover
cop in New York and was believed to be employed by Puffy Combs.
The ATF agent was investigating reports that Bad Boy Entertainment was involved in illegal gun sales. The two had abandoned their
surveillance on the evening of March 7 immediately after the Soul
Train Awards. It was the NYPD detective who had told the LAPD
that they needed to find and interview Officer Reggie Blaylock.

Blaylock, who said he had been recruited to work for Puffy
Combs by Kenneth Story at a gym where they worked out together,

gave investigators an account of the evening that ran to six pages, single-spaced, yet added little to what police already knew. The only real revelation was that Puffy Combs had loaded two young women into his Suburban before leaving the Petersen Museum's parking structure. Of all those who made up the Bad Boy security detail, Blaylock seemed most impressed by Eugene Deal, whom he described as "Biggie's personal bodyguard." Neither he nor Deal had observed any tension between Biggie and the Crips who approached the rapper briefly during the Petersen party, Blaylock said. The Inglewood officer agreed with Paul Offord that a white SUV had tried to pull between their black Blazer and the green Suburban Biggie rode in, and provided a definitive description of the vehicle driven by the shooter: "A late model Chevrolet Impala SS, black, with large wide tires" that was "very clean." He never saw the shooter's face, Blaylock said, only his hand as he stuck a semiautomatic pistol through the open window and fired off four quick shots, followed by another burst of three shots.

For the LAPD detectives, the part of Blaylock's story most difficult to swallow was that he tried to pursue the Impala, but the car had vanished by the time he turned right on Wilshire Boulevard. "There's no way Blaylock 'lost' the Impala," Poole said. "No experienced police officer could have lost that car that fast under those circumstances. I think he backed off because he knew it was going to be bigger than anything he had imagined. That's why he left that night without giving a statement. He knew he was in deep shit for working without a permit and didn't want to answer questions if he didn't have to."

Blaylock eventually would receive a twenty-four-day suspension for accepting private security work "without proper authorization," but Poole was far less interested in what happened to the Inglewood policeman than in persistent rumors that LAPD officers in the employ of Death Row Records had been at the Petersen Museum party, and might have been involved in the murder. "Normally, I would have just shrugged that stuff off," Poole said, "except for the reports I'd heard about Kevin Gaines's involvement in criminal activities connected to Death Row, and what I read in the report by the Long Beach detective who was working for the federal task force. Also, the interview with Reggie Blaylock made me realize that all of the cops who were working security for these rappers must have had the same thought at some point, 'If shit goes down, what am I going to do?' And when you look back at the El Rey Theater incident, what did they do? They ran like scared rabbits, instead of being witnesses. Because they needed permits to work for these rap labels and they didn't have them. Suge Knight had to have known all this. He's very shrewd and he knew police departments wouldn't let their officers work for him or his organization. So the ones who crossed the line and worked for them anyway—he had them by the balls. And when you have policemen in your pocket, you are one powerful gangster."

He wanted to follow up on the rumors of an LAPD–Death Row connection, Poole said, but Fred Miller dismissed them as "crap," and insisted that they concentrate for now on Biggie's associates and whatever evidence already had been assembled. Poole and other detectives assisting the investigation wasted dozens of hours reviewing more than thirty videotapes that had been seized from surveillance cameras at the Petersen Museum, from a nearby *am pm* mini mart, and from the City National Bank branch that was directly across from the shooting scene. The LAPD brass became very excited when they learned that a woman from Houston had called the television program *America's Most Wanted* to claim a friend of her daughter had videotaped the Biggie Smalls shooting. The tape in Texas would be "instrumental in solving the case," LAPD spokesman Ross Moen told reporters. When detectives flew to Houston to take a look, however, they discovered that all the videotape showed was Puffy Combs's Suburban leaving the museum's parking structure and heading north on Fairfax to the intersection with Wilshire. Gunshots could be heard in the background, but by the time the camera panned back to the green Suburban the black Impala was gone.

LAPD Crime Scene Logs for the early morning of March 9 did reveal that someone driving a black Ford Bronco had fired a single gunshot in the vicinity of the west side of the Petersen Museum about ten minutes before Biggie Smalls was murdered, and that LAPD officers were en route to the location when that black Impala pulled up next to Biggie's Suburban on the east side of the building. It looked at first like a planned diversion, but detectives who interrogated the young man they arrested for negligent discharge of a firearm decided he was simply a fool who had been showing off.

When the team of four detectives Miller had dispatched to New York City returned to Los Angeles during the last week of April, they had little to show for their trip. Gregory Young, who had been sitting right next to Biggie when he was shot, would provide the LAPD with no new information. "Young said, 'Puffy has told us that if our names even appear on a witness list, we're out of a job,'" Poole recalled. What made this threat amusing was that the very first name on the LAPD's list of witnesses in the Biggie Smalls case was "Sean 'Puffy' Combs." Puffy was no help to the LAPD detectives either, however. Interviewed at his attorney's Park Avenue office, Combs not only said he knew nothing about Biggie's murder, but denied even that there had ever been any "rivalry" between Bad Boy Entertainment and Death Row Records.

Damien Butler also offered little, although he did confirm that Biggie had attended a celebrity basketball game at Cal State Dominguez the day before his murder. D-Rock told detectives as well that Biggie had not moved out of the Four Seasons Hotel in L.A. because of security concerns, but because the management asked them to leave after a "loud altercation" between Biggie and his Philadelphia girlfriend, Tiffany Lane.

The L.A. investigators suspected that the women who were traveling with the Bad Boy contingent at the time of the shooting had included D-Rock's girlfriend Aysha Foster and three companions from Brooklyn, who had flown west to party with Biggie and his crew. Foster, though, insisted that she and the other three women were on the sidewalk outside the Petersen Museum when Biggie was killed, and heard the gunshots but never saw the shooter.

Paul Offord was the most forthcoming of the Bad Boy group, and the first to tell the LAPD that when Biggie came out of the Petersen Museum that night several young black men in the crowd began shouting and throwing West Coast signs. He was "uncomfortable and concerned," Offord said, which was why he focused so intently on the white SUV that tried to cut between his black Blazer and the green Suburban carrying Biggie. He did not even see the black Impala on the other side of the Suburban, Offord said, until he heard shots and turned to see the gun in the hand that was extended through the Chevrolet's open window.

All the LAPD detectives agreed that the most impressive of the New York witnesses was Eugene Deal, and that Deal had provided the only really compelling information. This involved Deal's observation of a black male wearing a bluish-gray suit with a bow tie whom he had seen standing on the east sidewalk of Fairfax Avenue as Biggie and Puffy were preparing to leave the Petersen Museum. The man, who appeared to be a Black Muslim, "seemed to be checking them out," Deal said, then walked north on the sidewalk in the direction from which the black Impala would come less than ten minutes later.

James Lloyd provided no more information about Biggie's death than did Puffy Combs, but L'il Caesar did give his most detailed description to date of Tupac Shakur's shooting at Quad Studios three years earlier. He and Biggie and Puffy were up on the eighth floor, waiting for Tupac, but not certain he would show up, said Lloyd, who stuck his head out a window and spotted Shakur approaching the building on the sidewalk. At Biggie's request, he went down to tell Tupac what floor they were on, Lloyd said, but by the time his elevator reached the ground floor, Shakur had been shot. He immediately pushed the CLOSE DOOR button and rode the elevator back up to the eighth floor to tell Biggie and Puffy. He knew Tupac believed that Biggie and Puffy were responsible, said Lloyd, who denied any knowledge of this. Unlike Puffy, though, L'il Caesar admitted that there was hostility between Bad Boy and Death Row, and that it had "caused us all trouble" in any number of cities where Puffy Combs's performers appeared.

* * *

On May 7, Poole and Miller flew to Las Vegas to consult with the detectives there who were investigating the murder of Tupac Shakur. The LAPD detectives had little doubt that Shakur's death was connected to the shooting of Biggie Smalls. "Suge Knight hated Puffy Combs, and anonymous sources had told us that Puffy was responsible for Tupac's death," Poole explained. "Knight had told people that Combs had Jake Robles killed, and even though Robles was a total thug, he and Suge were close. Biggie was close to the Crips, and the Crips were who had been implicated in Tupac's murder. No matter how many times Puffy denied it, we knew that Crips had worked as bodyguards for Biggie when he came to L.A."

The theory that the Crips were responsible for Tupac's murder was most strongly backed by the bloody gang war that broke out in Compton in the immediate aftermath of Shakur's shooting in Las Vegas. Everyone who lived in Crips territory understood "that since people thought Southside had killed Tupac, his people, the Mob Piru, would be riding in our neighborhood," a young man named Corey Edwards had explained to the LAPD in a sworn affidavit. "Tupac wasn't really from Mob Piru, but that's where Suge Knight grew up and Tupac was now part of Suge's group. We just warned everyone to be careful."

Not everyone was, however. On September 9, 1996, two days after Tupac was shot, a young member of the Southside Crips named Darnell Brims—"rumored" to have been in the white Cadillac with Shakur's killer two days earlier—walked into a liquor store near the intersection of Alondra Boulevard and Atlantic Avenue, right on the borderline between Crips and Bloods territory. Brims had just stepped inside when a Blood with a gun in his hand rushed through the door behind him and opened fire. Hit three times in the back and buttocks, Brim plunged to the floor. The Blood stepped forward to finish him off but hesitated when he saw that Brims had used his body to cover the critically wounded ten-year-old girl who lay under him. Whatever measure of humanity remained in the Blood prevented him from firing another shot, and both Brims and the girl, Lakezia McNeese, survived. So did a pair of Piru Bloods shot in a drive-by shooting on North Bradenfield Street the next day. A Blood, whose brother worked for Wrightway Protective Services, was shot several times at the corner of Bradenfield and Pino by Crips who rode in a blue Blazer; he also survived.

Thirty-year-old Bobby Finch was not so lucky. Corey Edwards had warned Bobby the day before that the Mob Piru would be riding through the neighborhood. But Finch, who worked private security with his brother, a Compton school police officer, knew that gang shootings almost never happened before two or three in the afternoon, and figured it was safe to drop off his ten-year-old daughter at his mother's home on Compton's Southside early on the morning of September 11. The girl had just gone inside when Bloods opened fire from a passing car and mortally wounded him.

Compton P.D. gang officers had raided a Southside Crip "safe house" on East Glencoe Street the day before, when they were tipped off that a weapons dealer had just delivered a duffel bag filled with guns to the location. Although some of the young men inside escaped, and one, Jerry "Monk" Bonds, was seen running from the house with a gun stuffed into the waistband of his pants, the Compton cops did seize an assault rifle, two handguns, a huge cache of ammunition, and "seven full-face black ski masks." On the evening of Bobby Finch's murder, Compton detectives were contacted by a citizen who said she had just seen several Southside Crips, including Keffy-D and Baby Lane Anderson, carrying weapons into a house on South Burris Street. When police responded to the location, they did not see Keffy-D, but Anderson *was* in the front yard. When Anderson ran inside, the police followed him through the door, where they discovered an AK-47 assault rifle, two shotguns, an M-11 assault pistol, and a .38 revolver, along with a good deal of ammunition.

Neighbors advised them that the Crips were warning people to stay off the street because "it's on," police said. The next day, Compton gang officers reported that their informants said the Neighborhood Crips, the Kelly Park Crips, and the Atlantic Drive Crips had joined Southside's army, while Mob Pirus had recruited the Leuders Park Pirus and Elm Lane Pirus to their side. "All Piru groups are aligned with Death Row Records," observed the Compton P.D.'s affidavit, which also reported that the members of Suge Knight's goon squad had been telling the other Bloods that Tupac Shakur's killer was "Keffy-D's nephew."

The next shooting in the gang war took place on September 13, the day Tupac Shakur died, when a pair of Piru Bloods were murdered by a Crip who approached them on foot. Shortly after the news that Tupac was dead reached Compton, two more Crips were shot on South Ward Street. Three other Crips were shot the next day on Chester Street, and then, suddenly, the shooting stopped and the war was over. Word spread on the street that maybe it wasn't the Crips who had killed Tupac after all.

The Las Vegas police certainly had their doubts, and just about all the detectives in Vegas seemed to be sure of was that they weren't likely to arrest Shakur's killer. "The Las Vegas homicide guys showed us this whole cabinet of clues that they had just sort of filed away, and weren't really following up on," Poole recalled. "We all talked about what a defense lawyer could do with all the contradictory evidence that had come in. But then the Vegas guys told us that the main reason they would never solve this case was that the politicians didn't want them to. They said the powers that be had let them know the city didn't need an O.J.-style circus. I was shocked, but my partner was yucking it up with them, and saying he feels the same way about the Smalls case. Fred said, 'These are just gangbangers with money.'"

The investigation of Tupac Shakur's murder by the police in Las Vegas already had been criticized by an assortment of observers as astoundingly sloppy. Many key witnesses were never interrogated, and those who were said the cops seemed a lot more interested in threatening them than in getting answers to their questions. The more Poole read about the case, the more convinced he became that the Las Vegas police had "messed up" from the very beginning, starting with the failure of the two bicycle officers, who were at the rear of the Death Row caravan when the shooting started, to secure the scene and detain witnesses. Instead, the bike cops had gone after Suge Knight's BMW, while cars continued to drive through the crime scene for at least twenty minutes and dozens of pedestrians trampled over evidence. In a large part this was because the first wave of detectives and canine units were dispatched to the wrong location. Then no aerial photos were taken, and the Metro police who were the first to arrive at the shooting scene alienated all but one of the eyewitnesses to Tupac's murder. That lone cooperating witness was Shakur's backup singer Yafu Fula, who assured police he could identify the killer if shown a photograph. Instead of detaining Fula, however, the Las Vegas police let David Kenner persuade them to release the rapper by promising to set up an interview that never happened. Two months later the nineteen-year-old Fula, his torso protected by a bullet-proof vest, was shot in the face in the hallway of a New Jersey housing project. He died nine hours later at Newark's University Hospital.

The Las Vegas police had also let Suge Knight skip town without talking to them, although Suge did return four days later for the brief interview that the Vegas homicide investigators described to the media as "not helpful." Russell Poole, however, was intrigued by what the Vegas police told him about their conversation with Knight. "They said the interview was very strange," Poole recalled. "Suge Knight had been cut on the side of the head by a piece of glass, but he kept pointing to it and telling them he was hit with a bullet. They thought it was an act, that he had cut himself. And he kept telling them it was the Crips who killed Shakur, which was weird, because these gangbangers never snitch on each other."

It was only after his trip to Vegas that Poole began to consider another theory of Tupac Shakur's murder that had been floating on the street and in the media: Suge Knight had arranged the hit. Knight hadn't helped to alleviate suspicions by telling ABC's *Primetime Live* the outrageous lie that a bullet fired by Tupac's killer was still lodged in his head. Then when the network's reporter asked if he had any idea who Shakur's murderer was, Suge answered, "I don't get paid to solve homicides." The rumor that Knight had orchestrated the gang war that began immediately after Tupac's slaying was fueled by the report of a police informant who said Suge had delivered an entire load of AK-47 assault rifles to Bloods gang members at the Nickerson Gardens housing project on the night before the shooting started.

Other than Orlando Anderson, the most interesting witness to Shakur's murder among those still alive was Tupac's bodyguard Frank Alexander. From the beginning Alexander had described the attack on Baby Lane Anderson at the MGM Grand as an incident that seemed staged. Anderson almost appeared to be waiting for the Death Row group when it emerged from the Tyson-Bruno fight, Alexander said, and the Crip had not tried very hard, if at all, to escape when Tupac, Suge, and their entourage of Bloods came after him in the hallway outside the hotel's auditorium.

Alexander's description of his dealings with Suge Knight in the aftermath of Tupac's shooting was curious as well. Suge brought him out to the Paradise Valley mansion that night, Alexander recalled, and the two met out by the red swimming pool, where the only lights were those illuminating the Death Row emblem that seemed to float like a ghostly stain on the water. When the Las Vegas detectives interviewed Alexander, Suge said the bodyguard should tell them that Orlando Anderson had snatched a chain off Tupac, and that this was what set off the attack on him. Anxious to get out of there, he agreed to whatever Suge wanted, Alexander recalled. On the afternoon of September 13, though, Suge brought him back out to the mansion, Alexander said, and this time adopted a more threatening attitude. David Kenner was at this meeting, the bodyguard recalled, and so was Death Row's head of security, Reggie Wright Jr. Before he realized what was happening, Alexander recalled, Suge began to blame him for Tupac's death, insisting that the bodyguard should have had a gun on him that evening, permit or no permit. The atmosphere became so ominous that he began to believe he might not leave the house alive, but just when he began to think about making a run for it, the phone rang. When Suge received the news that Tupac was dead, he seemed to forget that Alexander was there.

He never saw Suge again after that day, the bodyguard said. After Knight was pulled back into court to face the charge that he had violated probation by participating in the attack on Orlando Anderson, though, Alexander began to receive phone calls on a regular basis from Kenner and Milton Grimes. The lawyers wanted him to testify for Suge, but he answered that he would be a better witness for the prosecution than the defense, Alexander said. Soon after he talked to the Las Vegas police, Alexander was warned by a friend of his who still worked for Wrightway Protective Services that Death Row intended to have him killed. That same day, a security guard who was close to Reggie Wright Jr. confirmed what his friend had told him, Alexander said. The bodyguard made one more call, this one to David Kenner, who began to read to him from his interview with the Las Vegas police. He told Kenner that he hadn't said any of those things, recalled Alexander, who nevertheless admitted he was troubled by "all the shit that was off" on the day Tupac was murdered.

The police in Compton, however, continued to insist that their evidence pointed toward Orlando Anderson or one of the other Crips who was in Las Vegas as Shakur's killer. Almost all the evidence the Compton cops had against Anderson and the Crips, however, Poole noticed, was based on anonymous informants. Baby Lane Anderson was a clear cut above the average gangbanger, Poole discovered. He graduated from high school, attended Compton College for a couple of semesters, and had a half brother who graduated from Berkeley. Word on the street was that Baby Lane—who never had been convicted of a crime as an adult—was the only Southside Crip who didn't drink or use drugs. The kid didn't even have tattoos. Anderson was no choir boy, of course. He had fathered four children out of wedlock by the age of twenty-three, but never once held a job that required him to file a federal tax return. And whatever his involvement in the murder of Tupac Shakur, there was little doubt he had participated in the retaliatory attacks on Piru Bloods that resulted from the murder of Bobby Finch.

Tupac Shakur's estate named Anderson as one of two defendants when it filed a wrongful death lawsuit in the rapper's slaying. The other alleged killer named in the lawsuit was Jerry "Monk" Bonds, who reportedly had been spotted driving a white Cadillac into an auto body shop at White and Alondra in Compton. Corey Edwards, however, told the LAPD that if the vehicle driven by the killers of Tupac Shakur had indeed been the "late model" Cadillac he saw described in the newspaper, it couldn't have been Bonds's, because that battered old heap was an early '80s model.

Anderson, meanwhile, along with his family and friends, continued to deny that he been Tupac's killer. "I just want to let everybody know that I didn't do it," Baby Lane told CNN, claiming that he was afraid to leave his house for fear that he would be killed by someone out to avenge Tupac's death. A lot of things about the way Anderson had handled himself in Las Vegas struck not only Poole, but other detectives also, as curious. When the Vegas police tried to persuade him to fill out an incident report and file a complaint against Suge Knight, Tupac Shakur, and others who had participated in the attack against him at the MGM Grand, Anderson refused. "And the MGM security guards said that Anderson didn't want to tell them who had beat him up," Poole recalled. "They said his behavior seemed really odd, because he wasn't angry at all—he just wanted out of there." Corey Edwards told the LAPD that he saw Baby Lane in the bar at the MGM Grand right after the attack on him and that Orlando just told him "everything was cool." Anderson "didn't appear to be too upset about what happened," Edwards recalled.

"There was something fishy about that whole incident at the MGM Grand," Poole said. "I was starting to wonder if it had been staged. Suge Knight might have wanted it on videotape to set up a motive for the killing of Tupac Shakur that would point the blame at the Compton Crips."

If that was so, Suge had an ally in Compton's mayor, Omar Bradley, who publicly criticized the police in Las Vegas for not pressing their case against Orlando Anderson. "We arrested someone [for the murder of Tupac Shakur]," Bradley told reporters. "The Las Vegas police didn't want him. Compton police thought he was the one." Poole was not entirely surprised when he learned that Omar Bradley and Suge Knight enjoyed a cozy relationship. Knight had cooperated with Bradley on a number of "civic endeavors," and even met with the mayor to discuss financing his run for the Compton district's open congressional seat. Compton for years had been the most corrupt municipality in all of California, and Mayor Bradley's commitment to patronage politics was notorious. Among other things, the mayor had appointed his sister to a school board whose other members included a convicted felon and the key witness in a bribery scandal. In 1993, when the state Department of Education discovered that Compton's Unified School District was $20 million in debt, a subsequent investigation revealed a horrific level of failure throughout the small city's academic administration. Featherbedding was so extreme that six secretaries did the work of one, and school buildings had leaky roofs, broken windows, and walls that were literally covered with graffiti. Janitors ignored bathrooms so completely that the stench made state investigators gag when they tried to use them. Despite the fact that student test scores in Compton were by far the lowest in California, Bradley leveled the predictable charge of racism when the state took over administration of the city's schools. It was the same accusation he made against those who insisted upon "hounding" Suge Knight.

On May 27, 1997, Poole found this message on his desk in L.A.'s Parker Center: "Officer Knox of LAPD West Valley called. His informant will give you any info you need. The officer's captain will not allow Officer Knox to get involved. Call Officer Knox on 5/28/97 at 0700 hours and he will tell you how to get in touch with his informant." Poole had never heard of Senior Lead Officer Kenneth Knox before that day. Nor had he been told of the "civil abatement" action against Suge Knight's recording studios in Tarzana that Knox had undertaken almost a year earlier.

Knox's involvement began on June 21, 1996, when he was summoned to a meeting with an aide to Los Angeles City Councilwoman Laura Chick and members of the Tarzana Courts Homeowner's Association to discuss "numerous complaints about Death Row Records." The meeting was not without a certain droll humor. The small industrial park where Death Row leased its studio space was surrounded by town houses and condominiums occupied predominantly by wealthy Jewish people. During the past year these residents had experienced an astronomical increase in the number of assaults, auto thefts, and armed robberies in the area, most of them committed by black gangbangers from Compton. There had been a number of confrontations between gang members who parked their cars in private parking spaces and refused to move when asked. Residents complained that they were afraid to go outside after dark, and that even when they stayed indoors they were tormented by noise from the studio that was both excessive and continuous.

Two days later, Knox and three other LAPD officers arrived at the CAN-AM Recording Studios in Suite 211 at Pacifica Industrial Park "to verbally admonish Death Row Records." It did not go well. The studio manager, Kevin Lewis, son of the jazz musician Ramsey Lewis, "immediately threw up the race card," as Knox noted in his report, and blamed the company that owned the building for any problems the neighbors were experiencing. When Knox explained that many neighbors had complained about seeing "armed gang members" coming and going from the Death Row studios, Lewis answered that the people carrying guns were not gang members, but off-duty police officers. "Some are your guys," Lewis told him. If they were police officers, a skeptical Knox asked, why were they "dressed down" like gangbangers? Because the rappers they worked for, including Snoop Dogg and Tupac Shakur, preferred that look, Lewis answered.

In his report of this encounter, Knox described himself as "shocked," but he shouldn't have been. Five months earlier, on his very first visit to the Death Row studios, Knox had encountered in the parking lot a young black male he believed to be a gang member. The young man admitted he was armed, Knox recalled, but then claimed to be an LAPD officer who was working off duty as a security guard for the record label. Knox was unable to obtain the alleged officer's name, but described the encounter to Captain Robert Gale when he returned to the West Valley station. Gale said it was common knowledge among the department's brass that a number of black LAPD officers were working for Death Row.

The day after his first meeting with Kevin Lewis, Knox went back to the Death Row studios with Captain Gale and a West Valley sergeant. As the three strolled through the studios they saw Snoop Dogg, Tupac Shakur, and M.C. Hammer, each surrounded by known members of the Mob Piru Blood and Bounty Hunter gangs. Knox met no police officers on this visit to the Tarzana studios, however, and questioned Kevin Lewis on his claim that LAPD officers were working for Death Row. On many evenings, Lewis replied, an LAPD officer from Metro Division sat at the studios' front desk. When Knox said he doubted any LAPD officer would be foolish enough to work for Death Row Records, Lewis just smiled.

Knox went back alone three days later to tell Death Row's manager that the department wanted to officially register its concern that the presence of so many gang members, unlicensed "security personnel," and, possibly, off-duty police officers increased the possibility of "armed confrontations" in the neighborhood. A number of local businessmen already had complained that gang members were brandishing weapons at them. Kevin Lewis appeared "unimpressed."

A series of fruitless meetings ensued between representatives of the LAPD and Death Row Records. Assaults and robberies in the area continued, and on one occasion a pair of LAPD officers who were working the area's crime suppression detail became involved in a verbal altercation with four Crips in the Death Row parking lot that

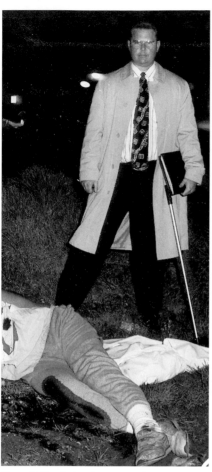

Russell Poole begins a murder investigation.

A young Russell Poole, with his wife, Megan, celebrates his hiring by the LAPD.

LAPD Chief Bernard Parks: How many secrets can one man keep?

Kevin Gaines: Shooting victim was more criminal than cop.

Undercover detective Frank Lyga probably saved his own life when he shot Kevin Gaines, but has been labeled an "out of control racist cop" in the L.A. media.

Suge Knight's estranged wife, Sharitha, was Kevin Gaines's girlfriend and Snoop Dogg's manager.

By the spring of 1997, Suge Knight, shown here with David Kenner, knew that the State of California finally intended to send him to prison, but not for murder.

The Death Row Family (*left to right*): Afeni Shakur, Frank Alexander, off-duty police officer/security guard Leslie Gaulden, Tupac Shakur, David Kenner, and Suge Knight.

Dre (seated) and Tupac with Nate Dogg, sound engineer, and assorted nonmusical "friends" in Death Row Studios.

Dr. Dre looked a lot more menacing after he gave up his spandex jumpsuits and joined NWA.

Like his Lakers jersey, Snoop Dogg was "more blue than red," as Suge Knight would learn the hard way.

SIMON GREEN-ENGLISH

(*above*) Tupac seduced Faith Evans, then publicly humiliated her to strike back at the singer's estranged husband, Biggie Smalls.

(*left*) Tupac arriving in a wheelchair at a Manhattan courtroom on December 1, 1994, to hear the jury's verdict in his sex-abuse trial: he had been shot at Quad Studios less than seventy-two hours earlier.

Biggie walking to a waiting police car outside the 6th Precinct in Manhattan on March 23, 1996, shortly after his arrest for attacking fans with a baseball bat.

Puffy Combs and Johnnie Cochran, cozy companions at the 2001 Essence Awards show in Madison Square Garden: Puffy had been acquitted one month earlier on gun charges related to a Manhattan nightclub shooting.

REWARD
$50,000.00
FOR INFORMATION ON
THE MURDER OF
CHRISTOPHER WALLACE
AKA: "NOTORIOUS B.I.G."
ON SUNDAY, MARCH 9, 1997

LOS ANGELES POLICE DEPARTMENT — MAY 19, 1997 — WILLIE L. WILLIAMS, Chief of Police

THE CITY OF LOS ANGELES AND CHRISTOPHER'S FAMILY ARE OFFERING A REWARD TOTALING $50,000 FOR THE INFORMATION LEADING TO THE ARREST AND PROSECUTION OF IE PERSON OR PERSONS RESPONSIBLE FOR THE MURDER OF RAP ENTERTAIN- CHRISTOPHER WALLACE.

MURDER VICTIM: CHRISTOPHER "BIGGIE SMALLS" WALLACE

ON MARCH 9, 1997, RAP ARTIST, CHRISTOPHER WALLACE, KNOWN AS "NOTORIOUS B.I.G." OR "BIGGIE SMALLS," WAS SHOT TO DEATH IN HIS VEHICLE AS HE LEFT A PARTY HONORING IOUS TRAIN AWARD' RECIPIENTS. THE PARTY HAD BEEN HELD AT THE PETERSEN MUSEUM AT FAIRFAX AVENUE AND WILSHIRE BOULEVARD IN THE CITY OF LOS ANGELES.

THE LOS ANGELES POLICE DEPARTMENT IS REQUESTING YOUR HELP IN IDENTIFYING THE PERSON OR PERSONS RESPONSIBLE FOR THIS SENSELESS MURDER. IF YOU KNOW WHO COMMITTED THIS MURDER, OR IF YOU HAVE ANY INFORMATION ABOUT THIS CRIME, PLEASE CALL THE LOS ANGELES POLICE DEPARTMENT IMMEDIATELY.

ALL INFORMATION WILL BE KEPT STRICTLY CONFIDENTIAL!

IF YOU HAVE ANY INFORMATION, CONTACT DETECTIVE'S FRED MILLER OR RUSS POOLE, ROBBERY-HOMICIDE DIVISION, AT (213)   MONDAY THROUGH FRIDAY, BETWEEN THE HOURS OF 7:00 A.M. TO 4:30 P.M. WEST COAST TIME. DURING NON-BUSINESS HOURS AND ON WEEKENDS AND HOLIDAYS, CONTACT DETECTIVE HEADQUARTERS DIVISION AT (213) OR TOLL FREE (984)

This investigation is filed under

Even when the reward for information that would solve the murder of Notorious B.I.G. was doubled to $50,000, no takers could be found.

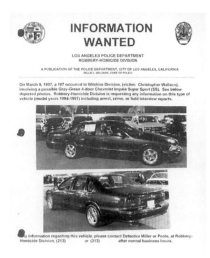

INFORMATION
WANTED
LOS ANGELES POLICE DEPARTMENT
ROBBERY-HOMICIDE DIVISION

A PUBLICATION OF THE POLICE DEPARTMENT, CITY OF LOS ANGELES, CALIFORNIA
WILLIE L. WILLIAMS, CHIEF OF POLICE

On March 9, 1997, a 187 occurred in Wilshire Division, (victim: Christopher Wallace), involving a possible Gray-Green 4-door Chevrolet Impala Super Sport (SS). See below depicted photos. Robbery-Homicide Division is requesting any information on this type of vehicle (model years 1994-1997) including arrest, crime, or field interview reports.

ly information regarding this vehicle, please contact Detective Miller or Poole, at Robbery- Homicide Division, (213)   or (213)   after normal business hours.

The Impala SS described by witnesses as the vehicle driven by Biggie Smalls's killer was an exact match to the one found later in David Mack's garage.

On March 9, 1997, at 0049 hours, Christopher Wallace, a.k.a. "Notorious B.I.G. and Big E-Small," a 24 year old "rapper", was shot and killed during a drive-by shooting shortly after leaving the Petersen Museum at Fairfax Avenue and Wilshire Boulevard. The victim was in his 1997 blue GMC Suburban northbound on Fairfax Avenue approaching Wilshire Boulevard when the suspect in a dark vehicle pulled alongside him and began shooting. The victim was transported to Cedar-Sinai Medical Center in his vehicle. Victim sustained multiple gunshot wounds and he was pronounced dead by emergency room personnel.

The suspect is described as a male Black, 20/25 years of age. Light complexion, fade haircut, thin mustache and well dressed in a business suit.

If anyone has any information please contact Wilshire Division Homicide. Detectives Cooper and Scott (213) 8457-399- or (213) 485-4022.

One of two composite drawings of the Biggie Smalls shooting suspect that were circulated by the LAPD.

Amir Muhammed, aka Harry Billups, aka Harry Muhammed: Why did the LAPD fail to investigate clues that may have linked him to the murder of Notorious B.I.G.?

A cache of realistic toy guns was among the items seized by police during the raid on the home of Rafael Perez. The corrupt cop and his cohorts apparently planted them on gang members they arrested. More interesting to Russell Poole were the bank bags, which may have connected Perez to David Mack's bank robbery, and the police radios (not shown), which might have provided a link to Suge Knight.

Rafael Perez at L.A. County Jail: One of the dirtiest cops in the history of the LAPD plays puppet master to an entire city, even after failing five polygraph tests.

Three Amigos: Sammy Martin, David Mack, and Rafael Perez (*left to right*) celebrate with fine cigars at a Lake Tahoe casino.

Suge Knight decorated the trunk of his own Impala SS with the Death Row logo, a hooded man strapped into an electric chair.

He Who Chases Monsters: a mural painted on the wall at the LAPD's Rampart Division Station.

nearly turned into a shoot-out. The officers backed off but then pulled the four over as they drove away because the vehicle they rode in was not registered. A computer check revealed that three of the four were on parole for armed robbery. When the car was searched, the officers found a semiautomatic handgun and two ski masks. They were friends with Tupac and Snoop Dogg, the four said, and had just stopped by for a visit.

On July 2, Knox informed Death Row Records that LAPD officers were not permitted to work for the record label. An annoyed Reggie Wright Jr. demanded either a meeting with the department brass or a formal letter outlining its policies. Two weeks later, Knox prepared a memorandum that was distributed department-wide, summarizing his investigation of Death Row Records and warning officers that a supervisor should accompany them "during all contacts" at the Tarzana studios. Knox also noted in his memo that no valid work permits had been issued for employment with Death Row Records.

Knox made no headway in his civil abatement action until the morning of July 30, 1996, when Kevin Lewis dialed 911 to report that he had been attacked by two men in Death Row's parking lot. He had just arrived for work and was walking from his car to the studios, Lewis said, when he heard footsteps behind him and turned just in time to see the baseball bat that struck him on the top of his head. When he fell to the ground, Lewis said, the man with the bat and another hit, kicked, and stomped him until he lost consciousness. Police interviewed the Death Row manager at a nearby hospital emergency room, where he received eight stitches to close the wound on his head, four more for a wound on his neck, and treatment for "various cuts and bruises on his body."

Until this attack, Lewis had been particularly arrogant and obnoxious in his dealings with the LAPD. When Knox had informed him that LAPD officers were not permitted to work for Death Row, Lewis responded that "they would make millions of dollars by recording an album about LAPD officers not being allowed to protect Snoop Dogg," as the officer's notes of the conversation described it.

In reply to a question from Knox about why Death Row hired only black officers, Lewis said that the only white employees at Death Row Records were the punk rockers he hired as his personal "slaves." Lewis's overconfidence, however, was shaken by his beating in the parking lot. Death Row's manager at first told police he knew both his attackers and the person who had sent them after him. The very next day, however, Lewis said he didn't know who had attacked him or why, then insisted that he no longer wanted to press criminal charges. A large man who had been a college athlete, Lewis made a considerable impression when he admitted he was frightened, and did not want to risk retaliation.

Lewis became increasingly cooperative after this, however, and Kenneth Knox began to rely upon him for inside information as his civil abatement action turned into an increasingly complex investigation. Knox spent hours on the phone with detectives from the Las Vegas Police Department after Tupac Shakur's murder. At the same time, he consulted regularly with the two federal agents heading up the task force probing Death Row Records, Dan McMullen of the FBI and John Ciccone of the ATF, who provided "intelligence information" on the alleged involvement of Suge Knight and Death Row Records in a gun-smuggling and narcotics-distribution ring that operated out of the Nickerson Gardens housing project. Compton detectives, meanwhile, helped Knox compile lists of gang members affiliated with the record label. He soon was considered to be such an expert on Suge Knight and company that Afeni Shakur's New York attorney, Richard Fischbein, phoned Knox to ask for "the hierarchy structure of Death Row Records." Reggie Wright Jr. became so accustomed to dealing with Knox that Death Row's director of security freely admitted to the LAPD officer that Suge's personal bodyguards were armed members of the Bloods gang. From the Compton police, Knox learned that there were three contracts out on Suge's life, and that the Rolling 60s Crips and the Bounty Hunter Kill Squad both had promised that Suge would be dead before Christmas. Knox observed that Knight now came and went from Death Row's studios in the middle of a five-vehicle caravan.

By the beginning of October, Death Row's Tarzana operation was finally getting the LAPD's full attention. On the first day of that month, eight LAPD officers responded to a "major disturbance" call at the Death Row Records studios. The security guard would not let them through the door, but he did step outside to say that an "altercation" had taken place inside and that he had struggled with a gang member who was trying to use a metal chair as a weapon. The officers saw a bloody towel at the security guard's desk, but the man was reluctant to provide any information, insisting that he did not know the names of the men involved and that they had left the location. The building's night manager, however, told officers that most of the gang members who had started the trouble were still inside and that he was concerned about the damage they might do if the police left. The LAPD officers then "evacuated" the studios and, in the course of this action, rounded up thirteen suspects, seven of them members of the Mob Piru Bloods. One man wore a bullet-proof vest, but if the gangbangers had guns, they were stashed inside.

On October 10, a female LAPD officer from West Valley Division informed Knox that a friend of hers had just sold Suge Knight a yacht, and that he believed Knight was using it to smuggle narcotics and firearms into the country from Mexico. That same day, Kevin Lewis, panicked by the murder of Tupac Shakur, admitted to Knox and an LAPD captain that Death Row had "an internal security problem," but he still seemed reluctant to discuss specifics. Five days later, a man who lived near Death Row's studios phoned the LAPD to report that he had observed prowlers outside his home who seemed to have come from the vacant house next door. When police arrived, they found the back door of the vacant house open and went inside to check, guns drawn. The prowlers had vanished, but the officers did discover bills of sales for two Glock semiautomatic pistols, a Department of Water and Power bill that had been sent to Death Row

Records, and a box from a nearby dry cleaners with a receipt bearing the name "David Kenner." The next day, three members of Tupac Shakur's Outlaw Immortalz were arrested and charged with attempting to rob a Decatur, Georgia, liquor store with a pistol that had been stolen from a home near the Death Row studios in Tarzana. Two days after that, Knox was advised that Suge Knight, detained as a possible prowler outside a condominium in Woodland Hills, had told police officers he lived there with his girlfriend and had lost his keys. The condo had been rented to David Kenner, police learned, and was occupied by a young woman named Latricia Johnson. The Jeep Cherokee and the Mercedes parked downstairs were registered to Kenner, not Johnson.

Knox had no clear picture of what had been taking place inside Death Row's studios, however, until Suge Knight was jailed for violating his probation, and Kevin Lewis began preparing to leave the record label. Almost immediately after Knight was locked up in County Jail, Lewis phoned Kenneth Knox to ask for police protection, offering in exchange to tell the LAPD a good deal about what he had seen happening around him in recent months.

He was a legitimate music producer who had been brought to Death Row in 1994 by Dr. Dre, Lewis wanted Knox to know, and only became involved with the record company because he did not realize that Suge Knight was more of a gangster than a music mogul. He had been planning to leave the rap label since early that summer, Lewis said, but made the mistake of confiding this to a couple of other employees at the record company. The attack in the parking lot took place only a short time later, Lewis said, but being beaten with a baseball bat was a lot less frightening than the mind games Suge Knight began to play with him. One of Suge's favorite forms of torture, Lewis said, was to keep him working late at the studio, let him go home, then phone at 3 A.M. to say, "I need you over here right now." When he complained that he had just gotten to sleep, Suge simply repeated, "I want you over here right now." He'd take a shower, get dressed, and drive to the studios, Lewis said, but each time he arrived Suge would say, "I just wanted to see if you'd come when you were called. See you later."

Suge also began to send around his crew of thugs to give him the evil eye, Lewis said. "Neckbone," "Heron," "Chili Red," "Rock," "Tray," "Hen Dog," "Lil Wack," and the others were all frightening characters, Lewis told Knox, but none compared to Alton McDonald— "Buntry"—who, with his brothers Tim and James, were known within Death Row as "Suge's killers."

In addition, there were a lot of Black Muslims around the studios, Lewis said, and especially at Suge's private parties. Suge himself professed to be a Muslim, said Lewis, whose relationship with Louis Farrakhan's son Mustapha, a childhood friend, had put him in good with Knight when he first went to work for Death Row. Most of the Muslims involved with Death Row, however, had adopted the faith in prison, Lewis said, and like everyone who was part of Suge's inner circle they considered the time they spent behind bars to be a badge of honor. For these guys, getting out of prison was like graduating from college was for most people, Lewis explained.

The atmosphere around the studios had become increasingly scary, Lewis said, since Jake Robles's 1995 killing in Atlanta. He'd been present at the Chateau Le Blanc during the assault on Mark Anthony Bell that December, Lewis said, and was stopped on Suge's orders when he tried to walk upstairs to see what was happening. Particularly unsettling was the way police officers and gang members mixed within Death Row's security detail, Lewis said. Some nights there would be as many as seventy-five Crips and Bloods in the building. Guns were everywhere, but the worst part was that you didn't know if the guys carrying them were cops or gangsters, because some of the cops acted more like gangsters than the gangsters did.

Tupac's murder had convinced him it was time to get away, Lewis said, but by then he had discovered that you didn't just *leave* Death Row. At one time he had believed his father's famous name, and the fact that his family's friends included Jesse Jackson (their next-door neighbor in Chicago), would protect him, Lewis said. But Suge

Knight didn't give two shits about any of that. Suge was a bad guy—no morals, no heart, no soul, Death Row's former manager explained. Gangbangers who looked like they wouldn't flinch if you put a gun to their heads, would leave his office bawling like babies. By the fall of 1996, the stories that circulated through the studios were the kind that you didn't want to repeat to anybody, for fear word would get out that you liked to talk. The whole company was built around fear, and the atmosphere was "insane," Lewis said. After Tupac's death, all he knew was terror, the Death Row manager explained. He went days without sleeping and would lie in bed at night wondering when they were going to come for him, and whether they would just beat him up or actually kill him.

When Knox asked about the black police officers employed by Death Row, Lewis said that Reggie Wright Jr. dealt exclusively with them, and that he knew very few of their names or what departments they worked for.

Lewis did know the name of the LAPD officer who worked the front desk at Death Row, however. And that, Kenneth Knox told Russell Poole, was Richard McCauley.

The connection between Officer Richard McCauley and Death Row Records had first come to the attention of the Los Angeles Police Department in October of 1995, when Lt. Anthony Alba of the LAPD's West Valley Division received a phone call from a Compton police sergeant. His department was concerned that one of their officers was working for Suge Knight, despite being ordered not to, explained the Compton sergeant, who asked Alba to visit the Tarzana address that evening and see if this officer was seated at the front desk. When Alba arrived at the Death Row studios, he did indeed discover a police officer stationed near the metal detector at the entrance. This was not the Compton officer he had come looking for, however, but Richard McCauley, currently assigned to the LAPD's Wilshire Division. When he advised McCauley that "it would be wise for him to terminate his employment there," Alba recalled, the indignant officer answered that he had a valid work permit. This was true; two months earlier, the LAPD's Human Resources Division had given McCauley permission to work off duty for Wrightway Protective Services. Wrightway had been founded with a $300,000 "investment" from Suge Knight, and provided security almost exclusively for Death Row Records, but the Human Resources Division made no real check into the company's background or affiliations.

Only when Lt. Alba persisted did McCauley agree to terminate his employment with Death Row Records. The officer's two lieutenants at Wilshire Division believed McCauley "fully understood the severity of the conflict of interest his off-duty employment posed for the department," and they recalled that the officer had made an impassioned promise to "sever all ties with Death Row Records." The lieutenants informed their captain that "McCauley appeared to be sincere and fully regretted his involvement with Death Row." The officer's disavowals of Suge Knight and his record label were "so strong," in fact, the lieutenants recalled, that they felt McCauley's pending promotion to sergeant should not be jeopardized by this one unfortunate lapse in judgment.

On November 1, 1995, McCauley was formally ordered not to work for Death Row or any company associated with it. His work permit was revoked by the LAPD one week later. But in September of 1996 the Las Vegas Police Department would inform Kenneth Knox that an LAPD officer named Richard McCauley had been in Las Vegas when Tupac Shakur was shot. Furthermore, the Vegas cops said, while Shakur fought for his life at the University Medical Center, McCauley was a guest in one of the rooms at the Luxor Hotel reserved by Suge Knight for Death Row Records personnel.

This was not exactly shocking news. McCauley had been under suspicion since the previous June, when Kevin Lewis showed Knox a work form for Death Row's security detail that included the name Richard McCauley. Knox informed his commander, Captain Valentino Paniccia, but the captain declined to contact Internal Affairs. Paniccia did say, however, that he would make a phone call to McCauley's captain in Wilshire Division, Lyman Doster.

Captain Doster told Paniccia that he believed McCauley had ended his employment with Death Row Records months earlier, and said the officer definitely had been ordered to do so. This was, however, a cop who had some problems, Doster added. McCauley was the object of several complaints by Community Watch block captain Tilly Jackson, the leading anticrime activist in the black community that made up the southern section of Wilshire Division. Jackson had impressed Doster by organizing a number of "anticrime marches," and had risked her life on several occasions to mobilize black neighborhoods against gang activity. The woman was more covert, though, in her efforts to close the business she considered the locus of organized criminal activity in her neighborhood. She wanted whatever she said about the Community Liquor Store to be confidential, Jackson had advised Captain Doster, because she feared what the people associated with it might to do her. Neighbors she trusted told her they had seen "a lot of guns" in the back of the liquor store, Jackson explained, and she believed weapons were being bought and sold there. Also, she had heard many reports of narcotics sales conducted inside the liquor store, Jackson told Doster.

One of the things that concerned her, Jackson explained, was the close relationship an LAPD officer named Richard McCauley seemed to have with employees of the Community Liquor Store. She believed McCauley was a "bad cop," Jackson said. He regularly frequented Roscoe's Chicken and Waffles Restaurant, where he was often seen sitting with the manager, a man who had a reputation as a major drug dealer. The LAPD had for some time classifed Roscoe's as a "problem location," mainly because the place stayed open until 4 A.M. on weekends, attracting a large and rowdy crowd. Reports of fights, disturbances, and shots fired in and around the restaurant had become regular occurrences.

After talking to Jackson, Captain Doster instructed McCauley's sergeant to "monitor" his connection to both Roscoe's and the Community Liquor Store. Perhaps this young man needed a talking to, Doster said. Only a short time later, Tilly Jackson phoned Doster to complain that the owner of the liquor store had told her he knew she was trying to get his business closed, and that he had threatened her life. The only way the man could have gotten this information, Jackson told Doster, was from a police officer.

In February of 1996, Doster told Captain Paniccia, after several conversations with detectives from the Compton Police Department, he had asked McCauley if the officer was still working for Death Row Records. McCauley insisted he had "severed his association with the company" back in October of 1995, Doster said. But now, four months later, Paniccia was saying that he believed McCauley had continued his involvement with Death Row. Doster advised the West Valley captain that McCauley already had one sustained allegation of "lying and denying" in his personnel package, and that he felt it was possible the officer might be on the verge of "going the other way."

The LAPD's Internal Affairs Division did not commence its investigation of Richard McCauley, however, until the Las Vegas police phoned Kenneth Knox three months later. To say that the department's investigation proceeded slowly would put it kindly, Poole and Knox agreed. Not until May of 1997 did Internal Affairs investigator Sgt. John Iancin travel to Las Vegas to collect statements from nearly a dozen witnesses who said they had observed McCauley working as one of the private security guards posted outside Tupac Shakur's room in the University Medical Center's Trauma Unit during the days before the rapper died. Four of these witnesses were hospital security officers who said McCauley had boasted to them about being an LAPD officer. Suge Knight had kept private body-guards in the Trauma Unit around the clock, the security officers explained, two per twelve-hour shift. McCauley's light complexion and green eyes made him stand out, they said, and so did his weight lifter's build. Also, several members of the hospital's staff had re-marked upon McCauley's late-model Mercedes sedan, wondering how a police officer could afford it. McCauley told them he worked regularly for Tupac Shakur, the hospital employees recalled, and that Suge Knight had brought him to Las Vegas from L.A. to provide "extra security" for the rapper.

McCauley himself was interviewed by Iancin two weeks later. By this time the LAPD had obtained work records from Death Row Records that showed McCauley had been posted at the front desk in the label's studios on numerous occasions during the spring of 1996, not only more than six months after his work permit was revoked, but also during a period of time when he was on sick leave from the department. During his interview with Iancin and another IA investigator on May 27, 1997, however, McCauley insisted that the evening in October of 1995 when he met Kenneth Knox was the only time he had ever worked at the Death Row studios. McCauley agreed that the signature on the LAPD Employees Report form in which he had pledged to "permanently sever his ties with Wrightway Protective Services" was his, and that he had kept this promise.

Yes, he had traveled to Nevada around the time Tupac Shakur was killed, McCauley admitted, but the purpose was to visit his grandmother in Henderson, about fifteen miles from Las Vegas. He did not attend the Tyson-Seldon fight, and was not inside the MGM Grand when Orlando Anderson was attacked, McCauley insisted, nor was he part of the Death Row caravan when Tupac was shot.

He came back to Los Angeles on September 8, McCauley said, but returned to Las Vegas two days later to spend time with a young woman he had met the previous weekend. McCauley could only recall the young woman's first name—"Renee"—and described her as an Asian with highlighted black hair. He could not remember her last name, her address, or her phone number, McCauley said, and had not heard from "Renee" since his second visit to Las Vegas. He was, after all, a married man.

Between September 10 and September 15, he had been either at "Renee's" or at his grandmother's house, said McCauley, who denied ever staying at the Luxor Hotel. When Iancin showed him a Luxor registration form that showed room No. 7050 had been occupied by a Richard McCauley of 1791 N. Sycamore in Los Angeles, McCauley said he used to live at that address but had never stayed at the Luxor. After thinking about it for a few moments, McCauley had an explanation: He had allowed his "best friend," Compton Police Officer James Green, to use his credit card to check into the Luxor. James was going through a divorce, and had filed for bankruptcy, so he wanted to help the guy out, McCauley said, then quickly amended this story to say that he had not given the credit card to Green, but rather had used it himself to open the room account so that Green could stay there.

McCauley also denied working security at the hospital where Tupac Shakur lay dying. He had gone only one time to the hospital, McCauley said, and that was to bring food to James Green, who *was* part of the Death Row security detail.

At this time Iancin informed McCauley he would be facing an additional charge of "knowingly providing false and misleading statements to supervisors who were conducting an official investigation." The IA man then explained that four security officers at the University Medical Center had identified him as part of the Death Row Records security detail, and that each of these witnesses recalled engaging in conversations with McCauley in which he had boasted about his job with the LAPD.

McCauley knew he was cooked, yet again he denied working security at the hospital. Maybe he came to the hospital more than once, McCauley said. Yes, now that he thought about it, he had stopped by two or three times to "B.S." with James, who took him up to see Tupac. The hospital security guys saw the two of them together and jumped to the wrong conclusion, explained McCauley, adding that he "might have" told those guys he used to provide private security for Death Row Records.

James Green backed McCauley's stories, both about the use of the room at the Luxor and about working security at the hospital. Problem was, the Compton P.D. had already told the LAPD that Green was not be trusted about anything. The accused officer's father, Richard McCauley Sr., however, was a respected LAPD detective with more than thirty years on the job. McCauley Sr. said he knew nothing about his son's off-duty employment or his association with Death Row Records. The older man also denied the allegation that he had phoned his son and pleaded with him not to go to Las Vegas to guard Tupac because it might cost him his career.

McCauley's grandmother was more equivocal, saying only that she was "pretty sure" Rich had visited her on the weekend of September 6th and 7th, but couldn't remember if he had stayed with her. She also didn't know if her grandson had worked for Death Row Records during his stays in Las Vegas, the woman said.

At this point McCauley perhaps had plausible deniability about working for Death Row in Las Vegas, but then IA investigators found the young woman who had accompanied the officer on his second trip to Vegas, Melissa Delgado. She had started dating Rich about a month earlier, Delgado said, after he pulled her over with his patrol car to ask her out. From the start Rich told her he worked as a bodyguard for Tupac Shakur and had been doing so for the past two years, Delgado said. After disappearing for about a month, the young woman recalled, Rich phoned to say he had been in Atlanta, working for Tupac at the Summer Olympics. He told her that Suge Knight was paying him good money, Delgado recalled, and that he was ready to make a commitment to her. Rich never mentioned that he was married, she explained.

He invited her to Las Vegas to attend the Tyson-Seldon fight, Delgado recalled, but only when they were about to leave did Rich explain that he was scheduled to "bodyguard Tupac" that weekend. Just before they left Los Angeles, Delgado said, Rich's father phoned to warn his son that he shouldn't work for Tupac that weekend, because it might cost him his job. She backed his father, but Rich insisted he needed the money, she recalled.

She and Rich drove to Las Vegas with James Green and one of her girlfriends, Delgado said, and stayed at the Excalibur Hotel that first weekend. After the Tyson fight, they went to the 662 Club, where Rich and James were to work security, but shortly after arriving they learned Tupac had been shot. The four immediately returned to their hotel room, Delgado recalled, where Rich took a phone call, then said Suge Knight wanted him to work as a bodyguard for Tupac at the hospital.

Rich drove her back to Los Angeles the next day, Delgado remembered, then said he was returning to Las Vegas to work for Suge. He would call her from his hotel, Rich said, and arrange for her to visit him there. On September 13, he phoned to say he would fly Delgado and her roommate to Vegas, the young woman recalled; they could stay at the Luxor Hotel and Suge would pay for everything. When Rich and James picked the two of them up at the airport, Delgado said, her boyfriend immediately told her he wanted to get married. They could have the ceremony performed by a justice of the peace the next day.

Tupac died that afternoon, but though he was shaken, Rich kept his promise to get married, and they were, on Saturday, September 14, said Delgado, who offered the marriage license and the names of the two girlfriends who had witnessed the wedding as evidence.

When they returned to Los Angeles, she asked her roommate to move out of their apartment so Rich could move in, Delgado recalled, but he never did. He had just made sergeant, Rich explained, and was working such long hours that most nights he slept at the station. One day at the law firm where she worked as a secretary, however, a woman who had just been hired saw Rich's photograph on her desk and said she knew him. When she told the woman Rich was her husband, Delgado recalled, the woman's mouth dropped open. Eventually, the woman revealed that Rich was already married to a woman named Becky. She lost control of herself so completely, Delgado said, that coworkers had to carry her to the ladies' room. When she had regained her composure, she phoned Rebecca McCauley and told the woman that she had recently married Richard McCauley. The woman on the other end of the line replied that she and Rich had been married for years and had two children together.

Richard McCauley phoned her only a few minutes later, Delgado recalled, and demanded to know why she had called Becky. She wanted to know the truth, Delgado replied. McCauley asked, "nonchalantly," Delgado recalled, what she intended to do with that. All she knew was that she never wanted to see or speak to him again, Delgado answered. Only a couple of days later, however, Delgado told McCauley's mother that she intended to press criminal charges. The officer's mother replied that she would make sure her son had a good lawyer.

Delgado phoned to say she wanted to change her story—at least the part about her marriage to McCauley—only a few hours after this first LAPD interview, however. The IA investigators weren't sure what to think. Twice before, Delgado had failed to show up for scheduled interviews with them, each time explaining to Iancin over the phone that she was being "pressured" by McCauley's mother and his friends not to cooperate with the LAPD investigation. That evening, Delgado told the IA investigators that Rich had been so drunk during their wedding that he had laughed all during the ceremoney, and that James Green practically carried the groom back to his car afterward. Back in L.A., Rich insisted they had to annul the marriage, Delgado said, although he never told her he was already married. When the IA investigators asked why she was telling them this now, Delgado replied, "I don't want Rich to lose his job."

Rich would, though, in part because Delgado never retracted the part of her story that had to do with McCauley's work for Death Row Records in Las Vegas. And within a few weeks the IA investigators had spoken with a number of former Death Row Records security employees who agreed that Richard McCauley had done a lot of work for the record label in 1996. A Westec Security officer remembered working a Mike Tyson fight with McCauley in Las Vegas, and said that he had seen the LAPD officer with the Death Row crowd during the weekend Tupac Shakur was shot. The same man recalled a meeting in Malibu that Reggie Wright Jr. had organized between his key people at Wrightway Protective Services and gang members who worked directly for Suge Knight. McCauley had shown up in a black-and-white LAPD patrol car, the Westec officer recalled, wearing his uniform.

An Oakland P.D. officer who had been employed by Westec until February of 1997 said he had worked with McCauley at Death Row's Tarzana studios on numerous occasions in 1996. The last time he heard from Rich was in December of 1996, the Oakland cop said, when the LAPD officer phoned to ask if he would be interested in working for a security company that required its employees to have a concealed-weapons permit or peace officer status. Two other Westec employees also described working with McCauley at the Tarzana studios.

The most interesting interview conducted in connection to the McCauley investigation, however, was with Reggie Wright Jr., who finished McCauley off with the first few sentences he uttered. Yes, McCauley had worked at Death Row's Tarzana studios "off and on" during 1996, agreed Wright, who acknowledged his signature on work sheets showing that McCauley was at Death Row's front desk during April, May, and June of that year. After that incident with Kenneth Knox in 1995, McCauley claimed that the LAPD had "lost" his work permit, remembered Wright (who was led to believe this investigation concerned only McCauley's presence in Las Vegas around the time of Tupac Shakur's murder).

Some Death Row employees referred to the company's security director as "Rona Barrett" behind his back, because the man talked too much, but Wright tried to say as little as possible to the Internal Affairs investigators. He made a major mistake, however, by producing a work sheet that listed the names of those assigned to Death Row's September 7 "security detail" at the 662 Club in Las Vegas. Richard McCauley's name was on it.

Wright also acknowledged that McCauley had been at the hospital where Tupac Shakur lay dying, but said the LAPD officer had come on his own, and that the only compensation he received was a free room at the Luxor Hotel. He knew that McCauley and James

Green were staying together, Wright said, because he spoke to both men when he phoned the room.

Green had asked to be paid "under the table," Wright said, but never received any money because the Compton P.D. had initiated an investigation of the officer soon after he returned to Los Angeles carrying Tupac Shakur's ashes in an urn.

For Russell Poole, what made Wright's interview so significant was the very last question he answered. Were there any other LAPD officers who worked for Death Row Records? Wright was asked. The label's security director at first refused to reply, but when threatened with a subpoena he "reluctantly" provided the names of three other LAPD officers who had "performed security work" for Death Row. They were Hurley Glenn Criner, David Love, and Kenneth Sutton. Wright, however, "was vague in explaining their actual roles with Wrightway Protective Services," noted Sgt. Iancin, who ended his notes of the interview by promising that "this information will be addressed in a separate investigation."

To Kenneth Knox's knowledge, though, it never was. "As soon as it was suggested that there were at least several and probably many more LAPD officers working for this gangster organization, the brass told Knox to back off and not get involved anymore," Poole explained. "He was very disturbed and frustrated, because he had become convinced that this was a giant scandal in the making. Knox agreed with me that McCauley and the other officers named by Reggie Wright were probably just the tip of the iceberg, and that Wright most likely had just given up the ones who were minor players. We both figured that the names of the guys who were deeper in would never show up in any paperwork. Suge Knight is too smart for that. He wasn't going to give up the guys he owned. We had already been told that some of these cops who worked for Death Row weren't considered security guards, but were more like confidants or troubleshooters or covert agents."

Like Poole, Knox was outraged by the intradepartmental memorandum, signed by Deputy Chief David Gascon, that concluded

Richard McCauley was the only LAPD officer working for Death Row Records. "This 'conclusion' was based entirely on the fact that McCauley was the only one either stupid or honest enough to apply for a work permit," Poole observed. "Instead of doing an investigation, they 'performed an audit.' They only found what they wanted to find."

Kenneth Knox was stifled a short time later, when his superiors ordered him not to discuss Death Row Records with anyone inside or outside the department unless authorized to do so. "They closed the lid on him," said Poole. "But not before he made me aware that the LAPD brass had known for some time that their officers were working for Death Row Records. The fact that Kevin Gaines was involved with Sharitha Knight and Death Row became a matter of record for the LAPD back in August of '96 when that 911 call incident happened. And the McCauley investigation started a month later. But they kept those two things separate and they kept them secret. The brass all knew about McCauley but they never told me. I had to find out from Knox. And they never gave me any information about this other supposed 'investigation' they conducted into the rest of the cops who were working for Death Row. I don't think there was any investigation. They kept it all buried in Internal Affairs, where the person who ultimately controlled the information was Deputy Chief Parks."

Bernard Parks had been promoted to Chief of Police by the time Richard McCauley was scheduled to appear at a trial board hearing where he faced six potentially criminal charges, each one related to the lies he had told about his work for Death Row Records. Shortly before that hearing, Parks permitted McCauley to resign "in lieu of dismissal," ensuring that none of the facts of the case against him would become public record.

"The truth got buried," explained Poole, "and that's what made me such a problem for the department's brass. Because they knew I wanted to dig it all up."

CHAPTER EIGHT

The biggest difference between the informants who implicated Suge Knight in the killing of Biggie Smalls and those who pointed blame toward the Crips, Russell Poole had noticed, were that the former gave their names. This alone did not make such witnesses credible, of course. Four of the six identified informants who had implicated Knight in Biggie's murder, in fact, were behind bars.

The first was an inmate at L.A. County's Wayside Detention Center named Wayman Anderson, who on April 4, 1997, told Wilshire detectives that Knight had offered him a contract on the rapper's life. The tip produced a flurry of activity, including a lie detector test administered to Anderson. Ultimately, detectives concluded that Anderson probably knew something about the murder of Biggie Smalls, but that he couldn't be relied upon as a witness in court.

Only a short time later, a county jail inmate named Antonie Sutphen—an employee of Death Row Records prior to his incarceration—told detectives he was one of Suge Knight's "closest associates" and could provide them with evidence that Biggie Smalls had been murdered by members of Suge's "goon squad." Detectives assigned to investigate Sutphen's story soon found their way to a young woman who told them that she had been the object of a romantic rivalry between Antonie and Suge's "personal bodyguard" Aaron Palmer, better known as "Heron." She chose Heron, the young woman said, after he told her that Sutphen was nothing more than a "waterboy" at Death Row. A short time later, the two men had a violent argument, the young woman said, and when Heron backed Sutphen down, Antonie had come up with a story for the police that would implicate Suge's man in the murder of Biggie Smalls.

A slightly more persuasive account of Biggie's slaying was offered by an inmate at Corcoran Prison. This man said that Marcus Nunn, a Mob Piru Blood who shared a cell with him at the time of Biggie Smalls's murder, had confided that Suge hired another Mob Piru to take the rapper out. The Corcoran inmate also claimed to know who had killed Tupac Shakur, and said Suge had been behind that, also. This was all at best secondhand information, however, and Marcus Nunn denied everything.

A Los Angeles County Jail inmate who gave only his first name—"Devin"—phoned the management company of Biggie's ex-girlfriend L'il Kim (after reading an article about the singer in *People* magazine), and said he knew for certain that the killer of Biggie Smalls was a Bloods gang member who had received $50,000 for the job from David Kenner. The shooter had fled to Chicago immediately after the killing, Devin said, but now was back in L.A. and working at Death Row Records. The problem for LAPD investigators was that "Devin" had identified the killer only as "Willie Williams"; when Poole ran the name through the LAPD computer, hundreds of convicted criminals with that name popped up on-screen.

Two current Death Row Records employees, one male, the other female, had contacted the LAPD during the first week after Biggie Smalls's death with information that linked the record label to the murder. That the two provided their names, addresses, and phone numbers made them at least interesting to the Wilshire detectives. Kelly Cooper, the black detective who had headed up the Smalls murder investigation during its first month, noted that he had been unable to find even a single Death Row employee who would talk about the beating death of Kelly Jamerson back in 1995. These two witnesses could not offer anything close to what would provide probable cause for an arrest, however. The male employee said he had heard Suge Knight boast about arranging Biggie's murder, while the female employee told police that she believed David Kenner had actually arranged the hit, and that she could provide information that Kenner was a "major drug dealer." In the end, detectives concluded that the woman's evidence was entirely circumstantial, and that the man's would be thrown out in court as hearsay.

Suge's rapper DJ Quik, whom many in the LAPD believed should have been charged with the murder of Kelly Jamerson, was briefly a suspect in the Smalls murder. Quik had shown up at the Petersen Museum party accompanied by ten Bloods, and the day after Biggie's death several witnesses reported hearing him say, "Fat motherfucker should not have been out here in the first place." Detectives received the tip that Quik's most trusted bodyguard drove a black Impala SS, but when LAPD officers attempted to locate the man they learned he recently had been murdered in what appeared to be a home invasion robbery.

A series of other promising leads took detectives nowhere. During July of 1997, the house in Woodland Hills, where Suge kept his girlfriend Stormy Randham and the child he had fathered by her was burglarized. Soon after this, Kenneth Knox informed Poole that the young woman's mother, Patricia Wright, only recently had been arrested in another home leased by Knight for the gruesome 1981 murder of her then husband, Willie Jerome Scott (whose body was found in an abandoned motor home with a large knife buried in his chest). An informant who came forward fifteen years after the fact, told police that Patricia Wright and her lover had killed the man to collect his life insurance. Detectives for a time thought they might use the pending murder charge to pressure either Wright or her daughter into cooperating with them, but in the end neither woman gave them anything they could use against Suge Knight. A call from an ATF agent in San Diego, who gave his name as John McNeil and said he had compelling evidence that M.C. Hammer had killed Biggie Smalls for Suge Knight, intrigued detectives—until they learned that the ATF had no agents named John McNeil in California. Some clues were simply puzzling; a former PR man for Death Row Records reported that his home in Louisiana had been burglarized, but that the thief took only some canisters of film he had shot while promoting the rapper Nate Dogg.

Many of the most intriguing clues connected to the murder of Biggie Smalls involved the theory that his killer had been either a Black Muslim, or someone dressed like one. A security guard who had been posted at the main entrance to the Petersen Museum on the night of the *VIBE* party told detectives that just before the party began he had spoken to a pair of men he believed were Muslims. Both sported short fade haircuts, the security guard said, and one wore an electric-blue suit. One of the videotapes seized from the museum's surveillance cameras had caught the image of a Muslim in a suit and bow tie standing just outside the front entrance with two other black males. There was the odd story—attested to by several witnesses— that Puffy Combs had been accosted by a Muslim at a restaurant in Century Plaza only a couple of days before Biggie's killing. When the man began to berate Puffy for how he had treated the Muslims in New York, witnesses said, Mustapha Farrakhan was forced to intervene. On the other hand, detectives from the LAPD, Compton P.D., and Inglewood P.D. all reported recent robberies and shootings in which the suspects had posed as Muslims in order to obtain access to private residences.

By far the most compelling claim of a Muslim connection to the murder of Biggie Smalls, however—and perhaps the best clue received by detectives involved in the Smalls murder investigation— had come from a jail inmate described by the Los Angeles County Sheriff's Department as an "ultra-reliable informant." This man already had solved two homicide cases for them, sheriff's deputies explained. The shooter in the Smalls case had been a contract killer who was a member of "the Fruit of Islam," the Sheriff's informant told the LAPD, and went by the name "Amir" or "Ashmir." He had been told that the killing was ordered by Suge Knight, the informant said, and that it had something to do with the death of Tupac Shakur.

Suge Knight now was among the numerous inmates at the California Men's Colony in San Luis Obispo who professed a devotion to Islam. Practice of his religion had become rather difficult for Suge, however. Sentenced by Judge Czuleger to serve the full nine years of his sentence for the assault on the Stanley brothers at the Solar Records studios, Suge entered the Men's Colony in June of 1997, and immediately was awarded a plum assignment to the prison's "yard detail." After the LAPD named him as a suspect in the murder of Biggie Smalls, though, Knight had been moved to Administrative Segregation. (The prison's administration at the same time posted one of the LAPD's "Wanted" posters looking for information about Biggie's killing in the "module" where Suge was housed.) As an "ad seg" inmate, Suge received his meals in a cell he was permitted to leave only for showers, and the "non-contact" meetings where he was separated by a thick glass wall from visitors, who were shuttled daily to the prison in a blood-red limousine. Without Knight's presence in Los Angeles, though, Death Row Records was rapidly becoming a shell of its former self. The label's first release after his incarceration, The Lady of Rage's *Necessary Roughness,* was a flop, and Snoop Dogg's disaffection from the label was becoming increasingly obvious. Death Row insiders also suggested that Suge had fallen out with David Kenner. Those who had been named as the "temporary heads" of Death Row Records in Suge's absence included not only Norris Anderson and Reggie Wright Jr., but also Sharitha Knight and the singer Michel'le, who, despite being the mother of one of Dr. Dre's children, had taken to identifying herself as Suge's wife and was ensconced in Knight's old office at Interscope. No one doubted that Suge was still running things, of course.

Despite the mountain of bad press he had received in recent months, the media's attack on Knight seemed to be softening. The attorney Suge hired to defend him against the government's racketeering investigation, Milton Grimes, had struck an effective blow by asking why the IRS and FBI were focusing entirely on Mr. Knight, while his corporate masters at Interscope, Time Warner, MCA, and EMI went unquestioned. Interscope, which had settled its share of Afeni Shakur's racketeering lawsuit with a payment of $3 million, plus the promise of royalties from posthumous albums created from Tupac's unreleased recordings, remained in business with Death Row, while MCA and its parent company, Seagram's, pocketed their share of the profits. Time Warner, whose CEO had announced the company's decision to sell its share in Interscope by declaring, "If music is being distributed in our name, we must bear responsibility for that music," quietly retained control of Death Row's music publishing rights worldwide. EMI already had paid a reported $50 million for a half-interest in Priority Records, a company that distributed many of Death Row's albums, and was angling to purchase the gangsta rap label outright. As such facts were contemplated in a series of newspaper articles published in Los Angeles during the second half of 1997, the revisionist history of Suge Knight advanced to the point that one article quoted an entertainment lawyer who said, "Suge was no different than any of the other head honchos in this business. There is a formula and he understood it. You step on others' backs to get where you need to go."

The news for Suge still was more bad than good, however. Perhaps the most alarming report he received was that Michael "Harry-O" Harris had been transferred to the Metropolitan Detention Center in Los Angeles, where he was said to be cooperating with federal agents investigating the claim that Death Row Records had been started with drug money. LAPD detectives could get almost no information out of the feds, however, other than that their investigation of Death Row Records was "ongoing."

Russell Poole remained convinced that the connection between Death Row and the police officers employed by the record label was in some way relevant to the Biggie Smalls case, but he was not encouraged by his superiors to pursue this aspect of the investigation. The conflict between Poole and his partner, meanwhile, intensified week by week. "Not long after we came back to L.A. from Las Vegas, Fred told me, 'We're not gonna solve this case. We'll go through the motions, but we're never going to make an arrest,'" Poole recalled.

"I told him I was sure we could solve the case, but I have to admit that I was wondering if anybody wanted us to."

The partners bickered over the dozens of hours Miller had invested in checking the records of cell phone calls that had been made in the vicinity of the Petersen Museum shortly before Biggie Smalls's murder. "A complete waste of time," Poole called it. There had been a flurry of such calls, Poole explained, and some of them were clearly "Death Row-related," but most of these conversations were conducted on "clone" phones, using numbers that had been stolen. "And by the time we called the numbers we thought were connected to Death Row, they were all out of service," Poole recalled.

When Poole asked his superiors what had happpened to the investigation of Derwin Henderson and the other black officers accused of interfering with the Gaines-Lyga investigation, his questions were met with either raised eyebrows, stony silence, or suggestions that he mind his own business. "We didn't know if Henderson was connected to Death Row or just a friend of Sharitha Knight's," Poole recalled. "It was an obvious investigation that needed to be done, but it never was. I was concerned that the cops who had been involved with Death Row were going to start disappearing back into the woodwork now that Suge was in prison. Nobody would even talk about the informant who had implicated Kevin Gaines in the Smalls's shooting, and I came to believe that this clue was simply quashed."

Poole couldn't be sure about that, however, because he was excluded from many meetings involving the case. "Here I am listed as one of the two lead investigators, and I can't get anybody to tell me what's being said behind closed doors," he recalled. "Fred kept reminding me that I had no pull. Now, among homicide investigators rank rarely matters. The point is to solve the case, and everybody helps everybody else do it. But suddenly in this case rank is everything, and I'm constantly being reminded that I have no power and should just keep my mouth shut."

Poole couldn't help but see a contrast in how the LAPD had responded to Biggie Smalls's murder and the shooting death of Ennis

Cosby, since both investigations were taking place at the same time. "In the Cosby case, there were about fifteen hundred clues that came in, from all over California, and we followed up on every one," Poole recalled. "I was sent way out into the desert to check on one of twenty-five clues in that case they gave me. Because in high-profile cases you get a lot of people calling up thinking they know who did it. From an investigator's point of view it's sort of like a lottery and you just hope you get the right clue. It turned out that the Cosby case was solved by a clue that came in from the *National Enquirer*, which was really a first. But in the Smalls case I saw lots of clues that were sort of being shunted to the side, even though I thought they were important, while a lot of time got wasted on stuff I knew wasn't going to pan out."

During the late summer of 1997, Poole struggled to keep his displeasure with his partner to himself. "Fred wrote the six-month progress report on the Smalls case all by himself," Poole recalled. "It was less than two pages long and a total summary. There was absolutely nothing in it that wasn't already public knowledge. When I let it be known that I thought a lot had been left out, the lieutenants and captains told me they knew Fred was a lazy ass who hadn't made a major arrest in years, but that I'd just have to deal with it. He was a Detective III supervisor with twenty-seven years on the job who seemed to have a lot of clout, so I wasn't in a hurry to challenge him, either. People don't want to take on a guy with that kind of seniority, because they know he has nothing to lose, while you have a lot to lose."

Poole soon would find himself engaged in an increasingly public dispute about the direction of the Biggie Smalls murder investigation. By the time it was over, Fred Miller's insistence that police officers could not have been involved would be backed by most of the LAPD brass, including the new Chief of Police, Bernard Parks.

Poole's theory of the case would become much more difficult to dismiss, however, after November 6, 1997, the day an LAPD officer named David Mack pulled off one of the biggest bank robberies in Los Angeles history.

* * *

Like Suge Knight, David Mack had grown up north of Alondra Boulevard in Compton, west of Wilmington Avenue and east of Leuders
Park, the territory of the Piru Bloods. And like Knight, Mack had left
the neighborhood on an athletic scholarship. During the early 1980s,
while at the University of Oregon, he won three PAC-10 conference
titles and an NCAA championship in the 800 meters. Mack was
ranked number one in the world going into the 1984 Olympics, but
a leg injury that wouldn't heal ended his track career before he could
compete for a gold medal, and in 1988 he joined the Los Angeles
Police Department.

Mack began his police career in Southeast Division, where the
combination of his athletic career and the fact that he had been personally recruited into the department by Bernard Parks gave him a
good deal more status than the average rookie cop. After only two
years on the job, he was turned loose on the streets as an undercover
narcotics officer. In 1993, Mack was awarded the LAPD's second-
highest honor, the Police Medal, for shooting a drug dealer who allegedly had pointed a gun at the head of Mack's partner, Rafael "Ray"
Perez.

Jesse Vincencio was holding a pistol in his right hand as he approached their parked car, Mack and Perez said. The two undercover
cops gave Vincencio $20 for a rock of cocaine, but the dealer threw
the money back into Mack's lap, they recalled, then asked, "Are you
Crips or Bloods?" The two denied being either gang members or drug
dealers, Mack and Perez said, but Vincencio (who later would test
positive for PCP) became so agitated that Mack slipped his own gun
out of his waistband and held it hidden under his shirt. Vincencio
suddenly raised his weapon and pointed it back and forth between
the two men in the car, pausing finally with the barrel of his weapon
aimed at Perez's head. Convinced he was about to be killed, Perez
would testify, he pleaded with Vincencio, "Come on man, I'm just a
basehead, take it easy. Don't shoot." At that moment, Mack pulled
his own pistol from under his shirt and fired four shots. Vincencio

had been hit, but was still on his feet, standing in the middle of Cambridge Street, according to Mack, when once again he raised his weapon. Mack said, he pushed his car door open and crouched behind it, firing off five more rounds. Vincencio was not yet down, however, according to Mack and Perez. The dealer turned left and began to run, reaching back to point his gun one more time at Mack, who fired off another four shots, making thirteen total. When the smoke cleared, Vincencio was dead and Mack was a police hero, credited by Perez with saving his life.

Little more than a year later, however, Mack had given up his prestigious assignment in the Narcotics Bureau to work the graveyard shift in West L.A. He needed more time with his wife, Carla, and their two children, Mack said. But the flexibility of his new schedule also allowed the officer to devote more hours to his extracurricular activities. Among these was his relationship with Errolyn Romero, who had been a nineteen-year-old ticket taker at the Baldwin Theater in 1990, when Mack first asked her out. Their subsequent affair lasted seven years. Romero's disapproving family insisted that she break it off with Mack, and the young woman told them she had, but she continued to sleep with the married man even after she went to work for the Bank of America. In August of 1997, Romero was transferred to the big B of A branch just north of the USC campus at Jefferson and Hoover. This bank was a huge operation, with twenty teller stations and a large wall of "ballistic Plexiglas" that separated the lobby from the vault area.

Normally the bank kept about $350,000 in currency in the vault, but slightly more than twice that amount had just been delivered by armored car on the morning of November 6, 1997, when a black male wearing a three-piece gray suit with sunglasses and a tweed beret walked through the front door and headed directly for the bulletproof door that divided tellers from customers. A security guard said he couldn't go back there, and the man explained that he simply wanted to get into his safe deposit box. After the man in the gray suit filled out a safe deposit box entry form, Errolyn Romero buzzed him through the first gate, then left her window and unlocked a second security door that opened into the vault area. Inside, two female employees of the bank had just begun to count the $722,000 (all in twenties, fifties, and hundreds) that sat in three separate bundles on a steel cart, sealed in plastic shrink-wrap.

The man immediately shoved Romero to the floor, opened his suit jacket to reveal the Tec-9 semiautomatic assault pistol that hung from a shoulder strap, took the gun out, pointed it at the two women who were counting the cash, and told them, "Don't touch those fucking pagers or I'll blow your fucking heads off! I want all the money Brinks just brought! Don't lose your life over money that's not yours, and don't give me any of that exploding bait! If it explodes on me, I'll come back and kill you! Don't look at me, and don't touch those pagers!" Both the tone of the man's voice and the expression on his face convinced them he was perfectly capable of following through on his threats, the two women explained later, and they immediately got on the floor.

The man let his weapon drop back into the strap under his jacket and scooped up the three bundles of cash. If they used their pagers to set off a silent alarm, or if a dye pack exploded on him, the man warned the three women again, he would come back and kill them.

The man in the suit appeared to be acting alone until an unarmed bank security guard saw him carrying the money as he left the vault. The guard ran to a telephone, but before he could dial he felt a gun barrel against his ribs, then heard a second man say, "Put the phone down, fool!" As it dawned on the bank's customers that a robbery was in progress, the man in the suit began to shout at them: "Close your eyes! Don't look at me! Get out of the way! I have a gun! I'll blow you up!"

"Stay there. Don't go anywhere," the second robber told the security guard, as he followed the man in the suit out of the bank door to a white van where a third robber sat behind the wheel. The van drove less than half a mile to a parking lot behind an apartment building on Ellendale Street. A USC student who lived in the building turned toward his open window when the van screeched to a stop.

He stuck his head out of the window when he heard what sounded like police radios, the student said, and saw two black men jump out of the van. "Let's get out of here," the one who carried a bag over his shoulder shouted, then both ran off on foot.

All three robbers had vanished by the time police arrived and discovered that the van was wiped clean of prints. The man in the gray suit and his accomplices had pulled off one of the biggest heists in Los Angeles history, but their execution would prove far superior to their planning. Within a week, the Bank of America's corporate security division informed the FBI that its USC branch had far more cash on hand at the time of the robbery than was authorized, and that the money had been ordered by assistant manager Errolyn Romero. The bank sent Romero to the LAPD's Parker Center headquarters on December 16, 1997, to take a polygraph test administered by an FBI agent and two detectives from the Department's Robbery-Homicide Division, Brian Tyndall and Gregory Grant. After telling Romero that she had failed the polygraph, the detectives showed the young woman a batch of bank security photographs of the robber who had been with her in the vault. Visibly upset, Romero did not answer yes or no when asked if she could identify the man, instead inquiring, "What if I can convince him to give the money back?" Was she afraid of this person? the detectives wondered. "Yes and no," Romero replied. She couldn't bring herself to say the man's name, but finally opened her purse, took out a business card, and pushed it across the table to the detectives, who were more than a little startled to see that it was emblazoned with an LAPD badge and the name of Officer David Mack.

Mack was carrying fourteen hundred-dollar bills in his wallet when he was arrested that evening. Police found another $2,600 in fifties when they searched his house, along with receipts and invoices for $18,000 in cash purchases that had been made in the six weeks since the robbery, all hidden under the carpet in a closet. Officers also recovered the Tec-9 pistol and shoulder strap Mack had used in the robbery.

What most interested Russell Poole was the black Impala SS parked in Mack's garage next to a wall that was decorated with Tupac Shakur posters and memorabilia; detectives described it as a sort of "shrine" to the slain rapper. "As soon as I learned that David Mack owned a vehicle that matched the one used in the Biggie Smalls killing, and that Mack had used it as the third car in the bank robbery, I asked to have it tested by our Scientific Investigations Division," Poole recalled, "but the brass said no, that they didn't want to 'step on the FBI's toes.' What bullshit! The LAPD has never cared about stepping on the FBI's toes. What they didn't want was to find out that one of our officers was implicated in Biggie Smalls's murder. Because there was no telling where that might lead."

Poole's interest in Mack only increased, however, with each new report he received from detectives working the bank robbery case. In Mack's house they had discovered thousands of rounds of German-manufactured 9mm ammunition, the detectives said, exactly the kind of bullets that had killed Biggie Smalls. Mack had grown up in the same Compton neighborhood with Suge Knight, where he was a legend for his foot speed, and like Knight, proudly professed to be a Muslim. Biggie Smalls's killer looked like a Muslim, witnesses said. Mack, it turned out, had been seen at numerous Death Row functions, and he was known for dressing in the same blood-red suits that Suge Knight and his entourage favored.

From the moment of his arrest, Mack had acted more like a gangster than a police officer, Poole was advised. Even as detectives from the Bank Robbery squad read him his rights, Mack smirked and told them, "Take your best shot." At the Montebello City Jail, where he was locked up after his arrest, Mack immediately informed the other inmates that they better not fuck with him because he was a member of the Mob Piru Bloods. Mack also boasted while in custody that the nearly $700,000 remaining from the bank robbery was "invested" in a way that would at least double his money by the time he was released from prison. He could do eight years standing on his head, Mack said, and would be a rich man when he hit the streets again.

A lot of what the police knew about Mack's plans they learned from the young man who had stolen the white van used in the bank robbery, Dale Williams. The FBI had interviewed Williams in January of 1998, shortly after he was arrested in Redondo Beach and told police there that he had important information about a major crime. He had known David Mack most of his life, said Williams, because his father, a former Arizona state sprint champion, had tried to convince Mack to attend USC rather than Oregon. During October of 1997, Mack had offered him ten thousand dollars to steal a van he could use in a robbery, Williams said. Mack also asked if he knew anyone who did "work" and could handle a lot of money, said Williams, who understood "work" to mean drug dealing. On November 5, 1997, he stole a white Toyota Sienna van from the Budget Rent-a-Car lot at the airport, Williams said, and delivered the vehicle to Mack that evening, along with a set of paper dealer tags from Crenshaw Motors. Mack initially said he was going to use the van to rip off a drug dealer, Williams said, but changed his story at some point and said an armored car carrying $900,000 in cash was the target. Mack slipped on the evening of November 5, though, and said something about "the bank" opening at 9 A.M. Williams knew Mack had a girlfriend who worked for a bank, because David had said several times she was going to make him rich. Mack admitted what he was up to at that point, Williams told police, and even showed him the Tec-9 he would carry into the bank on a shoulder strap, explaining that he planned to wear a suit and a wig during the robbery.

He was at his friend Darryl Dorberry's house the next morning at 11:40, about an hour and a half after the bank robbery, Williams said, when Mack showed up, threw $10,000 in fifty-dollar bills on the floor, and said they were square. After he learned that David had been arrested and was locked up in the Montebello City Jail, however, Williams said he became concerned about his own exposure, and decided they needed to talk. His method was simple: He and a female friend went to a mall in Montebello and started shoplifting until they were caught; when the local police locked him up, he and David had lots of time to talk. What worried him, Williams explained, was an article in the newspaper that described Errolyn Romero's part in the robbery and reported that she had identified Mack as the "mastermind." He was surprised and disappointed to learn that his old friend would put himself in a position to be ratted out by Romero, Williams said, because David had told him many times before, "Never trust a bitch."

Mack apparently planned to deal with Romero, Poole soon learned. While at the Montebello jail, Mack hired a Hispanic gang member to kill Romero, but the would-be hit man got scared at the last minute and went to the police. The FBI and the LAPD found his story credible enough to insist that Romero be transferred to the special housing unit at the women's jail downtown.

Romero now intended to use a "duress" defense at trial, claiming Mack had intimidated her into cooperating in the robbery. She had seen Mack resort to violence several times in bar fights, Romero said, and believed him when he told her that if he found out she had another boyfriend he would kill her, and no one would be able to prove he did it. Still, she had never believed Mack would actually go through with the bank robbery, Romero said. Afterward, his only response to her questions was to say she had better keep her mouth shut. "The weak and those who talk too much get eliminated," Mack told her, the young woman said. Several times during their relationship Mack had told her that he had no problem with killing someone to protect himself, and boasted that he had shot three people to death while working as an undercover cop. When Mack described the circumstances of one fatal shooting, Romero recalled, she said he should have aimed at the man's legs instead of his body. Mack's reply was that he didn't want that person to testify about the circumstances of the shooting.

On the basis of Romero's story, LAPD detectives performed a cursory reinvestigation of the shooting in which Mack allegedly had saved his partner Perez's life, and reported that they had found nothing improper. Poole, who noted that Mack and Perez had been involved in a total of five shootings (in a department where the majority of officers—himself included—went their entire careers without ever firing a gun while on duty), doubted that Jesse Vincencio's death had been thoroughly examined. He would be borne out when a pair of eyewitnesses the police had failed to interview came forward to say that Vincencio never drew his gun before David Mack shot him in the street. "I was sure that shooting was dirty," Poole recalled, "but I couldn't get any of the brass interested in taking another look at it."

David Mack would not become the primary focus of Poole's own investigation until shortly after he returned from a three-week vacation in January of 1998 and learned that the first person to visit the arrested officer in jail was a man who went by the name Amir Muhammed. "'Amir or Ashmir,' our informant had said was the name of Biggie Smalls's killer," Poole recalled. Amir Muhammed had been Harry Billups when he and Mack met as students at the University of Oregon, where Billups started at both tailback and wide receiver on the football team. A high school sprinter in California and Virginia (where he had grown up), Billups worked out regularly with the university's track team and lived with Mack in a dormitory dominated by athletes.

Poole took a deep breath when he saw the driver's license photo Muhammed had presented at the Montebello City Jail: While David Mack looked nothing like the composite drawing of the shooter in the Biggie Smalls's slaying, Amir Muhammed bore a distinct resemblance to the suspect. Muhammed had used a false address and social security number when he signed in as a visitor at the Montebello jail, and when Robbery-Homicide detectives did a computer search on the man, they turned up eight prior addresses, each with no forwarding.

A short time later, Poole examined David Mack's personnel file and was stunned by the dates of Mack's "family illness" leaves. "Most coppers very rarely take 'FI' days," Poole explained. "You only get a few and most of us save them for a major emergency." During the last eight months of David Mack's LAPD career, however, the of-

ficer twice had taken a series of family illness leaves. As Poole suspected it might, one series of "FI" days taken by Mack coincided with
the date of the bank robbery. Mack had taken an earlier series of family
illness leaves, though, on March 4, 6, and 7—immediately before the
weekend of Biggie Smalls's murder.

This discovery was followed shortly by Poole's reinterview of
Damien Butler. After about ten minutes of preliminary questions,
Poole showed Biggie Smalls's best friend a "six-pack" photo lineup.
"I'm sure this guy was standing just outside the door to the museum
as we were entering into the party," Butler said, as he pointed to a
photograph in the upper right-hand corner. It was David Mack's mug
shot.

From Russell Poole's point of view, the evidence already in hand
not only implicated David Mack in the Smalls shooting, but very
nearly nailed him for it. The detective's superiors in the department
did not see it that way, however. Not only did the LAPD fail to run
forensic tests on Mack's Impala, no search at all was made for Amir
Muhammed, aside from an aborted one-day stakeout and a single run
of his name through the department's computer system. "We were
kept from following these natural leads because they implicated a
cop," Poole said, "plain and simple. The brass told me, 'We're not
going that way.'

"All along I had tried to keep an open mind about whether police
officers were involved in the Biggie Smalls murder. I didn't know. There
were little clues here and there that pointed in that direction and made
me wonder. I asked again what had happened to the Gaines clue. The
only answer I got was that they made up a six-pack folder with Gaines
in it, but I never saw or heard any evidence that they showed it to any
of the witnesses. All I knew was that there was no mention of it at all in
the murder book. The clue had been completely purged.

"I thought the arrest of David Mack and the evidence that implicated him in the Biggie Smalls murder was our big break in the
case, but it was like everybody wanted to look the other way. And

once I got Mack ID'd at the Petersen Museum party, the whole investigation ground to a halt. Suddenly Fred is meeting with the brass on an almost daily basis while I'm being cut out of the loop. I went twice to my lieutenant to complain, but he was afraid to do anything, because he really didn't know which direction this thing was going to turn. There were captains and commanders coming in and out of his office, then reporting directly to the deputy chiefs. The brass wanted updates every day, so they could control whatever information was made public. I really couldn't grasp what was happening, because I'd never dealt with something like this before. All my commanding officers up to that point had told me to follow the case wherever it leads, and don't stop until you find the killer. That's how it works. One clue leads to another clue which leads to another clue which leads to another clue and that's how cases get solved. But that process had broken down completely during the course of the Biggie Smalls investigation.

"Whenever I pressed for an explanation of why we weren't investigating these clues that connected Mack and possibly other LAPD officers, I couldn't get any real answers. I was told, 'Don't go there. Just keep your mouth shut and do your job.'"

Poole understood that many of his colleagues in Robbery-Homicide now considered him a pain in the ass. The guy was irritatingly earnest, some felt. Among other things, Poole was the only detective in the division who kept "The Homicide Investigator's Creed" tacked to the wall above his desk. "No greater honor will ever be bestowed on an officer or a more profound duty imposed upon him than when he is entrusted with the investigation of the death of a human being," it read. "It is his duty to find the facts regardless of color or creed without prejudice, and to let no power on earth deter him from presenting these facts to the court without regard to personality." Some RHD detectives began to roll their eyes whenever they looked at the thing, joking to one another that even Poole's e-mail address was eaglescout-at-dot-something.

"The pressure was subtle," Poole remembered. "Looks, raised eyebrows, guys murmuring, 'Leave it alone.' I was becoming an outcast."

Poole received a clear signal of where he stood with his superiors on January 22, 1998, when a black detective who had played a relatively minor role in the Smalls investigation up to this point, James Harper, sent him this note: "Russ, Lt. Conmay wants myself and Haro to maintain control of the Mack clue book—Harper."

Even if the LAPD wasn't chasing them with much enthusiasm, clues continued to come in that linked David Mack to gangsta rap in general and to the Death Row Records label in particular. Most of the tipsters were other police officers. One was a detective who had seen Mack wearing a Nation of Islam pinkie ring. Another LAPD officer, who considered Mack a friend, said that David had offered him an off-duty job providing security for "the wife or girlfriend of an unnamed Death Row Records executive." A sergeant with the Beverly Hills P.D. recalled that during the previous summer he had taken an off-duty job working as a security guard outside the Wilshire Theater during the recording of a Def Jam concert for HBO. Security inside the theater was provided by Muslims from the Farrakhan sect, the sergeant said, who "were very uncooperative" until an LAPD officer pulled up in a black-and-white patrol car and spoke briefly with them. He later had recognized that officer from photographs in the newspaper as David Mack, said the Beverly Hills sergeant, who recalled that the Muslims inside the theater "were much more friendly" after Mack came and went. That same sergeant said he had seen Mack on two other occasions, once at a 7-Eleven store that had just been robbed and again at the end of a car chase that had started in Beverly Hills but ended in Hollywood. On both occasions, Mack seemed to show up out of nowhere, said the sergeant, who had the feeling "something was going on with the guy," but couldn't put his finger on it.

To Poole, it looked like the other LAPD detectives assigned to the Smalls case were just going through the motions. "They were piling up paper, but they weren't making connections," Poole said. "They'd ignore what I thought were the best clues we had, then run off after something that obviously led nowhere. It was incredibly frustrating to watch. I mean, we already had ten times more than we needed to write search warrants on Mack. Hell, we almost had enough to take Mack to trial."

But even the single supervisor in Robbery-Homicide whom Poole still trusted advised him to keep quiet. "I knew Brian Tyndall was a fine detective and an honorable man," Poole explained, "but he was also a guy who believed in following orders and doing what he was told. He'd tell me, 'Just relax a little, Russ. We're gonna work things out.'" Even though Poole had been excluded from the investigation of David Mack, he still was nominally listed as the lead investigator on the Biggie Smalls case, Tyndall reminded Poole. There were other avenues he could pursue. Suge Knight still was considered the main suspect—focus on him.

Frank Alexander didn't know much about Biggie Smalls's murder, but the bodyguard was only too happy to implicate Suge Knight in the shooting of Tupac Shakur. His first contact with Death Row had come in September of 1995, Alexander told Poole during an interview in Laguna Niguel, the same month Tupac was released from prison in New York. Before beginning work, the bodyguard recalled, he was interviewed by Reggie Wright Jr. at the offices of Wrightway Protecive Services in the city of Paramount. At 5'7" and 260 pounds, Wright did not impress Alexander, who had taken home more than fifteen first prizes in international bodybuilding competitions. Reggie and Suge Knight were "tight as brothers," however, Alexander said, and Suge often referred to Wright as his personal bodyguard.

Alexander recalled spending a few weeks at the front desk in the Tarzana studios, where the weapons he confiscated included Glocks, Tec-9s, and Bowie knives that were damn near the size of machetes. By Halloween, though, he was working full time as body-guard to Tupac.

The rapper had understood what he was getting into when he joined Death Row, Alexander said; Suge Knight was "the biggest, baddest brotha out there," and Tupac wanted all the power and protection his affiliation with Suge gave him. By the summer of 1996, however, Suge and Tupac were falling out on a regular basis, Alexander said. While he was filming the movie *Gridlocked,* Alexander recalled, Tupac fought with Suge over money on several occasions, and publicly accused Knight of stealing from him. And just before the MTV Awards show in New York, less than two weeks before he was shot, Tupac got into "a heated argument" with Suge over a woman, and the two almost came to blows. Money was the real prob-lem between the two, however, Alexander said. Tupac believed he was owed millions, and that Suge was doling out his royalties in order to maintain control and keep him tied to Death Row Records.

Alexander ticked off all the things that were "odd and off" on the day Tupac was shot in Las Vegas. First, he was concerned that Kevin Hackie had been fired and that no one had been hired to re-place him, Alexander recalled. Now assigned to protect Tupac all by himself, Alexander immediately learned that he didn't have a per-mit to carry a gun in Vegas, then was given a cell phone with a dead battery. And that whole incident at the MGM Grand had looked fishy to him, Alexander said, for several reasons. First, Orlando Anderson looked like he was waiting for them when the Death Row entourage came out of the auditorium at the MGM Grand. Two, Suge's home-boy Tray was the one who got Tupac to attack Anderson. Three, Anderson didn't try to escape when Suge and his thugs came charg-ing after him. The thing that really stuck in his mind, though, Alexander said, was that after Suge told everyone to scatter and dis-appear, he stopped to make a phone call before leaving the hotel.

He believed the entire assault on Anderson had been staged, Alexander said, and that it was entirely possible Suge had paid the Crip to take that beating, and then kill Tupac. The bodyguard's description of the shooting added a detail Poole had never heard before: That white Cadillac didn't just pull up "alongside" the car Tupac and Suge were riding in, Alexander said, but was actually a little bit ahead of the BMW when the killer opened fire, allowing him to shoot at an angle that made it possible to avoid hitting Suge with a stray bullet.

He believed that Suge, Reggie Wright, and Orlando Anderson had all been involved in Tupac's murder, Alexander said finally, but that he'd never admit it in public.

The bodyguard also told Poole and Miller that he knew there was one LAPD officer who had been especially close to Suge. He had never met the man and didn't know his name, Alexander said, but he did recall that Suge and Reggie referred to him as "Rabbit," because he was such a fast runner.

His interview with Alexander convinced Poole that he needed to interview Orlando Anderson, but locating the Crip was difficult these days. It would become impossible on May 29, 1998, the day Anderson was shot to death at a car wash on the corner of Alondra Boulevard and Oleander Avenue. The Compton police said the shooting (in which two other men were killed and a fourth man wounded) had been about money, but Poole was not inclined to believe anything the Compton cops told him at this point. "It just seemed a little too convenient," Poole explained. "Yafu Fula and Orlando Anderson, the best witness and the main suspect in the murder of Tupac Shakur, both shot dead, while the Shakur case remained unsolved."

Kevin Hackie advised Poole to look into a couple of other killings that had taken place in Compton and South Central. The victim of the more recent of these two murders was a bodyguard named Darryl Reed, who on January 21, 1998, had been murdered in a house owned by DJ Quik. Reed was a guy who may have known too much for his own good, Hackie said, during an interview at his office in the San Fernando Valley. The more interesting case, though, Hackie told Poole, involved the May 1996 murder of Bruce Richardson.

Richardson was well known in South Central L.A. as the owner of the Genius Car Wash at Crenshaw and 54th. He was even more famous, though, as perhaps the only major drug dealer who hired both Crips and Bloods. Though formally a Blood, Bruce was welcome among the Rolling 60s Crips, who treated him as one of their own. This was unusual, to say the least.

Richardson had attended high school with Suge Knight, and was a major figure in the black neighborhoods of southern Los Angeles County long before Suge Knight began to capture public attention. Among other things, Bruce was all but unbeatable in hand-to-hand combat. A legendary streetfighter with a black belt in karate, the tall and powerfully built Richardson intimidated just about everyone, including Suge Knight, who at one time had openly admired his former schoolmate. That changed, of course, when Suge became the CEO of Death Row Records. Even when Suge was the one with all the power, though, Bruce refused to kowtow. Calling Suge "a punk and a pussy," Richardson decided to become a manager of rap groups and beat Suge at his own game. One of Bruce's rappers, a kid named Dramacydal, became close friends with Tupac Shakur, who wanted Dramacydal to join his Outlaw Immortalz as a backup performer on the *All Eyez on Me* album. Bruce gave his consent, but only if Suge promised him a percentage of the album's royalties. After the album was completed, however, Suge not only refused to pay but persuaded Dramacydal to leave Bruce and sign on as a client with Knight's own West Coast Management.

An enraged Richardson confronted Suge a short time later at a nightclub where he astonished onlookers by slapping Knight around until three of his thugs jumped in and drove Bruce off. Publicly humilated, Suge made no secret of the fact that he wanted revenge.

Two weeks later, Bruce Richardson was shot to death in his home. Kevin Hackie named Suge Knight's thugs Neckbone and Buntry as the likely hit men—they were the guys that did this sort of thing for Suge, Hackie said—but a question remained about how the killers had gained access to Richardson's home. It was well known that Bruce's place was a virtual fortress, with reinforced steel doors, double dead-bolt locks, heavy bars on all the windows, and an elaborate alarm system. The evidence clearly indicated that Bruce had opened the door for his killers, engaging in a fierce battle with them only after they were inside the house. No way Richardson would have let a couple of Suge's thugs into his living room, Hackie and Poole agreed. He might have opened the door for a couple of guys in LAPD uniforms, however. There were, of course, other possibilities; at right around the same time Bruce was killed, three Bloods had gained entrance to the home of a drug dealer they robbed and shot by posing as Muslims selling bean pies door-to-door. It didn't seem likely that Bruce Richardson would have fallen for that sort of ruse, though.

According to the Rolling 60s Crips, Tupac Shakur had phoned Bruce Richardson's father shortly after Bruce's murder to say that he had nothing to do with it. Tupac hadn't been willing to say the same about Suge Knight, however.

Kevin Hackie proved to be the most verbose Death Row insider Poole had interviewed so far. He already had shared most of what he knew with the FBI, Hackie said, but was happy to repeat it to Poole and Miller. He first met Reggie Wright Jr. back in the late 1980s, Hackie recalled, when he was hired by the Compton Unified School District's police force. Reggie was working as a jailer at that time, but joined his father Reggie Wright Sr. on the Compton P.D. a short time later. Wright Jr. and his partner Smoky Burrell were notorious for ripping off drug dealers, Hackie said, and he believed that was how Reggie and Suge Knight had become involved. It was well known in Compton that Reggie was helping out Suge's homeboys when they got into trouble.

Wrightway Protective Services was created with $300,000 that Suge loaned Reggie in '93 or '94, Hackie said. Suge also was the one who encouraged Reggie to hire off-duty police officers, which, among other things, obviated the need to apply for concealed-weapon permits.

He realized that Death Row was more than simply a record label, Hackie told Poole, soon after joining Wrightway Protective Services in 1994. At the Tarzana studios, Suge's closest associates, after Reggie Wright Jr., were his thugs. He knew for certain that Buntry, Neckbone, and Heron were running drugs, Hackie said, and had heard Suge discussing how to obtain and distribute assault rifles on at least one occasion. Also, Hackie said, Death Row ran a money-laundering operation that took in as much as $80,000 per month.

Suge was a classic bully, but he was shrewd and nervy at the same time, Hackie said, with a real talent for psychologically manipulating the people around him. The cops still underestimated him; he was as powerful as any gangster in the country. Hackie used almost the same words that Frank Alexander had in describing Suge Knight's approach to business. "Both bodyguards said that Knight only let people get close if he had something on them," Poole recalled. "And that he always lets it be known that you will be killed if you cross him."

Suge met with Omar Bradley and Mustapha Farrakhan to talk about backing Bradley's run for a vacant congressional seat, Hackie said, yet at the same time treated the Compton mayor like one of his bun boys. And after Knight caught Bradley messing around with one of his girlfriends, Hackie added, Suge told the mayor that if he ever came near the young woman again he was a dead man.

David Kenner was "the brains of the company," Hackie said, and it was common knowledge at Death Row that the attorney provided connections to the organized crime families back east.

Although he was absolutely certain that Suge and Reggie Wright had been behind Biggie Smalls's murder, Hackie said, he had no real evidence that Suge was responsible for Tupac's slaying. He believed it was more than possible that Suge *had* been involved, though, Hackie added. Shakur and Knight were fighting over money all summer; when Tupac would ask for the royalties he was owed, Suge would respond by sending him a forty- or fifty-thousand-dollar bill for the expenses his family had run up at the Westwood Marquis. Everyone at Death Row recognized that Tupac was inching his way toward the door, and when he fired David Kenner, they knew the rapper was risking his life. In fact, Wright had turned on Hackie because Reggie and Suge believed the bodyguard was encouraging Tupac to leave L.A. and relocate to Atlanta. Tupac definitely did not want to go to Las Vegas on the weekend he was murdered, Hackie said, and changed his mind only because Suge went to work on him. He was unimpressed by the fact that Suge was in the car with Tupac when the rapper was shot, Hackie said: "Suge was bold enough to take that chance."

Frank Alexander wasn't the only one whose life was threatened after Tupac died, Hackie told Poole: Reggie Wright had phoned him to say, "I can have you killed at any time."

He believed, by the way, that Reggie had been behind the murder of Orlando Anderson, Hackie said; Wright owned a champagne-colored Chevy Blazer that matched the description of the "suspect vehicle" in that killing. And no matter what else they heard, Hackie told Poole and Miller, Reggie Wright was the one running Death Row while Suge was in prison. Reggie was Suge's "little bitch," and did his master's bidding without question.

Kevin Lewis had no evidence that Suge was involved in the murders of either Tupac Shakur or Biggie Smalls, but the former Death Row studio manager had no doubt that Knight was capable of killing anyone he wished to eliminate. The terror in his eyes was what made Lewis so persuasive. It had taken Poole months to arrange a sit-down with Kenneth Knox's main informant, who vowed that he would never set foot in Los Angeles again. A scheduled meeting in Chicago was aborted when Lewis phoned from New York to say he couldn't make it, and that he still feared Suge Knight might have him killed. And when Death Row's former manager finally rendezvoused with Poole in Chicago, he added little that he hadn't already told Kenneth Knox. Lewis did acknowledge for the first time that he had been present when Kelly Jamerson was beaten to death at the El Rey Theater, though, and said he in fact "stepped over the body" on his way to the nearest exit. Getting away with that murder, Lewis said, definitely emboldened Suge and his thugs. Lewis also spoke in greater detail than previously about the fights between the Crips and the

Bloods that had broken out in the Tarzana studios, and told Poole that Suge had seemed to encourage these near riots. Those battles had created a real dilemma for Snoop Dogg, who was "more blue than red," Lewis said, and might be the one important Death Row rapper willing to talk about what he knew. Eight months earlier, the Long Beach detective who infiltrated Death Row as part of the federal task force had told LAPD detectives that "Suge used to slap Snoop Dogg around like a little girl." He believed Snoop hated Suge enough to betray him, the Long Beach detective said.

What Poole didn't know when he spoke to Kevin Lewis was that Snoop already had hit back at Knight. On May Day, shortly after breaking with Death Row to join Master P at No Limit Records, Snoop had appeared onstage to perform one song with his new partner at a concert in the Universal Amphitheater. As soon as Snoop stepped away from the microphone, he was surrounded by five Bloods. When one of them punched him in the face, the rapper broke free and ran toward the metal detector behind the stage, where a pair of deputies from the nearby L.A. County Sheriff's substation were posted. After the deputies called for backup, it took another twenty deputies, along with four dozen security guards, to break up the mob of young black males that had grown to more than sixty. Once they got Snoop inside the substation, deputies did a pat-down search and found a baggie filled with marijuana in the rapper's hip pocket. The lieutenant who commanded the substation then interviewed Snoop personally, and eventually relayed his account to Poole.

"I think I know who killed Tupac," the lieutenant said.

"I do, too," Snoop replied. "The guy who was seated next to him."

"You mean Suge Knight?" the lieutenant asked.

"Yes!" Snoop answered. The rapper's explanation was essentially the same one given by Frank Alexander and Kevin Hackie: Suge owed Tupac $3 million and didn't want to pay it, especially if Shakur was going to leave his label.

Armed with what he had learned from Alexander, Hackie, and

Lewis, Poole once again approached his superiors in the Robbery-Homicide Division, seeking permission one more time for a full-scale investigation of the clues that implicated David Mack in the Biggie Smalls murder. Again he was rebuffed. "The only explanation I got was, 'Those clues aren't viable,'" Poole recalled. "When I asked why they weren't viable, and if there had been an investigation that exonerated Mack, I was told it was none of my business. That was a first. Here I am still listed as the lead investigator on the Biggie Smalls case, and the investigation of the person I consider the main suspect is 'none of my business.'"

Poole was beginning to believe that the explanation for this was very simple: "Criminal cops get protected because the department wants to avoid scandal and publicity." And that protection seemed to increase exponentially whenever the criminal cops were black.

The LAPD's new double standard was nowhere so obvious as in the different treatment received by Kevin Gaines and Frank Lyga. While Gaines not only escaped repeatedly from the consequences of his actions, and was sheltered from investigation even after his death, Lyga remained under a cloud long after the evidence submitted by Poole had demonstrated his innocence. Chief Parks ordered Internal Affairs investigators to comb through Lyga's personnel package, breaking down every use of force by Lyga during his ten years on the force into assorted categories, including the suspects' race. IA investigators twice ran tests at the Gaines-Lyga shooting scene to verify that it was a "dead spot" where Lyga's radio broadcasts couldn't be picked up at LAPD headquarters. Even after the LAPD's Officer Involved Shooting Unit and a three-man "shooting board" agreed that Lyga's actions had been within departmental policy, Parks authorized a costly, computer-generated 3–D video model of the shooting, then nullified the ruling of the first shooting board and convened a second, this one made up entirely of black officers. That board also cleared Lyga.

"I gave them my final follow-up report months before they finally approved it and exonerated Lyga," Poole recalled. "It was in delay mode for a long time, the longest I'd seen in my entire career. The whole thing was blatantly political. And I was shocked when I saw the Internal Affairs report on Gaines later that year. They kept a lot of things out, including that fifteen-seven report from Officer Guidry that Gaines was a posible dope courier for Suge Knight."

Frank Lyga's ordeal wasn't over, either. When the detective's personnel package had been sent to the City Attorney's office to prepare for the lawsuit filed by Johnnie Cochran, the documents inside disappeared for eighteen months. During that time, Los Angeles newspapers ran a series of stories detailing every complaint filed against Lyga during his career. There were four, and although not one of them was sustained, articles filled with verbs like "punched," "kicked," and "tackled" created a troubling impression, especially when coupled with Cochran's charge that Lyga was "a racist, out of control cop." Only when the LAPD's final report was presented in March of 1998 did the public learn that the first of these complaints, made by an arrestee who claimed Lyga bound his wrists too tightly with handcuffs, was filed eight months after the incident. The second complaint had been made by an arrestee who said Lyga had kicked him in the kidneys, but omitted that Lyga had just found a concealed pistol in the suspect's boot and had forced the man back to the ground only after he tried to stand up. The third complaint, filed by an arrestee whose nose had been broken when Lyga and his partner tackled him, was dropped when the man pleaded guilty to resisting arrest. The fourth complaint, filed by an arrestee who claimed Lyga had beaten him, was dismissed after the man's friend said he had made up the story and investigators learned that Lyga hadn't even been on the scene at the time the incident occurred. An embittered Lyga demanded to know why the newspapers didn't want to put *that* information on their front pages.

Lyga, like Russell Poole, was furious when he learned that Kevin Gaines's friend Derwin Henderson had gotten off with a slap on the wrist. "Henderson should have at least been fired, and could easily have been charged with interfering with an investigation," Poole said. "Instead he gets a five-day suspension for 'inappropriate conduct.' If the races were reversed in this case, and a bunch of white officers had gone out to question witnesses like he and his friends did, all hell would have broken loose. Heads would have rolled."

Whatever role race played in it, Poole remained convinced that the LAPD brass was intentionally covering up for the officers who had been involved with Death Row Records. "Each time I pushed to go down that road in the Biggie Smalls investigation," Poole recalled, "the brass told me, 'We're not going to get involved in that.' Their attitude was, 'Gaines is dead. Mack has already gone down for bank robbery. Let's not get involved in more controversy.'"

Poole believed more controversy was inevitable, however. Each time he reviewed his notes of the interview with Kevin Hackie, Poole would pause at the answer Hackie had given when asked to identify any members of the Los Angeles Police Department who were close to Suge Knight. All he knew, Hackie said, was that three LAPD officers had shown up regularly at the "private parties" Suge Knight threw for his inner circle. Kevin Gaines was the only one whose name he knew, Hackie said. The second man the bodyguard would identify a few months later as David Mack. Hackie did not identify the third officer until more than two years later, when he was shown a photograph of Ray Perez.

PART FOUR

INVENTING THE SCANDAL

Poole has performed his duties in an outstanding manner. He is a dependable, hard-working and loyal employee. His investigations are always thorough and related reports are well-written . . . Poole maintains a good attitude in the midst of the present turmoil with the Department. He is extremely loyal to the LAPD and proud to be part of this organization. He works diligently to instill this attitude in those he works with and strives to achieve the Department goals.

—From the "Performance Evaluation Report" filed on Detective Trainee Russell Poole for the period 9/1/91 to 2/29/92

CHAPTER NINE

Poole had first heard of Ray Perez on February 6, 1998, when he was given a list of LAPD officers who were closest to David Mack. At the top were Sammy Martin, a detective trainee in the Rampart Division who was the godfather to one of Mack's children, and Perez, an anti-gang detective assigned to Rampart who once had been partnered with Mack as an undercover narcotics officer. Perez had been involved in an officer involved shooting, Poole was advised early on, in which Mack killed a drug dealer.

When he looked at Mack's personnel file and read the official account of Jose Vincencio's shooting, Poole was struck by a statement from Perez to the effect that he owed his life to David Mack and would do anything for the man. The lead detectives in the bank robbery, Tyndall and Grant, had called Perez in for questioning within forty-eight hours of Mack's arrest. A short time later, the detectives learned that Perez and Sammy Martin had left with Mack for Las Vegas two days after the bank robbery, staying in a $1,500 a night suite at Caesar's Palace, and blowing through $21,000 in a single weekend. On a similar excursion to Lake Tahoe, the three had posed together for a photograph, Mack in his blood-red suit, flanked by Martin and Perez, each of them holding unlit cigars. Like Kevin Gaines and David Mack, Poole soon discovered, Perez had for some time enjoyed a lifestyle that was impossible to support on the $58,000 annual salary he earned as a police officer. He drove expensive cars, took Caribbean cruises, lost thousands at the blackjack tables in Las Vegas, and apparently thought nothing of spending four or five thousand dollars in an evening to entertain one young girlfriend after another.

During April of 1998, Perez realized that he was under surveillance by officers from the Internal Affairs and Robbery-Homicide divisions. He assumed this was because the department suspected he had been involved in the bank robbery with David Mack. Perez responded by marching straight in to tell his commanding officer that he had nothing to do with it. His fellow cops, however, weren't tailing Ray Perez on account of his possible involvement in the bank robbery (although they strongly suspected he had been one of Mack's accomplices), but because they believed he had stolen a large quantity of pure cocaine from the LAPD's Property Division.

The investigation began on March 27, 1998, when a property officer at the LAPD's Evidence Control Unit realized that more than six pounds of cocaine checked out on March 2 still had not been returned. In early April, LAPD Officer Joel Perez was startled by an Overdue Property Notice reminding him to return three kilos of cocaine he had checked out more than a month earlier. He hadn't checked out any three kilos of coke, Joel Perez replied. Shown a sign-out sheet bearing his name and badge number, the officer insisted it was a forgery.

LAPD Property Officer Laura Castellano said she couldn't specifically recall the transaction in which she had released the three kilos, and didn't recognize the photograph of Joel Perez she was shown. She did remember handing over a carton of narcotics to another Officer Perez, however, Castellano said. Rafael was his first name, Castellano told detectives. She remembered the man mainly because he had been so "rude and arrogant," and she had remarked upon his obnoxious attitude to another property officer, who said he was always that way. Castellano also recalled the name of the supervising officer who released the coke to her. A check of LAPD records soon revealed that the three property officers had worked together on only one day in their entire careers—March 2, 1998. "If Rafael

Perez had picked up the cocaine on any other day he never would have been detected," admitted Richard Rosenthal, the assistant district attorney who was eventually chosen to prosecute the detective. "It was just bad luck."

On April 16, LAPD detectives discovered that a second carton of cocaine was missing from the Property Division, this one containing a pound of coke that on February 5, 1998, had been sent by courier to Rampart Division, where it was signed for by Officer Armando Coronado. He had made no request for cocaine, said Coronado, who reacted viscerally when detectives asked him about his relationship with Ray Perez. Perez despised him, Coronado said, mainly because of his refusal to cut corners in dealing with informants and when searching suspects. Perez called him a "company man," Coronado said, and on one occasion had threatened in the presence of several witnesses to "kick my ass."

Russell Poole was less intrigued by the enmity between Coronado and Perez than by the identity of the undercover detective who had booked the missing coke into evidence—his name was Frank Lyga. Poole became convinced—as did several other Robbery-Homicide detectives—that Ray Perez had targeted Lyga's coke as retaliation for the shooting of Kevin Gaines. "We all agreed this was just way too big a coincidence," Poole recalled.

Suddenly, the Los Angeles Police Department became very interested in knowing who and what they were dealing with here.

Born in 1967, in Humacao, Puerto Rico, of African and Hispanic ancestry, Rafael Perez had never known his father. His mother, Luz, moved her three children to Brooklyn in 1972, and quickly relocated to Paterson, New Jersey, where Rafael spent most of his childhood. The family moved again just before Rafael started high school, this time to a very tough neighborhood in North Philadelphia, where they stayed in the home of an uncle who dealt drugs for a living. Despite his difficult background, Rafael Perez was a straight-arrow teenager who joined the Marine Corps immediately after high school. While stationed at the Marine barracks in Portsmouth, New Hampshire, he met and married (at age eighteen) a young enlisted woman from the nearby Pease Air Force Base. Lorri Charles was black and assumed, based upon his features and complexion, that Rafael was also. It was an early example of Perez's remarkable capacity for shape shifting, especially along racial and ethnic lines. When his bride was discharged from the Air Force, her husband moved her to the Marine Air Corps Station in Tustin, California, Lorri's home state. The couple broke up only three years into their marriage, when Lorri discovered Rafael's infidelity.

In June of 1989, shortly after his wife had left him, twenty-one-year-old Rafael Perez was accepted into the Los Angeles Police Academy. He did his probationary stint in the LAPD's Harbor Division, then was transferred to patrol duty in Wilshire Division, where he first began to introduce himself as Ray. Driven and intense, Perez had a lithe body and a face that was remarkably handsome, except for eyebrows that grew in an almost solid line across the bridge of his nose. He advanced quickly within the LAPD, taking advantage of his fluency in Spanish to win an assignment as an undercover narcotics cop after only a year of patrol duty.

The West Bureau Buy Team was made up of eight to ten younger officers who could convincingly pose as drug buyers in neighborhoods all over the city. While other members of the unit worked the beaches and busted Rastafarians, Ray Perez and David Mack accepted the most dangerous of duties, purchasing narcotics almost exclusively in notorious gang neighborhoods and housing projects. Like most members of the buy team, Perez loved the work. "Just by its nature there is constant danger, a constant go, go, go, a constant rush," the detective who ran the buy team, Bobby Lutz, would explain to the *Los Angeles Times*. "Those guys were on the edge all the time . . . they lap it up, they relish it."

Russell Poole, like a lot of LAPD officers in more mainstream positions, regarded undercover narcotics officers as freelancers who made their own rules and regularly became untethered from such niceties as due process and probable cause. The worst of them were the best examples of how the War on Drugs had ravaged law enforcement in the United States. There was a distinctly ends-justify-the-means attitude that tended to blur the line between cops and criminals. Most undercover officers remained honest, but a lot didn't, believed Poole, who was convinced that both Ray Perez and David Mack had gone bad as members of the West Bureau Buy Team. "During the first briefing I received on Mack," Poole recalled, "I was told that he allegedly had been involved in several rip-offs of drug dealers. And since Perez was his partner, it seemed pretty likely that he had been involved also."

In 1994, soon after David Mack left the Buy Team to transfer to West L.A., Ray Perez applied for a job with the Chino Police Department. Everyone who knew about this was astonished when Perez didn't land the position. Ray's boss Bobby Lutz, figuring the yokels out in Chino should consider themselves lucky to land a top LAPD officer, phoned the smaller police department to ask what was going on. When the Chino cops said they couldn't talk about it, Lutz surmised that Perez had failed a test—either a polygraph or a psychological exam. It was a red flag that no one chose to wave, and only a few months later Ray Perez moved onward and upward to the Rampart Division's CRASH unit.

CRASH (which stood for Community Resources Against Street Hoodlums) was the LAPD's elite anti-gang unit, and Perez joined it at a time when the department estimated that Los Angeles was home to 403 distinct gangs claiming nearly 60,000 members. In 1994, the year Perez joined CRASH, gang members committed almost 11,000 crimes in the city, by the LAPD's accounting, including 408 homicides. Gang violence had become the number one problem in most citywide citizen polls, and about 10 percent of all Los Angeles's gang crimes were occurring in the Rampart Division, turf of the notorious 18th Street Gang.

Rampart was eight square miles of decaying apartment buildings and scabrous storefronts between Hollywood and downtown, encompassing the Pico-Union and Westlake districts. These neighborhoods were the most densely populated in Los Angeles, and home to perhaps the highest percentage of illegal immigrants in the state. Vendors who peddled big sacks of oranges and dealers who sold small bags of cocaine worked the sidewalks side by side. Nannies and gardeners who sent half their minimum-wage paychecks back across the border waited for buses all along the perimeter of McArthur Park, which had become the largest open-air drug market in the United States. And most of that drug trade was controlled by the 18th Street Gang.

The 18th Streeters were by far the biggest gang in a city that had become the nation's capital of gang activity, claiming as many as 20,000 members who were scattered in subgroups, or "cliques," up and down the West Coast from Tijuana to Portland, Oregon. The gang wove together layers of criminal enterprise that deployed a system of "tax" collection to link drug trafficking all the way from the powerful, prison-based Mexican Mafia at the top to the small-time independent dealers at the bottom. More than 150 murders were linked to the 18th Street Gang between 1985 and 1995. Citizens all across the city, and especially in the neighborhoods most affected, wanted the gang dealt with, and the members of Rampart's CRASH unit were on point in the LAPD's battle against the 18th Streeters, an engagement that would come to a climax in August of 1997, when the Los Angeles City Council won a court injunction against the gang that made it illegal for members to associate.

In this context, joining CRASH during the mid-1990s was more like becoming a special forces fighter in a wartime army than anything resembling traditional police work. CRASH unit members were there to "take back the streets" and an officer's performance was judged almost exclusively by how many gangsters he could put behind bars. Rampart's CRASH team had not only its own logo—the Aces and Eights of Wild Bill Hickok's "dead man's hand"—but even its own headquarters in a detective substation a mile from the main division station. "We Intimidate Those Who Intimidate Others," read the motto above the main entrance. Officers worked mostly at night and without any real supervision. If an officer made arrests that led to convictions, he was doing a good job; if not, he was considered to lack the "initiative" that anti-gang work required.

Ray Perez had been a top "producer" as an undercover narcotics cop, and he continued to make a high number of arrests when he joined Rampart's CRASH unit. And perhaps no other detective on the LAPD could match his effectiveness as a witness in court. Public Defender Tamar Toister would recall her feeling of helplessness as she watched Perez testify against her client Javier Ovando in early 1997. It was a case where Toister figured that both judge and jury might feel a certain sympathy for her client. Perez and his partner Nino Durden had shot Ovando three times in the process of arresting him, and the nineteen-year-old was left paralyzed from the waist down. Ovando had to be wheeled into court on a gurney at his preliminary hearing, and would be confined to a wheelchair for the rest of his life. After Perez described how Ovando (whose gang nickname was "Sniper") had attempted to ambush him and his partner with an assault rifle though, the 18th Streeter's fate was sealed. "Perez was unbelievably good on the witness stand," Toister recalled. "He was better than any police officer I've ever cross-examined, smooth, sincere, articulate, with just the right amount of emotion. You couldn't bait him, you couldn't trip him up, you couldn't get him to react." Duly impressed, Judge Stephen Czuleger sentenced Ovando to twenty-three years in state prison, even more time than the prosecutor had asked for. "That was entirely due to how good Perez had been on the stand," Toister recalled. "I have to admit, I believed him myself."

By June of 1998, Ray Perez was the target of a special LAPD unit. Though later made famous in the local media as the Rampart Task Force, back then it was known simply as the Robbery-Homicide Task Force, and its creation was largely a response to the detective work of Russell Poole. "The connections that Russ Poole had made between the David Mack bank robbery and the Biggie Smalls murder, including the possibility that an LAPD officer, or officers, might be involved, were the origin of the task force," agreed Richard Rosenthal. The assistant district attorney's recollection was ironic, since by the time Rosenthal came aboard, Det. Poole viewed the task force more as the vehicle for a continuing cover-up rather than as a means for arriving at truth.

During the last two weeks of May, Poole had engaged in a series of public confrontations over the handling of the Biggie Smalls case, first with Fred Miller, then with Lieutenant Pat Conmay, and finally with Captain Jim Tatreau. "I told Captain Tatreau, 'I've never seen anything like this,'" Poole recalls. "'If you want the Biggie Smalls case solved, you've got to give it to me alone.'" Several days later, Poole found a hand-drawn cartoon on his desk showing a toilet and the plumbing pipes connected to it. The words "You Are Here" were connected by an arrow to a turd lodged in the pipes. Poole recognized the handwriting as his partner's.

Two days later, Poole flew to Chicago to interview Kevin Lewis. While he was gone, another senior detective filed a complaint against him, alleging that Poole had been derelict in monitoring the autopsy of a Los Angeles Unified School District police officer who had been killed by a shotgun blast to the face. Poole's lieutenant ordered him transferred out of Robbery-Homicide, then reversed himself when the complainant's partner backed Poole. "For the first time in months I sort of had an upper hand," Poole recalled. "The lieutenant had made all these accusations against me without waiting to hear my side of the story, and now he was afraid I'd file a complaint against *him*."

Poole had been under an administrative cloud since the previous December, when the department had brought charges against him for the first time in his career as an LAPD detective. The incident seemed so inconsequential at the time that Poole hadn't realized how it might be used against him later. He and his wife had separated for five months at the end of 1997, mainly because Megan was fed up with her husband's devotion to his duties as a police officer. "Living with a homicide detective is tough," Poole admitted. "Getting calls in the middle of the night, working long hours and only coming home to catch a few hours of sleep, being so absorbed in a case that you don't see what's happening in your personal life. I felt, 'Look, it's a major responsibility to be a homicide detective. There's killers on the loose and it's my job to find them.' My wife wanted me to put my family first, and she was right, but I didn't see it at the time." While separated from Megan, Poole began dating a secretary who worked for the Los Angeles Police Commmission. Ten days before Christmas, the pair attended a Robbery-Homicide Division holiday party at Little Pedro's, a downtown restaurant favored by the LAPD. "All of us coppers drove our take-home cars," recalled Poole. "The woman I was dating and I only stayed about forty-five minutes. I was exhausted. I had been up for almost two days, with maybe three hours sleep in that time, and I had to get up early the next morning to fly back east. I didn't even have a drink. All I could think about was getting up at four the next morning." When they left the restaurant, Poole asked the young woman to drive while he took a nap. When she said yes, he kissed her on the cheek, then rolled over against the passenger-side door and fell asleep. What Poole didn't realize was that his car was being tailed by an LAPD commander who would file a complaint against him for taking a department-owned car to the restaurant, permitting a civilian employee to drive it, and kissing her on the cheek in public.

"When I went on vacation the week before Christmas, I figured I was facing the lightest slap on the wrist they could give me," Poole recalled. "For one thing, there were at least two dozen other police vehicles in the parking lot of that restaurant, most of them driven by people of higher rank." Over the holidays, Poole reconciled with his wife and moved back into the family home. He came back to work in January feeling rejuvenated and was startled to learn that he faced a disciplinary hearing. "I expected the captain and lieutenant to go to bat for me and say this is chickenshit," Poole recalled. "All the RHD detectives drove their take-home cars to places they shouldn't—bars, golf courses, whatever. I didn't even know what the rules were, because they were so loose. My supervisors were aware the parking lot of that restaurant had been filled with cop cars. I wasn't going to roll over on anybody, but they all knew." The investigation continued, however, and Poole knew by March that he would receive suspension days. "I couldn't comprehend that they were spending so much time and effort to make a case against me for such a trivial thing, when they had all these guys working for Death Row who were walking time-bombs in terms of bad publicity for the LAPD. I felt like it was the ultimate disrespect to me and all the other honest cops in the department."

Poole eventually concluded that his supervisors wanted leverage. "What the LAPD brass does to detectives working downtown is wait for you to make a mistake, then let you know that they've got you by the balls," Poole explained. "The message is, 'You will do as we say, or we'll use this against you.' When they think they have you under control, they put you in a position where you can be helpful." The detectives assigned to the Robbery-Homicide Task Force in the spring of 1998, Poole would observe, included one who had been caught using the word "nigger" over the radio and another who had been accused of beating his wife. Poole's lieutenant, meanwhile, had attempted for months to bait him into filing a complaint against Fred Miller for dereliction of duty. "Conmay would come to me and ask where Fred was," Poole recalled. "My answer was always the same: 'I don't know where he is now, lieutenant, but I can page him for you.' I could see the frustration in Conmay's eyes. He was hoping I would tell him Fred was on the golf course. But I wasn't going down that road. I knew the veterans would crucify a snitch." When the LAPD brought him up on charges for misuse of his take-home car, "they thought they had me," Poole recalled. "It really pissed them off when I admitted what I did, signed the papers, and took my suspension days. I wasn't going to let them hold it over me."

Poole's colleagues in RHD were sympathetic at first, but as word spread that he was trying to make a case against cops in the Biggie Smalls murder investigation, many of his fellow detectives began to observe that Mr. Goody Two-shoes had feet of clay. "There were a lot of innuendos of a sexual nature, because the woman I'd been dating was in the car with me," Poole recalled. "And that was painful, because I was back with my wife and wanted to put that whole period in my personal life behind me. And the guys who were still on my side were keeping quiet, waiting to see how this whole thing would play out. So I felt more and more isolated."

After the first attempt to oust him from the Robbery-Homicide failed, Poole's supervisors realized that having him around put them at risk. "So they got me out of RHD by offering me a more prestigious assignment," Poole recalled. "Captain Tatreau came to me and said, 'Russ, how would you like to join the task force and be in charge of Biggie Smalls and the connections to Mack and the bank robbery?' I said, 'I'd love to. But am I going to have some power and leeway to do this right?' I told [the brass] that time was of the essence, because once Suge Knight went to jail, it was a perfect cover for the cops involved to get out of the organization. They promised I would have the power to get all the subpoenas I needed, but almost as soon as I joined the task force, they told me I was off the Smalls case."

Fred Miller was embarrassed and had insisted that the Biggie Smalls murder investigation belonged to him, Poole was informed. "So now the brass wants me to concentrate on Perez," Poole recalled. "When we were first forming the task force, the main targets were supposed to be David Mack and any other police officers who might be involved in either the bank robbery or the Biggie Smalls case. And Perez was sort of an afterthought. That's what they said and that's what they wrote, but it was all bogus. They wanted that on the record as the official intent, but once we started they completely abandoned David Mack and Kevin Gaines and Biggie Smalls and the whole Death Row Records investigation. We didn't work on anything else but Perez. It was like the whole thing got transformed overnight. I knew it was coming down from the top, but nobody ever told me why we were doing what we were doing. I had to figure it out on my own."

The other members of the task force also seemed uncertain about the parameters of their investigation. Just how large a criminal conspiracy were they dealing with? detectives wondered. "Perez and Durden and Sam Martin were meeting for lunch every day," Poole recalled. "Then they'd reconnoiter in the middle of the night in Griffith Park behind a urinal stall. We didn't know if they were talking about the bank robbery, the stolen coke, the Biggie Smalls murder, or all three."

By the time Poole joined the task force, detectives working the coke-theft case realized that Perez had for some time been taking advantage of the LAPD's absurdly loose system for checking out drugs as court evidence, especially when the amounts involved were a pound or less. Essentially, all an officer had to do was make a phone call to the Property Division, give his last name and badge number, then ask that the dope be sent to him by courier. The drugs had to be returned, of course, but no one at Property Division ever checked to find out if what they got back was pure cocaine or a bag of baking powder. How much coke Perez had stolen remained in question, but there was little doubt he was supplying a significant number of street dealers.

During July of 1998, while still under surveillance, Perez was photographed in a "romantic embrace" with a juicy-looking Honduran nightclub singer he knew as Bella Rios. Her real name was Veronica Quesada. Poole and another task force detective were assigned to watch the woman's apartment, wait until she was alone, then ambush her with a request for an interview. "Veronica Quesada knows English, but she wouldn't speak to us," Poole recalled. "She kept saying, 'no comprende.' She hung tough during questioning. She's no easy mark, I can tell you that." Quesada's composure dissolved, however, when her brother Carlos Romero walked into the apartment carrying a quarter-pound of cocaine. "The brother was so dumbfounded that he just stood there," Poole remembered. "It might have been the easiest coke bust in history."

During a subsequent search of the apartment, the detectives opened a drawer in the living room console and discovered a framed photograph of Ray Perez wearing a blood-red sweatsuit and flashing the West Coast gang sign. "I remember thinking, 'I knew it,' Poole recalled.

Within a couple of weeks, detectives from the task force had established numerous links between Perez, Quesada, and Romero. The most significant of these was that both Quesada and Romero had been convicted of felonies during the past year for dealing cocaine, yet each had received a suspended sentence. In both instances this was because the judges who heard the cases received requests for leniency from the estimable Det. Ray Perez. At the time of her arrest in April of 1997, detectives learned, Quesada was in possession of "pay/owe" sheets bearing the initials "RP" and the phone number for the Rampart Division. And on the date that the two kilos of cocaine were checked out of the LAPD's Property Division, supposedly by Officer Joel Perez, Ray Perez had made a total of eight phone calls to Veronica Quesada and Carlos Romero. The detective made more than 160 calls to the same numbers between November of 1997 and June of 1998.

When questioned, Perez explained both his requests for leniency and the phone calls by claiming that Quesada was a "former informant" with whom he had, unfortunately, become sexually involved. "The guy was cool under questioning," Poole recalled, "but when I saw him one afternoon soon after that at the Police Academy, you could tell he was scared shitless. He was looking around all the time, over his shoulders, behind his back. He knew we were closing in on him."

By the time of the drug bust in Veronica Quesada's apartment, Russell Poole had become convinced that the main intent of the task force created by LAPD Chief Bernard Parks was not to expand the investigation, but to limit it as completely as possible. "First, Chief Parks wanted us—me—to drop everything pertaining to Biggie Smalls, Kevin Gaines, David Mack, and Death Row Records, and to concentrate on Perez," Poole recalled. "But then it turns out that we're not supposed to look very deep into Perez's background, either. I was starting to get the feeling that this entire investigation was going to end up as nothing more than a coke bust."

On his own initiative, Poole read through more than a hundred reports written by Ray Perez in connection to drug arrests the detective had made. "It's like this guy is superman," Poole recalled, "like he has X-ray vision or something, because he's making all these fantastic busts and dope seizures where he seems to see through walls." Again and again, Poole noted, Perez would report that suspects had signed "Consent to Search" forms. "He had all these dope dealers telling him where their stash was even before they confessed," Poole recalled. "That never happens. You bust a dealer, they figure, 'Fuck you, find the shit yourself.' And every one of these reports was the same. They were like boilerplates where you just fill in a new name and date. Any veteran cop would look at them and know they were fake, because any veteran cop knows that no case is identical to any other." Poole took the reports directly to LAPD Commander Dan Schatz. "He called them 'suspect,' but wouldn't add falsifying police reports to the charges against Perez," Poole recalls. "That was when I first began to realize that the main objective of the task force was to protect the higher-ups, starting with Chief Parks."

At almost the moment he began to think in this vein, Poole's supervisors reduced his role in the Perez investigation so that he could concentrate on an incident involving another member of the Rampart CRASH unit. This was Brian Hewitt, who had been accused of viciously beating 18th Street Gang member Ismael Jimanez during an interrogation. On February 26, 1998, Hewitt and his partner Daniel Lujan had picked up Jimanez and his friend Eduardo Hernandez in front of a tattoo parlor and "detained" the pair on

suspicion of grand theft auto. The real reason the two were transported to the Rampart detectives' office, though, was the complaint
of excessive force filed by Hernandez's mother against two other
Rampart officers. Both Jimanez and Hernandez said they were taunted
and threatened by Hewitt, who, after separating the pair, demanded
that Jimanez "find me a gun"—lead him to an 18th Street Gang
member he could arrest for illegal possession of a firearm. When
he refused, Jimanez said, Hewitt grabbed him by the throat and
forced him backward until his head struck a wall. "You're not fucking hearing me," Hewitt told him, according to Jimanez, whose
hands were cuffed behind his back. "I will book you for anything.
You had better tell me tonight where I could find a gun." When
Jimanez didn't answer, the powerfully built Hewitt punched him
with a clenched fist several times in the chest and once in the kidneys. "All I want is one little gun," Hewitt said, then turned and
walked out of the room. A few seconds later Jimanez vomited blood
on the carpeted floor and nearly passed out.

When Rampart officer Ethan Cohan walked into the interview
room a few moments later, Jimanez told him he couldn't breathe and
had vomited blood, then pleaded with Cohan to remove his handcuffs. Cohan looked at the bloodstain on the floor, said, "Oh shit,"
then quickly turned and left. Cohan came and went twice more,
Jimanez said, before finally removing the cuffs and telling him he was
free to leave. He vomited repeatedly during the mile-and-a-half walk
back to the tattoo parlor, Jimanez said, where friends told him he
looked really bad and drove him to Good Samaritan Hospital. Doctors in the hospital's emergency room reported the alleged assault to
Rampart Division's Watch Commander, who sent a sergeant to take
Jimanez's statement. A scrap of carpet was collected as evidence and
the case was turned over to Internal Affairs, "which basically did
nothing for the next five months," said Poole. The detective was
startled to discover that the IA investigators had not even ordered
DNA testing of the blood on the carpet. "All that takes is one phone
call," Poole explained. "I made that call as soon as I found out that

they hadn't checked to make sure the blood belonged to Jimanez. And it turned out, of course, that it was Jimanez's blood."

One claim after another made by the gangbanger and his friends checked out. At the same time, Poole heard troubling descriptions of Officer Hewitt's violent disposition. "It became clear pretty fast that Hewitt was a sadist," Poole recalled. "He really liked beating people up. He got off on it, almost in a sexual way."

Though he didn't quite comprehend it at the time, Poole's investigation of Hewitt would mark a major turning point in the task force's mission. Up to that point, all of the officers under investigation for criminal conduct were black, except for Perez, who was half black. Hewitt, however, was a blue-eyed blond. And the case against him was not for murder, robbery, or drug dealing but for brutality.

"It seemed very strange and mysterious when they moved me over to the Hewitt case," Poole recalled. "First, I was gonna go after Mack and Gaines and all the cops who were suspect in the Biggie Smalls case, then I was supposed to work the dope case against Perez, and the next thing I know they have me on the Jimanez beating. I kept wondering, 'What is this about?' Then they partnered me with an investigator from Internal Affairs. I asked the lieutenant, 'Isn't this a conflict of interest?' I mean, I was supposed to be investigating criminal charges and she was supposed to be investigating administrative ones. But the lieutenant said, 'No, you're both members of the task force.' I said, 'Okay,' but then they assigned the very detective who had tried to run me out of RHD with those bullshit charges about the autopsy to supervise the investigation. And right away he accuses me of trying to fabricate a case against Hewitt."

Poole went to the task force leader, Lt. Emmanuel Hernandez, and asked him to assign a new supervisor to the case. Hernandez, however, refused, "even after I told him that the guy's attitude was going to screw the case up if it ever went to court," Poole recalled. "What I didn't realize then was that Chief Parks didn't want this case to go to court, because the brass were still trying to cover up an earlier investigation involving Hewitt and Perez that they should have used to clean up Rampart Division way back in September of 1995."

In that case, Hewitt, Perez, and a female officer named Stephanie Barr were accused of criminal retaliation against three 18th Street Gang members suspected of slashing the tires on Hewitt's vehicle. After an entire squad of cops beat the three gangbangers senseless, Hewitt, Perez, and Barr stripped them down to their boxer shorts, the 18th Streeters said, and made them walk nearly naked through a crowd made up largely of young women their own age. Actually, only two of them walked. The third, nineteen-year-old Carlos Oliva, was in a wheelchair, paralyzed from the waist down by a shooting four years earlier.

Thoroughly humiliated and feeling he had nothing left to lose, Oliva filed a complaint the next day. The man who took that report was Lt. Emmanuel Hernandez, then a Rampart supervisor. Nothing much happened until December, when Oliva was arrested (by Stephanie Barr's partner, Walter McMahon, for allegedly driving a stolen car. Though released after five days on that charge, Oliva was rearrested a month later by Barr, McMahon, and Hewitt, charged this time with possessing fifty-five rocks of crack cocaine for sale. He had found the dope on Oliva when he arrested him on the auto theft charge that had been dismissed back in December, McMahon said.

Mainly due to the good work of his public defender, the case against Oliva was shown to be badly flawed and probably dirty. His arrest kept Oliva behind bars for three months, however, until the district attorney's office reduced the charges against him from a felony carrying a sentence of five years in state prison to a simple possession misdemeanor that allowed Oliva to avoid prison by entering a drug diversion program.

Oliva's complaint against Officers Hewitt, Barr, and Perez, meanwhile, was now being handled by the Internal Affairs Division, under the control of then Deputy Chief Bernard Parks. Internal Affairs moved the Oliva investigation along as slowly as was humanly possible, not even bothering to interview the alleged victim until eight months after he had filed his complaint. In the meantime, the young man who had joined Oliva in the complaint was turned over to the Immigration and Naturalization Service by a group of LAPD officers that included Hewitt and Perez, then deported to Honduras. Not until late 1997, almost two years after the original incident, did Internal Affairs officers file a report recommending that several officers, including Brian Hewitt and Stephanie Barr, be given letters of reprimand, a slap on the wrist that did not even delay Barr's promotion to homicide detective. Ray Perez was not disciplined at all for his part in the incident.

"That whole quote, investigation, unquote was about letting the statute of limitations run out so that no charges could be filed and the thing could be kept from the public," Poole said. "And that's how they wanted the Jimanez beating handled. It came to the task force originally in order to protect Parks from any connection to the Oliva thing. The IA investigator they partnered me with and I were supposed to put together a case that would let them fire Hewitt from the department and bury the whole thing internally. Only I thought criminal charges should be filed. So pressure was constantly being applied to back off. But I wasn't going to back off. And when they saw that I hadn't learned my lesson, they thought, 'Oh, no, we have a real problem here.' I figured, 'Yes, you do.'"

CHAPTER TEN

Russell Poole wasn't the LAPD's choice to be the officer who arrested Ray Perez, but the department continued to place the detective in the right place at the wrong time.

Poole and a female narcotics investigator named Diana Smith were assigned to perform surveillance on Perez's house in Ladera Heights on the morning of August, 25, 1998, shortly after the department's brass decided it was time finally to charge the CRASH detective with grand theft. "We were sitting out front when we saw the garage door come up," Poole recalled. "Denise Perez backs her BMW out and leaves for work. SWAT is supposed to make the arrest, and an hour later they're working their way toward us, but on the radio we hear that our cover may have been blown. One of the chiefs had ordered that Denise Perez be pulled aside at work and asked if her husband is at home. That tips her off. She goes back to her cubbyhole and calls home.

"Ray Perez comes out a few minutes later, climbs into his red Ford Expedition, and takes off. We catch up and follow. Diana is driving. I call in a request for an air unit and backup, because we are gonna pull him over. We're going north on La Brea by now. We pull up next to the Expedition, I point and hold up my badge. Perez gets this wild look in his eyes for a moment, and I think maybe this is going to turn into a pursuit or even a shoot-out, but then he pulls over to the curb, just as the air unit and a black-and-white show up. I take

Perez over to my car and put my cuffs on him. I can see his heart literally pounding through his shirt, but he won't make a sound. That's when I notice the briefcase in his vehicle and ask what it's for. He says, 'That's for my lawyer. I was on my way to my lawyer's office.' He's a cop, so he knows he has at least a legal argument to suppress if we open the briefcase and find evidence against him. I wanted to open it anyway, but when I phone the D.A., Rosenthal, he says no. It was a stupid mistake, but Rosenthal ended up making a lot of stupid mistakes. And Perez wouldn't say another word."

For Poole, his arrest of Ray Perez was considerably less significant than his role as evidence coordinator during the search of Perez's home nineteen days earlier. The search had produced a trove of 228 "suspicious items" stashed in nooks and crannies all over the house. In terms of the drug theft, perhaps the strongest evidence was a carton of papers that included receipts for thousands of dollars in cash deposits to a Wells Fargo Bank account, records of large purchases on an array of credit cards, documents related to the purchase of real estate in Puerto Rico and California, eight pages of cellular phone records, plus assorted phone and address books. Poole was most interested, however, in the fifty-nine items recovered from cardboard boxes in the basement of the house. These included not only hundreds of rounds of live ammunition that ranged from 12-gauge shotgun shells to .22 caliber rifle bullets, but a large assortment of folding knives and a perplexing collection of "replica" firearms that included an Uzi air gun, a .357 Colt Python with a plugged barrel, several realistic-looking cap guns (one with a screw-in silencer), as well as 9mm and .38 caliber models. These plastic weapons were stage props and children's toys, but they looked convincing in photographs, and Poole believed, correctly, that this was their purpose. "It turned out that Perez and his buddies were planting them on suspects," Poole explained, "taking photographs at the scene, and using those as evidence in court." Perez had cached a huge quantity of stuff stolen from the LAPD, including nearly two dozen keys to police vehicles, several "raid jackets," and three crowd control helmets. What caught Poole's attention, though, were the police scanners Perez kept concealed in his basement. "Since starting on the Biggie Smalls case, I had kept coming across these crime reports in which the perpetrators used police radios and scanners," Poole recalled. "Mark Anthony Bell said Suge Knight and his thugs had used them to monitor the cops while they had him locked in that room upstairs, and the USC student said he had heard Mack and the other two bank robbers listening to police scanners. There were all these reports of the Death Row people using them in and around their studios in Tarzana. Perez certainly didn't need them for framing suspects, and there was no evidence he used them in his dope dealing. For me, this was a possible link to Mack and to Death Row, but once again I couldn't get anyone interested in pursuing it."

Shortly before the search of the Perez residence, Fred Miller had responded to increased pressure to make something happen in the Biggie Smalls murder investigation (and silence Poole) by orchestrating a series of raids on the offices of Death Row Records production companies, and on assorted homes and businesses owned by Suge Knight. "A fishing expedition," Suge Knight's latest attorney, Robin Yanes, called it, and Russell Poole agreed. "I warned everyone that was the wrong way to go," Poole recalled. "To get to a guy like Knight you have to go from the bottom up, and the cops who worked for him were the best way to do that. Those guys were the weak link and I think a lot of them would have rolled over if they'd been brought up on charges, criminal charges especially. I've seen it before—once these guys are in the court system and know they're facing prison time, they will talk. Cops understand better than anybody that once arrests are made it becomes a race to see who can cut a deal first. But all those raids accomplished was to make everyone scatter." The LAPD trumpeted its seizure of an Impala SS owned by Suge Knight, and let the news media know that forensics tests had turned up gunshot residue around the driver's-side door. But that SS was red, not black, and the gunshot residue had been found nearly a year and a half after the Biggie Smalls shooting.

Poole's refusal to abandon his interest in the Biggie Smalls murder was making his position on the task force, and his assignment to the Robbery-Homicide Division as well, increasingly untenable. "I was complaining that we had had a series of incomplete investigations and that it was orchestrated to be that way," Poole explained. "I had become convinced that LAPD officers affiliated with Death Row Records had been involved in the conspiracy to kill Biggie Smalls and none of the brass wanted to hear that."

It didn't help that Poole persisted in pushing the investigation toward even more untested theories of police involvement. When he learned that the bloody clothing and shell casings that the prosecution considered its most important physical evidence in the murder case against Snoop Dogg had been either lost, stolen, or discarded while in LAPD custody, Poole inquired as to where those items had been held. He was informed that they had gone from West LA to Pacific Division before disappearing. "David Mack was at West LA and Kevin Gaines was at Pacific," Poole observed. "I know from my own experience that virtually any police officer can gain access to evidence held in the property room at an LAPD station, and that they have access to the computers that can be used to authorize destruction of evidence, also. I thought it should be looked into, but no one would even talk to me about it."

Poole also was intrigued when Brian Tyndall told him that one of the first people to communicate with David Mack after he was arrested for the bank robbery was the flamboyant racing and rock concert promoter Mike Goodwin. The note Goodwin sent to Mack at the Montebello City Jail read simply, "If you need anything, give us a jingle." What made those words interesting was that Goodwin for years had been the prime suspect in one of L.A.'s most famous unsolved murders, the 1989 slaying of the legendary race driver and former world land-speed record holder Mickey Thompson. Thompson had been shot to death in his driveway in what LAPD detectives described as "an assassination" by "professional hit men." A number of witnesses had seen the suspects fleeing on bicycles from

Thompson's secluded home in the hillside community of Bradbury, and identified the pair as black males in their mid- to late twenties. When Poole ordered up the composite drawings that had been made of the suspects, he decided that they looked a lot like David Mack and Amir Muhammed, who were twenty-eight and twenty-nine years old at the time. Descriptions of the suspects' heights and weights also matched Mack and Muhammed.

"I was reaching, obviously," Poole conceded, "but then that's how cases get solved." Again, he could not initiate an investigation. "I heard one more time that I didn't have sufficient probable cause," Poole recalled. "But how could I get that probable cause without authorization to investigate? It was the same catch-22 logic they had been using to block me all the way back to the Kevin Gaines investigation. Of course I couldn't demonstrate that Mack and Billups [Muhammed] had been Mickey Thompson's killers, but I felt certain there was a legitimate basis for looking into that possibility. Nobody in the upper echelons of the LAPD wanted to hear it, though."

Poole also was making a pest of himself in his pursuit of criminal charges against Brian Hewitt for the beating of Ismael Jimanez. As he pursued this investigation, Poole heard more and more reports of abuse involving Rampart officers, including claims that CRASH detectives were beating suspects with impunity, planting guns or knives on the gangbangers they rousted, having sex with prostitutes, and ripping off drug dealers. "You hear this stuff all the time, but it sounded a lot more credible than it usually does," Poole recalled. "These gangbangers could tell you names, dates, and times." He became convinced that, at a minimum, the Rampart CRASH officers "had their own retaliation group" to handle citizen complaints of police abuse. "If somebody reported one of them, they'd send out different officers to bring in the gangbangers who filed the complaint on false charges," Poole said.

Poole warned the LAPD brass that many of the marginal 18th Street Gang members were being mishandled by the Rampart CRASH team. "Fair and firm is what works with gangbangers," he explained. "Because not all of them are hard-core, and the ones who aren't will talk, if they know you're a decent cop." The 18th Streeters, Poole warned, were being "beaten down to the point where they didn't have anything to lose and might retaliate against cops." The detective looked like a prophet in August of 1998, shortly before the arrest of Ray Perez, when a CRASH officer from the Southwest Division, Filbert Cuesta Jr., the father of two young children, was shot dead in what police described as an "ambush" outside an apartment building. A note found at the scene stated that the 18th Street Gang was tired of being "disrespected" by the LAPD.

The climax of Poole's tenure with the task force came one month later, when he was summoned to a September meeting attended by Lt. Hernadez and Chief Parks, then was asked to give them an update on the Hewitt investigation. "I told Parks, 'It's much more than this case, chief,'" Poole recalled. "'You've got a bunch of vigilante cops at Rampart.' And everybody went silent all at once. The chief didn't ask me a single question. He just sat there, and so did everybody else."

The most uncomfortable moment in that meeting, however, came when Brian Tyndall brought up the Biggie Smalls case. "I had been told by Hernandez in advance not to say a word about Biggie Smalls, or Mack and Gaines," Poole recalled. "But near the end of the meeting Tyndall says, 'Chief, Russ still believes Mack had something to do with the Biggie Smalls case.' Tyndall didn't have to do that, and it took some balls. But he really believed deep in his heart in what I had to say, and he's a very good cop, so he spoke up. But Parks just clammed up. He wouldn't say a word, wouldn't even look at anybody. It was like Tyndall hadn't spoken. It was very bizarre. And then a few minutes later the meeting was over. When Parks finally spoke to me, all he said was, 'I don't want you to investigate any more. Give me a report in two weeks.'"

The report Poole turned in was on time, but hardly what Chief Parks had hoped for. Only a short time earlier, Poole had submitted his "Chronology" of the Biggie Smalls murder investigation. Thirty-one pages long and extremely detailed, it made a persuasive case that the LAPD had failed to pursue its best leads, dating all the way back to the implication of Kevin Gaines. Poole argued strenuously that David Mack should be considered a prime suspect in the murder, and that Mack's relationship with Ray Perez was perhaps the most important unexplored territory touched upon by the investigation.

The involvement of LAPD officers with both Suge Knight and the Bloods gang was not speculation, Poole insisted, but a fact that had been demonstrated overwhelmingly by evidence that the department had been sitting on for more than three years. Even though he had been listed for fifteen months as the lead investigator of Biggie Smalls's slaying, Poole's "Chronology" was rejected by his superiors and never included in the Murder Book that was the LAPD's official record of the investigation. The report he delivered to Chief Parks in early October of 1998—forty pages long, single-spaced, and barely margined—picked up right where his "Chronology" had left off, however. Combined, the two documents laid out an investigation that began with the Gaines-Lyga shooting, passed through the Biggie Smalls's murder and the Ray Perez dope bust, and culminated in his investigation of the Ismael Jimanez beating. What they described was a contamination of the LAPD that had spread from a crew of black cops affiliated with Death Row Records into the Rampart CRASH unit, which had become "basically a police gang."

"Hernandez was furious," Poole recalled. "He tells me, 'We can't use this. The chief doesn't want this stuff in there.'" Poole's forty-page report was edited to two pages by Hernandez, who put his own name on it before sending it to the district attorney's office. "They also purged most of the supporting documents I had given them," Poole recalled. "The D.A.'s office still doesn't know what was kept from them."

The *Los Angeles Times* published the first substantial media account of Ray Perez's arrest on August 29, 1998. OFFICER'S ARREST TRIGGERS CORRUPTION PROBE, read the headline. From Poole's perspective, that sounded promising. It soon became obvious to the detective, though, that the *Times* knew only what Chief Parks wanted it to know, and that the rest of the media in Los Angeles either followed the city's one daily newspaper or reacted to it. LAPD detectives were "focusing on several" officers who worked with Perez, according to the *Times*'s unnamed source, and were interviewing both "former and recent partners" of the accused detective "in an effort to determine whether there are other 'dirty cops' on the force," the newspaper reported. The only other suspects named in the article, however, were Veronica Quesada and Carlos Romero, while a careful reading of the story made it clear that the "probe" would be focused on alleged drug dealing by officers assigned to the Rampart Division. Also evident upon careful inspection was that the *Times* had depended upon a single source, identified in the article as "a police official close to the investigation." Although it could never be confirmed, rumors spread among both members of the news media and local government officials that the *Times* source was Bernard Parks.

Little of substance was added during the next several months of news coverage. There was no mention in the *Times* of David Mack or of Ray Perez's alleged involvement with Death Row Records. Perez was "Rafael Antonio Perez" in newspaper accounts of his arrest, and none of the city's media informed their readers, viewers, or listeners that the officers who were the focus of the investigation—David Mack, Sammy Martin, and Nino Durden—were all black. The *Times* did not report either that, prior to the theft of two kilos of cocaine he was charged with, Perez had stolen a pound of coke that had been checked into evidence by Frank Lyga. And while Det. Lyga claimed to have been told by Brian Tyndall that the wiretap placed on Perez's residence between August 2 and August 11 strongly suggested that the pound of cocaine had been targeted as payback for the death of Kevin Gaines, no mention even that the wiretaps existed was made by the Los Angeles media. In November, Deputy District Attorney Richard Rosenthal filed court papers explaining that he would not introduce the wiretap tapes as evidence at trial, meaning that they would never become public information.

Chief Parks described the arrest of Perez as "sad and tragic," while the accused officer's own attorney, Johnnie Cochran protégé Winston K. McKesson, told reporters his client was "shattered" by the charges against him. The story soon faded to such insignificance that when Perez's first trial ended on December 23, 1998, with the jury hung, the *Times* story ran on the fourth page of an inside section.

The case had been rushed to trial over the assistant D.A.'s objections, according to Richard Rosenthal. "I wanted to wait for the financials on Perez," the prosecutor explained, "but LAPD was anxious to get things over." Chief Parks and virtually everyone associated with the Robbery-Homicide Task Force understood what a disaster it would be for the department if the investigation that had led to the arrest of Ray Perez was closely examined by the local media. And Winston McKesson had at least an inkling. "This case has made everybody in the LAPD nervous," Perez's attorney remarked to the *Times*. "Nobody wants to be associated with this."

McKesson, born and raised in South Central Los Angeles, cut quite a contrast in court as compared to Rosenthal, a UC Berkeley grad in his mid-thirties who was best known in the D.A.'s office as a whip-smart wonk skilled at crunching numbers and making cases out of circumstantial evidence. "Rosenthal had absolutely no street smarts, though," Russell Poole would observe, "and that's what made him so wrong for this case." The media later would accuse him of botching the prosecution of Perez, but Rosenthal insisted, "Our case went well." Still, the prosecutor allowed, "it was a downtown jury, and Perez was a good-looking, likable guy of mixed ancestry. And he testified very well. I believed he was lying through his teeth, but he did it very convincingly."

Perez lied so convincingly that four members of the jury, all black or Hispanic women, voted to acquit him. "That hung jury changed the whole outlook of the investigation," Russell Poole recalled. "Parks wanted this thing over by the end of the year, but when they lost that first trial, the chief panicked, thinking, 'Oh, shit, what are people gonna think now? We gotta do something fast.' So they started pushing to make a deal with Perez."

What pushed Perez was that his potential prison sentence increased each time a new count was added. And new counts were being added on a regular basis after the task force began testing the drug packages returned to Property Division to see if the cocaine inside had been replaced with something else. Almost immediately investigators found several quarter-pound packages that had been switched. "We would have found more," Rosenthal said, "except that a lot of the smaller drug packages had been destroyed." Also, Rosenthal now knew that Perez's bank records showed unexplained deposits of $49,000 in cash during the same period the missing cocaine was checked out.

Now facing as much as twelve years in state prison, Perez gave McKesson permission to negotiate a deal in May of 1999. Rosenthal's best offer was a five-year prison sentence in exchange for full disclosure. The prosecutor added the condition that Perez submit to a polygraph examination, and that the results could be admitted in court at his sentencing hearing. The prosecutor also asked for a proffer of Perez's testimony.

"We sat down together at the counsel table in the courtroom," Rosenthal recalled, "and Perez told me, 'I was involved in a use of force that may or may not have been unlawful, but what was unlawful was that we planted a gun on the guy afterward.'" The next day, Rosenthal and his team went through every shooting case involving Perez, "and we knew right away that it was the Javier Ovando case he had been talking about," the prosecutor recalled. Rosenthal spent nearly all of that Friday with Perez, who admitted that Ovando had been unarmed when he and his partner Durden shot the gangbanger, and that they had planted the assault rifle on him to cover up their mistake. LAPD detectives interviewed Ovando in state prison over the weekend, and on Monday Rosenthal filed to free Ovando with the first writ of habeas corpus ever obtained by a California prosecutor. The day after that, Rosenthal sat down again with Perez, who this time gave the prosecutor a list of all the Rampart officers who were "in the loop"—that is, willing to frame gangbangers with manufactured evidence and then to perjure themselves in court.

By the time Perez finished talking, his confession was fifty hours and two thousand transcript pages long. More than seventy of his fellow officers had been implicated in crimes that included shooting unarmed suspects, planting guns or drugs on them, and beating gangbangers senseless with clubs, fists, and feet. Perez described how one gangbanger was used as a human battering ram until his head punched through a wall, and how another was hung from a fire escape by his ankles until he talked. He and other Rampart CRASH officers routinely picked up gangbangers they thought might give them a problem and delivered them to the INS for deportation, said Perez.

Only one incident truly haunted him, though, Perez said, and that was the shooting of Javier Ovando. He and his partner Durden were on stakeout inside a vacant apartment in a building on South Lake Street that was a known hangout for 18th Street Gang members, Perez recalled, looking for a cache of weapons that had been stolen from a residence in Orange County. They had been lying in wait for about three hours when Durden heard footsteps and the two of them turned toward the apartment door just as Ovando opened it and stepped inside. Durden immediately opened fire, hitting Ovando three times. Perez shot the gangbanger once himself, he said, then helped Durden plant a sawed-off rifle on Ovando and concocted the story that the critically wounded man had attempted to ambush the two detectives.

Perez also accused an East Indian officer named Kulin Patel of accidentally shooting an unarmed man during the raid of an apartment building on Shatto Place, recalling that he and his fellow officers arrived at the building in a commandeered gypsy cab with tinted windows that let them drive right up to the front door without being spotted by the gangbangers inside. When Brian Hewitt and his partner Doyle Stepp planted a gun on the dead man, Perez said, "nobody said a word."

Rampart CRASH maintained its own organized system for covering up crimes by police officers, one "quarterbacked" by Sgt. Edward Ortiz, according to Perez, who told Rosenthal that officers could join "the loop" only if they were "sponsored" by someone already inside. Officers who were in the loop received playing-card plaques whenever they shot somebody, a red deuce if the suspect lived and a black deuce if he died, said Perez, who claimed to have been rewarded with a two of hearts for crippling Javier Ovando.

Though he insisted it was sheer torture to rat out men who had trusted him, no one was more heavily implicated by Perez than his own partner. While Brian Hewitt was brutal, Nino Durden was vicious, Perez said, the kind of guy who thought it was amusing to spray pepper mace into the eyes of a passed-out drunk or shoot a cornered suspect in the mouth with a bean-bag shotgun. Durden once "outed" an informant in front of his fellow gang members, Perez recalled, chuckling later as he imagined what they must have done to the snitch.

Durden could be slick, though, Perez said; once Nino bought a mailman's uniform and used it to bluff his way past a group of paranoid crack dealers he wanted to rip off. It was Durden who first talked him into stealing drug money, Perez said. In March of 1997, they made an undercover buy from a dealer at the corner of 2nd and Serrano, Perez recalled, then seized $1,500 from the guy after his arrest; Durden palmed a thousand of that, and gave Perez half. That summer, the two of them busted a bunch of people who were cooking up crack in the Wilshire Division, Perez said. Back at Rampart Station, a pager belonging to one of the dealers went off and he and Nino set up a sale, supposedly to arrest the guy. When they arrived at the meet, though, Durden said, "Screw it. Let's just sell it to him." He "totally agreed," Perez recalled, and eventually went in with Durden on two more coke sales to the same person, all from a stash they kept in an Igloo cooler that sat in a corner of the cot room at Rampart Station. They cleared $5,000 apiece.

Perez rambled on and on, recalling how one officer chugged a pint of vodka at the Rampart crew's "crash pad" apartment in the

Valley, then vomited off the balcony onto the head of an older woman who lived downstairs, transitioning from that into a description of how Sgt. Ortiz had used a piece of chrome fender to cover for a female officer who fired at an unarmed man. Perez came across as entirely forthcoming about his own career as a drug dealer. Except for the three kilos that had led to his detection, all of the cocaine he stole from Property Division was delivered to him by courier at Rampart Station, Perez said. He had replaced all of that couriered dope with Bisquick, except for the pound checked into evidence by Frank Lyga, said Perez (who claimed that in this one instance he ditched his return package because he thought he was being followed). "The three kilos he was afraid to ask for by courier," Rosenthal recalled. "Also, they might have tested an amount that large."

He neither believed nor disbelieved Perez, Rosenthal said. "I learned from the trial not to judge Perez by his demeanor," the prosecutor explained. "I don't know when people are lying, and Perez is an exceptionally good liar." He was still waiting to see the results of the polygraph tests, Rosenthal recalled.

Russell Poole was aghast when he learned that the D.A.'s office had cut a deal with Perez. "My hunch had been proven right, but I was devastated," Poole said. "Because I knew we could have taken care of it cleanly if they just let me do what was right. We didn't need to make a deal with Perez, who should have been sent to prison for the rest of his life. The whole investigation was flowing toward some grand conclusion that was going to tie it all together. At least that's what I believed. But as soon as they made the deal with Perez, it was like he became in charge. He decided what parts of the investigation were going to stay alive and which weren't."

Perez had implicated almost every detective he worked with at Rampart Station, Poole noted, yet insisted Sammy Martin was clean. "The same Martin who was meeting with Perez and Durden in the dead of night once they knew there was an investigation," Poole observed. Even more dubious was Perez's insistence that he knew of no criminal activity by David Mack. Chief Parks himself would tell the media that he believed Perez was not telling the whole truth about Mack.

Because the inquiry into Perez's activities had become so vast, Rosenthal decided to conduct five separate polygraph examinations of the disgraced detective; the last two would focus on Perez's relationship with David Mack and on "other shootings not disclosed by Perez."

Perez submitted to the series of lie detector tests on separate days between November 30 and December 16, 1999. Rosenthal received the results on December 19, two days before Perez was to face sentencing. The timing was no small problem for the prosecutor, because Perez had failed all five of the polygraph examinations that he took.

"It was very disturbing news," Rosenthal admitted. "Frankly, my feeling had been that even if Perez lied, he would pass the polys, because he was such a good liar at trial. And I never dreamed he would fail all five."

The prosecutor promptly won a two-month delay of Perez's sentencing hearing, and spent much of that time searching for a polygrapher who would explain how Perez could fail all five polygraph exams and still be telling the truth. He eventually found a professor in Minnesota who said the polygrapher who administered the five exams had made a crucial mistake during the first session by springing a question on Perez that he wasn't expecting. "And that could have screwed up the other polys," Rosenthal explained, "because Perez felt he couldn't trust the polygrapher." Rosenthal declined, however, to ask that Perez submit to examination by a different polygrapher. "First, we had spoken to the judge in chambers and he made it clear that he gave no credence to polygraphs," the prosecutor explained. "Secondly, I felt that Perez would have a built-in excuse if he failed again.

Perez *would* have failed again, said Russell Poole, "so it was easier just to say the first polygrapher fucked up and give Perez his deal." Perez would do five years, less time served, for the cocaine thefts, Judge Robert J. Perry ruled, and receive immunity for all other crimes to which he had confessed. This meant that, with time off for good behavior, Perez could be a free man again before the end of 2002.

Perez's statement at his sentencing hearing on February 25, 2000, would be published by newspapers around the world. It was a model of contrition that began with the disgraced cop's admission that nothing he could say "would be strong enough or genuine enough to warrant my pardon." The "atrocities" he and other officers in his CRASH unit had committed, Perez told the court, were the result of an "us-against-them ethos" that allowed those in the loop to believe "we were doing the wrong things for the right reasons." At the end of his statement, Perez quoted the mottoes that were posted above the entrances to the LAPD's CRASH units, then said he would like to add one of his own: "Whoever chases monsters should see to it that in the process he does not become a monster himself."

Most of the spectators in the courtroom looked moved, and a few wept openly. Among those closest to the investigation, however, there was a palpable sense of unease. Perez had been just as convincing, they all knew, and every bit as emotive, when he perjured himself at trial after trial during the past several years. This was the best liar they'd ever seen in a courtroom, both prosecutors and defense attorneys agreed, and yet the vast legal web in which they found themselves caught had been woven with little more than his word. While Perez tearfully apologized for what he had done to Javier Ovando and insisted his guilt about it had driven him to confess, those who had been in court when Ovando was sentenced to state prison recalled that the detective's immediate response back then was a snicker.

"No one is ever going to know for sure how much of what Perez said is true and how much is made up," Russell Poole observed. "Just like we'll never know how much he revealed, and how much he kept to himself. The guy is like some human two-way mirror; he can see out, but we can't see in."

CHAPTER ELEVEN

Russell Poole's own police career already had wound down toward its sad conclusion. "My weakness was that I let it all get to me," Poole said, "this pattern of sabotaging the investigation that I saw again and again. The way it all piled up really affected me emotionally. For the first time in my career I was witnessing a cover-up and an obstruction of justice in the LAPD, and the whole thing was being orchestrated from the highest levels. I knew the chief was behind it, and that Internal Affairs was in on it with him. So who could I go to—the FBI?"

All through the autumn of 1998, Poole bit his tongue and bided his time, watching as Ray Perez escaped conviction in court and the assorted investigations that had led to the Rampart detective's arrest languished. "My one hope was that when the criminal case against Hewitt got filed, I would be called as the main witness for the prosecution and finally get a chance to tell the truth," Poole said. "But it didn't happen that way." First, the same senior detective who had attempted to have Poole thrown out of the Robbery-Homicide Division back in May was "slowly worked into position to testify as the authority on the case, even though I was the one who had put it together," Poole recalled. "Finally I went to Commander Schatz and asked, 'What's the status of the criminal case against Hewitt and Cohan?' He said, 'Well, I don't think we're going that route. Having them fired is good enough. I talked to the state attorney general's office and they agreed.'

"But neither the state attorney general nor the district attorney had all the information. Important documents were purged from the file that went to the D.A.'s office and that was what the attorney general's office got. So they deceived both offices."

Poole made the audacious move of visiting two deputy district attorneys he had worked with on earlier cases and telling them how frustrated he was by the way his investigation had been thwarted. "They were nervous and didn't want to put themselves in the middle of this," he recalled. "They told me, 'Let's wait and see how this plays out before you make any more allegations.'"

"Russ was stressed out and exhausted and very disillusioned," recalled George Castillo, who had prosecuted several homicide cases with Poole's assistance. "I knew him to be one of the best LAPD detectives I had ever worked with—probably *the* best—and one of the most honorable people I've ever met. The guy is a total straight shooter, so I never doubted for a second that he was telling the truth. But the whole thing was very complicated and it wasn't entirely clear where the LAPD was going with all this. So my advice was to wait and see. But I think Russ believed he'd waited long enough. I felt for him."

As soon as word got out that he had attempted to circumvent the LAPD's chain of command, what little support Poole enjoyed in the upper echelons of the department was withdrawn. During November of 1998, he was asked first to leave the task force, then to transfer out of the Robbery-Homicide Division altogether.

"I knew I would be a marked man for the rest of my career," Poole said. "'Disloyalty' is the one sin the LAPD won't tolerate. But at the same time my record was a real problem for them. I had dozens of commendations and years of rating reports that very few detectives could match, and one of the things I'd been praised for over and over again was my dedication to the department. So getting rid of me wouldn't be easy, and they knew it. It was a stalemate situation."

Poole seriously considered submitting his resignation and taking his case to the media. Instead, he decided to use the enormous backlog of "sick time" he had accumulated to consider his options. "I had taken hardly any sick days in my nineteen years on the LAPD, so I had about 900 hours of time saved up," he explained. "I talked to my dad about the situation and he agreed I should take a couple of months off to rest and reflect on what I was going to do." Poole's doctor provided him with a diagnosis of "job-related stress," and the LAPD did not challenge it. Poole's eleven-week leave began shortly after Thanksgiving.

"I was just trying to recharge my batteries for most of that period," Poole recalled. "I spent more time with my kids than I had since they were born and my wife and I really got reacquainted. I was working out five days a week. I took some long hikes with my dad in the desert."

Poole's father was dealing with some major stress of his own. Two years ealier, Ralph Poole's other son, Gary, had disappeared without a trace. It was a complete mystery.

Police could find no evidence of a violent abduction, yet it did not seem likely that Gary Poole would take off on his own accord. His apartment was intact and his bank accounts were untouched. The only thing Gary owned that was missing was his Ford F-250 pickup, and the vehicle never had been recovered. The thirty-six-year-old man had no criminal record and there was no suggestion that he was involved with dangerous characters. In fact, Gary had been much more introverted than his older brother and their two sisters. "The artist," everyone in the family called him, because all through school his favorite activities had been painting and drawing. "When I did an inventory of his home, I found many artist's notebooks filled with his sketches, and they were amazingly good," Russell Poole recalled. "Somehow that was the hardest moment for me." Gary had made a good living as a master tile-setter, doing mostly custom jobs on expensive homes—he'd recently been hired to do a bathroom at Bob Hope's place in Palm Desert, a job he seemed to regard as his Sistine Chapel.

"We'd never had any kind of tragedy in our family or anything that was even close to having a family member disappear," Russell

Poole recalled. "So it hit us all very hard. We'd have these family meetings to try to figure out what might have happened, and everyone was blaming themselves, even though we didn't know what it was about.

"I did a lot of thinking about my brother during that time I took off. I started thinking that maybe I should use my skills as an investigator to work on finding out what had happened to him. I really didn't believe in the LAPD anymore. For years I'd been able to tell myself that I might not make a lot of money, but at least I had a job that let me work on the side of truth and justice. Honor and integrity of the case were always what mattered most to me, but once I went downtown I learned that the people who actually ran the department didn't give two shits about any of that. To them it was all about politics."

During one of their hikes in the desert, Ralph Poole told his son about his darkest hour as a Los Angeles County Sheriff's deputy. Right after he was promoted to detective, the older man recalled, he had been assigned to the Internal Affairs Division and immediately caught a case in which another deputy, working by himself, had killed a burglary suspect. A preliminary investigation revealed that the suspect had been unarmed, and that the deputy had planted a gun on him to justify the shooting. Homicide investigators quickly realized what had happened, but transferred the case to Internal Affairs so they could avoid filing charges against one of their own. He had no choice but to make the arrest himself, Ralph Poole said, and to testify against the accused officer as the lead witness for the prosecution. The day he arrived at the courthouse to take the stand, he got caught alone near an elevator, the elder Poole recalled, and was immediately surrounded by seven or eight friends of the defendant who told him he was a rat, then began to close a circle around him. He would have taken a beating for sure, Ralph Poole said, if not for his veteran partner, who showed up to stand beside him, and convinced the others that they would be killing their own careers if they didn't back off right now.

Cops were always going to protect one of their own, Russell Poole's father told him; it was the real police code of honor, part of the us-against-them mentality that the job produced in almost any-body who did it. The only protection an honest cop could count on was the support of his superiors. And if they were corrupt, too, you were all by yourself.

"I never thought I'd hear him say it," Russell Poole recalled, "but my dad told me he thought I ought to resign."

While still on leave, in December of 1998 Poole returned to the LAPD's Robbery-Homicide Division, armed with signed res-ignation papers that he presented to Captain Tatreau. "I told him why I wanted to quit," Poole recalled. "I laid out all the corruption I'd witnessed in detail. And Tatreau made me feel as if he was going to take some action and talked me out of resigning. I remember him telling me, 'Russ, you're very intense and that's okay, I'm very in-tense, too.' Like we were sort of cut from the same cloth." At the same time, however, Tatreau made it clear that Poole would not be returning to the task force. Neither Lt. Hernandez nor any of the other supervisors wanted to work with him, said Tatreau, who advised Poole once again that it would be best if he transferred out of RHD altogether. In the meantime, the captain said, he could join the Bank Robbery Squad.

"So I said, 'Fine, I'll go to bank robbery,'" Poole recalled. "But they never assigned me any cases. After a week or so of sitting at my desk and doing nothing, I figured, 'Okay, I'll find myself another job.'" Being back with the LAPD, even as a glorified observer, made Poole think of all that he loved about the job. He remembered what it had been like as a trainee officer to stop a car and approach it at night on a side street in South Central, the way a day of total monotony could turn into sheer terror ten minutes before you finished a shift. Easily the most frightening and exhilarating part of the job in those days had been vehicle pursuits, Poole recalled: "The suspect is running red lights, so you have to go through, also. As a probationer you don't get to drive, so you're on the radio, but some of the partners I had were a lot more aggressive behind the wheel than others. Just going through an intersection with one of those guys was unbelievably scary, because there were some really close calls. You just can't understand the adrenaline pump you get when you're chasing armed felony suspects until you start to do it. It's indescribable."

Poole decided to try returning to what he knew, and phoned Lt. John Dunkin at his old unit, South Bureau Homicide. Dunkin said they didn't have any openings but would take Poole "on loan" from RHD until a spot became available. Poole went to work at South Bureau Homicide in January of 1999, and was permanently assigned to the unit two months later. He continued to follow the investigation of police corruption that now was split between the Robbery-Homicide and Internal Affairs Divisions.

"Brian Tyndall always made me feel there was hope that this all would be made right," Poole recalled. "Even after I was assigned to South Bureau Homicide, he was trying to get me back on the task force, but Lt. Hernandez and Commander Schatz refused to consider it. They felt that letting me take the witness stand in any criminal case connected to any part of the investigation would result in a major embarrassment for the department." Tyndall remained a source of information and inspiration for the disaffected, however. The senior detective not only confided to Frank Lyga that the wiretap on the Rafael Perez residence yielded persuasive evidence that Perez and his Blood associates had targeted the undercover cop to punish him for killing Kevin Gaines, but advised Russell Poole that Brian Hewitt had made a bid to blow the task force investigation wide open. This had happened during an interview by Internal Affairs investigators who were looking into allegations that Hewitt had stolen marijuana seized from an 18th Street Gang member. "Tyndall, who had heard the tape, said Hewitt stopped the interview and told the IA guys, 'Look, if you want a story, I got some things that will blow Rampart out of the water.' And the IA investigators said, 'No, we don't wanna know about that, we just wanna know about this one incident.' I was stunned when I heard about this. Hewitt knew a lot, and I think he was ready to tell it if he could get a deal. Tyndall and I both couldn't believe that they never asked Hewitt about this again. Tyndall wasn't going to challenge the brass, though, and that's where he and I parted company."

For Poole, the lawsuit filed by Johnnie Cochran against the City of Los Angeles on behalf of the Gaines family had become his last best hope for a full airing of truths that the LAPD seemed determined to suppress. Even though he was now at South Bureau Homicide, the City Attorney's office had named Poole as the chief witness for the defense. In May of 1999, the detective was riding in an elevator with Corey Brente, the assistant city attorney who was handling the case, when Brente answered a call on his cell phone and was informed that Cochran, Chief Parks, and City Attorney James Hahn had negotiated a settlement.

It was one of the most cynical deals in the city's history. Because municipal bylaws required every legal settlement in excess of $100,000 to be approved by the Los Angeles City Council, Hahn had structured the deal so that Gaines's wife and two daughters each would receive separate settlements of slightly less than that amount, totalling $250,000 in all. Even then the payments were broken into twelve parts, so as to further shield them from the scrutiny of overseers. The retired Superior Court judge who had presided over the settlement negotiations was outraged, however, firing off a letter to Chief Parks stating that he believed the settlement was "political" and intended to avoid significant adverse publicity for the department. City Council members Laura Chick and Joel Wachs almost immediately blasted the deal as "deplorable" and "unconscionable," but admitted they lacked the power to overturn it.

Hahn, Cochran, and Parks all refused to comment, but each had gotten what he wanted. Hahn was a bland political hack whose only real asset was his last name. Former Los Angeles County Supervisor Kenneth Hahn was a legendary figure in Los Angeles's black community, and justifiably so. In 1965, shortly after the Watts riots, the elder Hahn had been the only white politician in L.A. courageous enough to meet Martin Luther King Jr. at the airport when the civil rights leader arrived to survey the damage. His son Jimmy stood for nothing more than the advancement of his own career, but ever since entering politics he had depended upon overwhelming support from the black community to win election. James Hahn now was running for mayor of Los Angeles and understood that preserving his relationship with the city's black leadership was essential to his chances for success. And no black leader in Los Angeles was more influential at this moment in time than Johnnie Cochran, who not only would pocket a third of the money from the Gaines deal, but also could tell his supporters in South Central that he had stuck it to the mothers one more time. By going along, Bernard Parks had prevented a public airing of Kevin Gaines's conduct and of the LAPD's failure to deal with it. The chief also had made sure that Det. Russell Poole would not be on the witness stand telling people about the cross-pollination between the city's black gangs and its black police officers, and about how Parks had stifled his investigation of the black cops who worked for Suge Knight and Death Row Records.

Poole's disenchantment with the LAPD now was nearly complete. "Parks goes in with Hahn and Cochran on a deal to pay off Gaines's family when they know that Gaines is a criminal, a dirty cop, and a maniac, not to mention totally in the wrong in this case," Poole fumed. "How can he get away with this?"

Corey Brente attempted to set the record straight, telling reporters, "Frank Lyga adamantly opposed a settlement. He wanted a trial. He wanted the truth to come out. Cochran and [cocounsel] Carl Douglas had no evidence against him, despite all their efforts."

"That was good of Corey Brente, but Frank Lyga still had a cloud hanging over him," said Poole. "They had been promising him his day in court, then they took it away from him. Of course the guy is going to be bitter."

That Lyga was. "Parks and Hahn, in concert with Johnnie Cochran," Lyga said, "laid me out as a racist killer, a reputation I still have to fight every single day." He did indeed. During the next two years Lyga would be named as a defendant in twenty-two Rampart-related lawsuits, even though he had never worked in that division.

Like Poole, Lyga was infuriated to learn that the LAPD's task force had abandoned the theory that Ray Perez stole his cocaine in retaliation for the Gaines shooting. "We already knew that Perez called up Property Division and gave them the ID numbers for the dope that Lyga booked into evidence," Poole said. "That tells you he knew what he was after." It was quite a coincidence, conceded Richard Rosenthal, but Perez insisted he had no idea who Frank Lyga was. Impossible, said Lyga; apart from the enormous publicity that surrounded the Gaines shooting, Lyga once had supervised a narcotics operation that Perez worked on: "There's no way he doesn't remember me."

The same month that the Gaines family settled with the city attorney's office, May of 1999, Rafael Perez made his deal with the Los Angeles County District Attorney. When Poole learned of it later that summer, he knew that any hope for rectification was officially dead. "Rafael Perez is a pure scumbag," Poole said. "To see him crying on the stand about all the terrible things he's done. I bet he laughs all the way back to his cell."

Almost as soon as news of the deal with Perez was announced, Poole observed, Fred Miller and the other senior detective who was his new partner submitted their resignations to the LAPD. "I think they thought Perez was going to spill on the Biggie Smalls case, and it would come back to them," Poole said. "But I knew Perez would never betray Mack. Perez knows for certain that if he rolls over on Mack and Knight they will track him down and have him killed."

David Mack would face sentencing for bank robbery in September, only a few days before the "confessions" of Ray Perez were made public in a series of articles published by the *Los Angeles Times*. Despite overwhelming evidence, his conviction had been a close call. At one point during their deliberations, eleven of the jurors signed a note sent to the judge in which they complained that the twelfth member of the panel was refusing to discuss the evidence and had decided to vote not guilty before the trial began. To no one's surprise, this juror was black, and the other members of the panel—Hispanic, Asian, and white—wrote that they were being hung up by "a race issue." Only after a stern warning from Judge Robert M. Takesuki did the jury deliver a unanimous verdict of guilty.

Mack's attorney, Donald Re, had offered the court dozens of letters praising his client, including one written by Olympic track great Carl Lewis, in a vain attempt to have him released on bail. His wife and children wrote especially emotional letters that had the odd effect of making Mack seem both more sympathetic and more contemptible. Mack also received letters of support from Sammy Martin, who praised his former partner's "professional manner," and from the former Harry Billups, aka Amir Muhammed, who lauded his college friend for remaining "true to his convictions and dedicated to the principle for which they stand," then signed off as "Harry Muhammed."

At the sentencing hearing, Re made what is known in the law as a "tragic personal history" argument, citing Mack's "lack of guidance as a youth" and "disadvantaged upbringing." The assistant U.S. attorney who prosecuted the case replied by reminding the court that David Mack and his wife had a combined income of six figures at the time he committed his crime. This was a defendant, the prosecutor noted, who "has embraced his offenses, has never apologized for them, and evidently intends to keep hundreds of thousands of dollars." Before passing sentence, Judge Takesuki gave Mack a chance to tell the government where the money "could be located." On the advice of his attorney, he declined, said Mack. Takesuki then sentenced the defendant to 171 months in federal prison. Mack's request to be incarcerated in Southern California was refused, after the Bureau of Prisons reported that it would be unable to meet his "security needs" at any of its West Coast facilities, and placed him at the federal prison in Waseca, Minnesota.

Errolyn Romero, who had been the main witness against Mack at trial, received a sentence of thirty months in prison and would be eligible for parole within sixteen.

Ten days after Mack's sentencing, LAPD Chief Parks held a news conference to announce that he had formed an internal board of inquiry to examine the quality of the department's investigations into officer involved shootings. Parks's announcement coincided exactly with news reports that two civilian witnesses to the shooting in which David Mack allegedly had saved the life of his partner, Ray Perez, were claiming that the victim, Jesse Vincencio, did not have a gun in his hand before Mack killed him. The pair had never been interviewed by the LAPD.

Ray Perez continued to insist that the shooting of Vincencio was justified. "As far as I'm concerned," he told the *Times*, "David Mack was a hero that night." LAPD detectives who had interviewed Perez said they all were impressed by how determined he had been not to implicate Mack in any crimes. They viewed this less as a reflection of Perez's loyalty to his former partner, however, the detectives said, than as evidence that their informant was "terrified of Mack." Russell Poole agreed. During his investigation, Poole had been amazed by the level of fear Mack appeared to inspire in those he dealt with. "Mack must be some piece of work," Poole said, "because rarely do you see people so convinced that crossing a guy will get them killed. It wasn't at quite Suge Knight levels, but it was close."

Suge had been removed from the California Men's Colony in San Luis Obispo back in May, right around the time Ray Perez was cutting his deal with the district attorney's office in Los Angeles. He now was at Mule Creek State Prison, a facility that was somewhat less strict but also a lot farther from Los Angeles. The nearest town was Ione, population 2,667, a former gold-mining camp forty-three miles southwest of Sacramento, where residents could not help but notice the limousines that showed up on Thursday and Friday evenings, when inmates were allowed to receive visitors at the prison. Among those dropping by was Michel'le, who continued to identify herself as Suge's wife. Michel'le's album was Death Row Records' biggest release of 1999, heralded by company publicists as evidence that the label was determined to change its image as the home of gangsta rap. Suge also had found God, his spokespersons said.

"If that's the case, maybe he'll be moved to confess to the murder of Biggie Smalls," Russell Poole observed. Knight remained the main suspect of an investigation that was going nowhere. Police in both Los Angeles and Las Vegas reminded reporters that murders went unsolved all the time. "Murders don't go unsolved when the victim is a celebrity who gets shot dead in the street in front of dozens of witnesses who can identify the killers," Poole answered. "Remind me of any recent cases where that has happened, other than Tupac Shakur and Biggie Smalls. Murders like that only go unsolved if the police don't want to solve them."

Poole was feeling free to speak his mind because he knew his career as an LAPD officer was at its end. In August of 1999, the department announced that it was disbanding South Bureau Homicide, in response to a plummeting murder rate in Los Angeles and the rest of the country. "We were given a list of places we could transfer to, and one of them was the Organized Crime Unit," Poole recalled. "I was all set to go there when a lieutenant who had just transferred in from Robbery-Homicide intervened and said they didn't want me. I went to Lt. Dunkin to ask what happened, and he told me the lieutenant had told him, 'We're not going to accept Poole because of what happened while he was on the task force.' My complaint that they obstructed justice was considered a betrayal."

Poole transferred to Harbor Division Homicide, but one month later the deal Ray Perez had made with police and prosecutors became public. Poole was so disgusted that he felt he now had no choice but to resign from the LAPD. Before doing so, however, he took care of some unfinished business. He had been haunted, Poole said, by a story Kevin Hackie had told him about the 1993 murder of two Compton police officers. One of the slain men was Smoky Burrell, Reggie Wright Jr.'s former partner. "Hackie said that it was common knowledge that Burrell and Wright were robbing dope dealers of their money and narcotics on duty," Poole's notes of the interview read. "'They were notorious for stealing money.' Hackie says that the person who killed Burrell, Regis Thomas, may have been robbed by the two officers (Burrell/Wright) on previous occasions." Before submitting his resignation, Poole took his notes to two LAPD lieutenants, a captain, a commander, and to the office of Chief Parks. "What worried me was that the guy who killed Burrell had gotten the death penalty," he explained, "yet may have thought he was protecting himself from another rip-off or even defending his life. I wanted to make sure this was investigated before the guy got executed, but nothing was ever done."

Poole also delivered his investigative files on the Biggie Smalls murder—including the evidence that implicated Suge Knight and LAPD officers associated with Death Row Records—to William Hodgeman, the assistant district attorney who had become a public figure during the O.J. Simpson trial but was best known within the local law enforcement community as the liaison between Los Angeles County and the federal government. Hodgeman also was the prosecutor who had gotten Suge Knight sentenced to state prison. "I still hoped somebody someday would make use of this stuff," Poole explained.

It wouldn't be Poole, however. On October 25, 1999, Russell Poole submitted his letter of resignation to the LAPD. It contained just enough information to let Chief Parks and the rest of the department's brass know that he believed he had the goods on them. "The issues and circumstances [of my resignation] have to do with how some investigations I was involved in were handled," Poole wrote. "My concerns were addressed to my superiors, but were swept under the rug."

PART FIVE

HEAT FROM
A COLD CASE

Poole is a team player who makes himself available to assist others without regard to the time of day or night. Poole is a quality person who has found his calling. He has become one of the finest young detectives on the Department.

—From the "Performance Evaluation Report" filed on Detective Trainee Russell Poole for the period from 3/1/89 to 9/30/89

CHAPTER TWELVE

Shortly after his resignation from the LAPD, Poole agreed to cooperate with the *Los Angeles Times*. This would be, he eventually concluded, one of the worst mistakes he ever made. "The *Times* reporters, [Matt] Lait and [Scott] Glover, had been phoning me for months, trying to get me to talk," Poole recalled. "A couple of days after I turned in my detective's shield, I finally called them up and said, 'Okay.' I gave those guys everything I had, and then they came out with this story that was completely fucked-up."

The *Times*'s story seemed simply sensational when it ran on the morning of December 9, 1999. "A former Los Angeles police officer already in prison for bank robbery is among the suspects in the 1997 slaying of rap star Notorious B.I.G., according to sources and confidential LAPD documents obtained by the *Times*," the article began. "Among the theories [LAPD] investigators are pursuing is that ex-Officer David A. Mack conspired with Death Row Records founder Marion 'Suge' Knight to arrange the contract killing of the 24-year-old rap sensation whose real name was Christopher Wallace, according to a former detective on the case.

"Specifically, detectives are trying to determine whether Mack arranged for a longtime friend to carry out the attack outside the Petersen Automotive Museum on March 9, 1997, according to sources and Los Angeles Police Department documents. Police would not say whether they have been able to locate or question the man they suspect of being the gunman under this theory. He is Amir Muhammed, who was known as Harry Billups when he and Mack were college classmates at the University of Oregon, according to sources and documents. Muhammed apparently dropped from sight after visiting Mack in prison on December 26, 1997."

The *Times* article was vague about what police had done to "pursue" the theory that Amir Muhammed was the killer of Biggie Smalls, describing Muhammed as a shadowy figure who was impossible to locate: "Detectives searched for Muhammed, but many of the addresses that came up in a background check were either false or led to post office boxes, according to LAPD robbery-homicide documents. Police surveillance of some of those locations failed to find him. Numerous attempts by the *Times* to locate Muhammed through public records and a former friend were unsuccessful."

The "former detective on the case" who had been the *Times* reporters' main source couldn't finish the article the first few times he tried. "I was just in shock when I read it," Poole recalled. "They made it sound like the case was about to break wide open, instead of describing how the investigation had been thwarted. It was like the LAPD was on the brink of arresting this Amir Muhammed for the murder of Biggie Smalls. What I had told them was that nobody ever really looked for Muhammed, because the brass didn't want to conduct an investigation that might lead to LAPD officers, and that the clues that implicated David Mack were basically discarded. I tried to get those guys to do another story that got it right, but they wouldn't."

The *Times* would "do another story" almost five months later, but this article read more like a veiled retraction than a clarification of its earlier report. The newspaper's May 3, 2000, article was written by business reporter Chuck Philips. MAN NO LONGER UNDER SCRUTINY IN RAPPER'S DEATH, read the headline. PROBE: MORTGAGE BROKER HAD BEEN INVESTIGATED IN NOTORIOUS B.I.G.'S SLAYING, BUT POLICE SAY THEORY IS NOT BEING PURSUED.

The main source for Philips's claim that the LAPD had rejected the idea that Muhammed might be involved in the murder of Biggie Smalls was Dave Martin, identified in the *Times* article as "the lead detective in the case." "We are not pursuing that theory and have not been for more than a year," Philips quoted Martin as saying.

Philips also interviewed Amir Muhammed himself, who told the reporter, "I'm not a murderer, I'm a mortgage broker." The *Times*'s earlier article "made it sound like I was some mystery assassin who committed this heinous crime and then just dropped off the face of the earth—which is the furthest thing from the truth," complained Muhammed. He had not left his house for three days after the article ran, Muhammed said, for fear that one of Biggie Smalls's fans might be provoked into an attempt on his life.

Philips's article actually raised many more questions than it answered, but almost no one in the local media seemed to recognize that fact. Muhammed's attorney told the *Times*'s reporter that, one week after the first article ran, LAPD detectives had assured him that his client was not a suspect. They would like to interview Muhammed, the detectives said, "but never followed through with their request," the *Times* reported. Why not? was the obvious question, but if Philips had asked it, there was no evidence of this in his article. Amir Muhammed himself cited the failure of the LAPD to interview him as proof that "they obviously realized at some point it wasn't true" that he had been involved in the murder of Biggie Smalls. All it really proved, though, was that the LAPD had abandoned a viable theory without even a perfunctory investigation.

Philips's article also did not offer any explanation of why the LAPD had rejected the theory that David Mack—and possibly Amir Muhammed, as well—were involved in the murder of Biggie Smalls. There were no questions or answers about how Mack and Muhammed had been eliminated as suspects, or what the scope of the LAPD investigation had been. No one was asked to explain why Russell Poole's requests for warrants to search Mack's home, to run forensic tests on his car, and to examine his financial records were refused, despite an enormous amount of probable cause. Among the most obvious questions that Philips apparently hadn't asked Amir Muhammed was this one: Why, if your visit to David Mack in jail was an innocent contact between two old friends, did you use a false address, a false social security number, and an out-of-service phone number when you signed in at the jail? And the biggest question, of course, was why—if what Amir Muhammed said was true—he hadn't sued the *Los Angeles Times* for libeling him.

In New York, these questions would have been asked the first day and every day afterward, until reporters got answers. But Los Angeles was a long way from New York. The West Coast city had only one daily newspaper, but even worse, it had an "alternative" press that was more driven by political agendas than journalistic obligations. The rest of the local media not only failed to demand answers from the *Los Angeles Times* and the LAPD, but instead made a mob attack on the city's one real newspaper for running the first article that named Amir Muhammed as a suspect in Biggie Smalls's slaying. The firestorm of criticism was ignited by an article in the online edition of *Brill's Content* that accused the *Times* of running Philips's article as a way of avoiding the full retraction owed to Amir Muhammed. The claim that Muhammed was a suspect in the murder of Biggie Smalls "turns out to be dead wrong," *Brill's Content* reported, and the *Times's* failure to acknowledge this only compounded the newspaper's sins.

The *LA Weekly* promptly published an article (under the headline A B.I.G. MISTAKE) that chronicled the behind-the-scenes battle in the *Times's* newsroom. After Philips's story was ready for publication, the *Weekly* explained, the reporter and his editor in the Business section, Mark Saylor, were beset by editors from the Metro section "who reportedly wanted to play down elements of Philips's story that raised questions about what (Matt) Lait and (Scott) Glover had reported, and were successful in watering it down." Saylor, who had engaged in a public screaming match with the *Times's* executive editor Leo Wolinsky shortly after the *Brill's Content* piece was published, told the

Weekly that the atmosphere in the newsroom was "tense and uncomfortable." Saylor resigned from the newspaper shortly after this.

The *Weekly* did at least speak to Russell Poole, reporting that the "retired detective" admitted he was the only member of the LAPD who had wanted to pursue "the theory that Mack and Knight had convinced Amir Muhammed to shoot Wallace" and that he advised Lait and Glover that "he hadn't been able to check out the theory in any detail" because the department's brass refused to grant permission. "In fact, Poole says, the reluctance of his partner and supervisors to take the Mack-Muhammed theory seriously was one of the reasons he quit the force in disgust," the *Weekly* reported. The paper then dismissed the evidence linking Mack to the murder of Biggie Smalls as "gossamer thin," however, and the implication of Amir Muhammed as "even more tenuous." Since the paper had done absolutely no independent investigation of "the Mack-Muhammed theory," though, all its editors knew was what they read in the *Times*.

The *Weekly*'s reporting was top-notch compared to that of the *New Times of Los Angeles*. The city's other "major" weekly told its readers that Amir Muhammed was "an innocent mortgage broker" who had not been a suspect in the murder of Biggie Smalls for at least seven months before the Lait-Glover article that identified him as such ran in the *Los Angeles Times*. The *New Times* quoted an unnamed police source who said the LAPD had not pursued the Mack-Muhammed theory "because top investigators felt it wouldn't hold up," but provided absolutely no explanation of why not. The paper then leveled the inevitable charge of racism, quoting unnamed "cynics inside the paper" who believed "the *Times* would never have embraced such flimsy evidence if the target had been a prominent white businessman, instead of a Nation of Islam member." The *New Times* sank even lower by illustrating editor Rick Barrs's column with a drawing of Amir Muhammed being lynched by two white male reporters.

The most predictable and audacious comments on the Mack-Muhammed theory came from Suge Knight's latest attorney, Robin J. Yanes. This whole idea had come and gone a year ago, Yanes said, and was being recycled by the LAPD "to cover their butts." Yanes then said, "Suge doesn't know" David Mack. Suge most certainly did, however, as more than one witness already had told the LAPD.

For Russell Poole, the media fiasco that had ensued following the publication of the Chuck Philips article was perhaps even more disillusioning than what he had witnessed as a member of the LAPD. "It was like the cover-up had been covered up, this time by the media," Poole explained. When one took a close look at what actually was said in the avalanche of articles that castigated the *Los Angeles Times* for its original story on the Mack-Muhammed theory, they boiled down to this: Amir Muhammed could not be a murderer because he was a mortgage broker; David Mack had been cleared as a suspect in the murder of Biggie Smalls because the LAPD said it wasn't investigating that possibility; and the only reason these two had been singled out for mention was that they were black.

"The *Los Angeles Times*'s credibility was out the window, as far as I'm concerned," Poole said. "And this Rick Barrs guy at the *New Times*—what a stupid shit. None of these papers, not even the *Times*, did any probing whatever. They didn't ask the right questions, so how could they get the right answers?"

The idea that Amir Muhammed must be innocent because he was a mortgage broker especially infuriated Poole. Back in 1994, the detective had arrested a mortgage broker named Willie Darnel Hankins for shooting a man to death in an office on Wilshire Boulevard. During the course of an investigation that involved the subsequent murder of the accused man's father, Willie Hankins (whose real estate loan business had made him one of the wealthiest men ever to emerge from the South Central Los Angeles ghetto), Poole was astounded by "how skilled these guys were at manipulating and covering up in financial deals." Working as a mortgage broker "is a perfect way to make dirty money look clean," he explained, "and that's what a lot of them do." He had heard a number of stories back then, Poole recalled, about mortgage brokers who were helping gangsta rappers and other members of the Bloods gang launder the money they made from drug and weapons transactions.

Poole also recalled that the investigations of Kevin Gaines and Rafael Perez had shown that both men boasted about the large real estate portfolios they were able to accumulate. "I realized that there might have been a connection there to Harry Billups, or Amir Muhammed, or whatever he calls himself," Poole said. "For me, the fact that he's a mortgage broker only raises a lot of new questions. It was really painful to find out that not only the LAPD, but also the *Los Angeles Times*, doesn't want those questions answered."

The *Los Angeles Times* had been serving for months as the principal publicist for the accusations of Rafael Perez. The story that Perez had made a deal and was talking to the cops became public on September 16, 1999, one day after Bernard Parks held a news conference to announce that a total of twelve LAPD officers already had been relieved of duty on the basis of what Perez said. Nino Durden was the only one named. "It's not a good day," said Parks, who only a few hours earlier had handed out eighteen Medal of Valor awards to employees of the police department.

For the *Times*, the most important revelation to emerge was bannered across page one of the paper's Metro section: EX-OFFICER SAYS HE SHOT UNARMED MAN. Prosecutors at that moment were attempting to have Javier Ovando released from state prison, the *Times* informed its readers. The headline on the story in the next day's edition of the *Times* announced that Perez had implicated another officer in a second shooting AS CORRUPTION PROBE WIDENS. Even at this early stage, the newpaper reported, the "probe" had become "the most extensive inquiry into LAPD conduct" since the 1930s.

LAPD CORRUPTION PROBE MAY BE TEST FOR CITY LEADERS, read the headline on the *Times*'s next article. Already the paper was framing the story in the context of the Rodney King beating, the brutalization of minority victims by blue-suited brutes, and a police department that required the oversight of civil rights activists to protect them. The Los Angeles County District Attorney's office announced that day that it was suspending enforcement of its anti-gang injunctions against more than one hundred members of the 18th Street Gang. The day after that, the *Times* published a lengthy interview with Rafael Perez, under the headline, EX-OFFICER CALLS CORRUPTION A CHRONIC "CANCER." What he had done to Javier Ovando haunted him even in his dreams, Perez told the paper: "I go to sleep with it and wake up with it. It's something I have been living with for almost three years, and I wanted to find some closure for me, and, in a sense, a beginning for Mr. Ovando. . . . This is something that I'm doing for me and for my God, and something that I need to do to make me whole."

Bernard Parks addressed the Los Angeles City Council the next day and told them that many more officers than the twelve already suspended would be subject to investigation. "We take Rafael Perez at his word," said the chief, whose admission that "we may end up with a lot of information we can't prove" seemed to slip past the ears of most listeners. "Horrifying," the council's most left-wing member, Jackie Goldberg, called the contents of the chief's briefing. "We're not going to put blinders on to these allegations," an anonymous official of the U.S. Justice Department advised the *Times*, which reminded readers that federal officials "have been monitoring the LAPD for the last several years."

A week later, attorneys for Javier Ovando's two-year-old daughter, Destiny, filed a $20 million claim against the City of Los Angeles. On and on it went, for weeks and then months.

No one watched with more dismay than Russell Poole. Ray Perez, one of the dirtiest cops in the history of the Los Angeles Police Department, was playing puppetmaster to the whole city. "The politicians and the media not only didn't question Perez, they used what he said in every way they could to destroy the LAPD," Poole lamented.

The public parsing of Perez's "confessions" had become a kind of cottage industry for the political left in Los Angeles. The *LA Weekly* and *New Times* published story after story that attacked both the officers and the administration of the LAPD, while at the same time celebrating the murderers, drug dealers, and thieves who had become the official victims of the police abuse attested to by Rafael Perez. "How many innocent people are imprisoned because of false testimony by Los Angeles police officers?" asked USC law professor Erwin Chemerinsky in the first sentence of a "commentary" published by the *Los Angeles Times* in December 1999. The answer was that there was no way of knowing, since the only LAPD officer proven to have perjured himself in court was Rafael Perez, upon whose allegations Chemerinsky's question was based. "An independent task force needs to be created immediately to ensure unbiased review of all the possibly tainted cases," Chemerinsky asserted later in his commentary. This task force should be composed of "prosecutors, defense attorneys and others with experience in the criminal justice system." In other words, people such as himself.

Ramona Ripston, the executive director of the American Civil Liberties Union of Southern California, also cited the allegations of Rafael Perez in the commentary she wrote for the *Times*, asserting that, because of them, "long standing claims that such abuses exist beyond Rampart are increasingly plausible." Ripston proposed creating the position of "permanent prosecutor" to investigate and prosecute police misconduct, a kind of in-house Kenneth Starr who would not only usurp the authority of the district attorney's office, but create a new bureaucratic bailiwick as well. One subject Ripston didn't want to discuss was her close friendship with Nick Salicos, the LAPD captain who had been running the Rampart Division when most of the corruption alleged by Rafael Perez occurred.

Kathleen Spillar, national coordinator of the Feminist Majority Foundation, and Penny Harrington, the former Portland, Oregon, police chief who headed the foundation's National Center for Women and Policing, published a February 18, 2000, op-ed piece in the *Times* challenging the assertion that reduced hiring standards (in the name of affirmative action) had contributed to the Rampart scandal. "It is not that the men in blue were hired too fast," the pair wrote. "It's that the wrong men were hired. And not enough women." Perhaps Spillar and Harrington hadn't heard about the allegations against Stephanie Barr and against Melissa New, one of only two Rampart Division officers (other than Nino Durden) accused by Perez of an improper shooting that later was covered up.

No one took better advantage of the Rampart scandal than Tom Hayden, who was regularly using the op-ed pages of the *Times* (as well as the TV appearances they generated) to become the public face of advocacy on behalf of Javier Ovando and other members of the 18th Street Gang who had been victimized by the LAPD. Hayden was not an opportunist, of course, but an idealist, as he'd been demonstrating ever since he had used his movie star wife's money to win election to the California State Senate almost two decades earlier. Term limits were about to force Hayden to give up his senate seat, however, and since he had no chance of prevailing in a statewide election his only hope for a continuing political career was to win a seat on the Los Angeles City Council. Like virtually everyone involved in local politics, Hayden was aware that minorities were becoming a majority both in Los Angeles and all across California. Hispanics had outnumbered "non-Hispanic whites" in L.A. since 1990, and the disparity was mounting day by day. White people now were less than 50 percent of the population statewide, as well, and with skin as pale as Tom Hayden's or James Hahn's, a politician needed a very broad ethnic base to win public office.

The Hispanic citizens of the Rampart district, however, didn't seem to understand that they were supposed to be more afraid of police officers than of gang members. Polls consistently demonstrated the depth of support for the police in Hispanic communities. Almost immediately after Rafael Perez's allegations were published in the *Los Angeles Times*, local citizens staged a well-attended and wildly enthusastic pro–Rampart Division rally outside their LAPD station. A rally to protest police abuse that was scheduled to take place the next day fizzled for lack of participation.

The allegations of Rafael Perez, though, were embraced with ferver by the *Los Angeles Times*. A May 2000 editorial published by the paper began, "The Los Angeles Police Commission and its staff face a task that would have been unimaginable as recently as a year ago— restoring credibility to a department that long rested on its reputation for incorruptibility, a reputation we now know to be hollow." The *Times* apparently knew this because Perez had told them so.

It was unlikely anyway that the Los Angeles Police Commission would restore credibility to the LAPD, at least not as long as its president was Gerald Chaleff, a former defense attorney who only a few months earlier had remarked during a news conference that "all cops are liars."

Chaleff was a major supporter of the "consent decree" proposed by Bill Lann Lee, the chief of the U.S. Justice Department's Civil Rights Division, who in May of 2000 threatened Los Angeles with a "practice and pattern" civil lawsuit unless the city agreed to give control of the LAPD to federal "auditors." In September of 2000, the Los Angeles City Council voted 12–3 to accept the consent degree. "We all felt we neded all the help we could get, reforming the LAPD," explained Jackie Goldberg.

City Attorney James Hahn, still the city's leading candidate for mayor, avoided the subject of the consent decree as long as possible, but was compelled during an appearance before the City Council to answer a question about whether the city could be sued by the federal government if Los Angeles's powerful employee unions failed to abide by it. "We feel that what we are proposing is something we should be able to reach agreement on, if we roll up our sleeves and really work at it," was Hahn's non-answer. Los Angeles apparently was going to get the leader it deserved.

For most of L.A.'s interested parties, the real question had become how much this scandal was going to end up costing. The city's loosest cannon, civil rights attorney Stephen Yagman, had obtained from the LAPD a list of 9,845 cases involving twenty-seven Rampart officers implicated in wrongdoing by Rafael Perez, and by the end of 2000 he had filed nearly two hundred lawsuits in federal court. The *Times* quoted "legal experts" who warned that the cost of settling the pending lawsuits against the LAPD would be "significantly more" than the $125 million projected by James Hahn. The cost certainly would be more if Johnnie Cochran had anything to say about it. In February of 2000 Cochran had hosted a meeting of more than two dozen civil rights attorneys to discuss coordinating lawsuits, telling reporters afterward, "If we band together, we can get a lot done." In light of the $15 million settlement paid by the city to Javier Ovando, it looked as if a lot would be "done" whether the lawyers worked together or not.

By the spring of that year, either damage control or exploitation of the scandal had become the tactic of almost every important political figure in Los Angeles. Chief Parks and District Attorney Gil Garcetti, each of whom had been pointing his finger at the other in private for months, let their feud break into the open during March of 2000. Parks took the first swing, issuing an order to his detectives that they were to deny prosecutors access to any information regarding the Rampart investigation. Garcetti had given him bad legal advice, Parks said, was dragging his feet about prosecuting the cases already delivered to his office, and no longer could be trusted. Garcetti struck back two weeks later with an offer of amnesty to LAPD whistleblowers, an idea Parks already had rejected when it was proposed by the Police Protective League.

For Russell Poole, the final straw was Parks's criticism of Garcetti for not filing charges against Brian Hewitt in the beating of Ismael Jimanez. "Parks and the LAPD never wanted Garcetti to file charges in that case and were happy when he didn't," a seething Poole said. "Now they want to blame the D.A. for not filing. I know for certain that Garcetti didn't have all the information he should have had, because Chief Parks kept it from him."

Poole had spent the past year living in two parallel worlds. On the one hand, he spent more time with his wife and children than he had allowed himself to during his entire career as an LAPD detective. Poole also had launched a successful business that helped high school athletes obtain college scholarships. He was free to visit his parents at their home in Palm Springs, and to coach his children's baseball and softball teams. "My life was better," Poole said, "but I couldn't have peace as long as I thought I had let Chief Parks get away with what he did during that last year and a half I was on the department."

The more he thought about how the LAPD brass had treated him, the angrier Poole became. He had heard some of what was being whispered about him at Parker Center, suggestions that he was an emotionally unstable troublemaker who had betrayed his loyalty to the LAPD by going over the heads of his supervisors to the district attorney's office. Brian Tyndall advised Poole that his letter of resignation had circulated in photocopy throughout the Robbery-Homicide Division, even though it was supposed to be a confidential document.

Poole knew that his final Peformance Evaluation Report was being withheld so that the LAPD wouldn't have to explain what his problems were, especially in the light of an outstanding past record. The last evaluation Poole had received from the Robbery-Homicide Division, in October of 1997, was the most vague and elliptical he had ever seen. He had been been rated "strong" (the LAPD's highest rating) in each of the seventeen areas in which officers were evaluated, Poole noted, except one—the box labeled "judgment and common sense" had been left blank.

The same commanders and chiefs who suggested he was not right in the head, however, had asked for Poole's help when it became apparent that the LAPD's internal prosecution of Brian Hewitt and Ethan Cohan was going to fail. In June 1999, Poole had been subpoenaed at the last minute to appear at the departmental "trial board" hearing, where his testimony resulted in the dismissal of Hewitt and Cohan from the LAPD. "Apparently when they needed me I was no longer a nut case," he observed.

Ultimately, it was not being able to sleep at night that drove Poole to act. "I decided I had to get the truth out in the one way that was left to me," he explained. On September 26, 2000, eleven months after resigning from the LAPD, Poole filed a civil lawsuit naming Chief Bernard Parks, the Los Angeles Police Department, and the City of Los Angeles as defendants. The suit specifically accused Parks of violating his First Amendment right to go public after Poole "began to uncover evidence suggesting the involvement of other LAPD officers in criminal activity."

Chief Parks responded with a press release in which he described Poole's claims as "totally false." He could not comment on any specific allegations by former Detective Poole, Parks explained, but then did, chiding Poole for his failure to "make his complaints known at the time they occurred" and asserting that Poole's forty-page report on a scandal-in-the making had not been discarded or ignored, but rather was "edited of all conjectural materials." Interestingly, Chief Parks referred repeatedly to Poole's work on "The Rampart Task Force," without once mentioning what the group had been called back when Poole was assigned to it. "Chief Parks turned 'The Robbery-Homicide Task Force' into 'The Rampart Task Force' in order to cover up all that had led up to the arrest of Perez," Poole said, "and because of my lawsuit, he's going to have to explain why he did that. That's what scares him."

It was a favor of fortune that Poole's claim against the LAPD had been filed just as a number of people in Los Angeles noticed that the empire of lawsuits, suspensions, and scandals built on the word of Rafael Perez was beginning to crumble all around them. The first crack in the facade of repentance that Perez had constructed around him appeared in February of 2000, when the *Los Angeles Times* finally reported that "the ex-officer turned informant has failed a polygraph test." Actually, it was five polygraph tests that Perez had failed, five months earlier. The *Times*'s understatement was buried deep inside a story that ran under the headline POLICE IN SECRET GROUP BROKE LAW ROUTINELY, TRANSCRIPTS SAY, but, nevertheless, a lot of readers found it the most significant revelation in weeks.

Gradually, an assortment of other facts began to undermine the ex-officer turned informant's credibility. Perez's own admission that he had lied thousands of times under oath in court, and that he had done so quite convincingly, finally began to make at least a few observers wonder why they should believe anything he said now. So did the news that he had cheated on his wife so routinely that he couldn't remember his girlfriends' names unless investigators showed him photographs. Perez even had lied on his marriage license, it was discovered, swearing that Denise Perez was his first wife. Perez was essentially a chameleon, an LAPD officer who had worked with him at Rampart Division explained to reporters: "When he wanted to be Latino, he was Rafael. When he wanted to be black, he was Rafe." The LAPD detectives who had interrogated him all said Perez asked them to address him as "Ray." Most tellingly, though, a close examination of Perez's "confessions" revealed that by far the most despicable crimes he described had been committed by himself and by his partner Nino Durden. Much if not most of his other allegations amounted to stuff you could watch Andy Sipowicz doing any Tuesday night on *NYPD Blue*.

The inconsistencies in Perez's story emerged slowly. First, an LAPD search for the "crash pad" apartment in the San Fernando Valley that Rampart officers supposedly had used for their debaucheries ended in failure, convincing investigators assigned to the case that Perez had invented the story. He couldn't recall the address of the apartment, Perez explained, or the street, or even the neighborhood. He did recall attending a drunken party at which Officer Kulin Patel had been present, Perez said, and even was able to provide a date. But when Patel's attorney produced photographs and documents that utterly refuted Perez's story, the LAPD's charges against Patel were withdrawn. "All this proves is that he's human," said Winston K. McKesson. What it proved was that he couldn't be trusted. That became even more evident when Perez apeared at an LAPD trial board to testify against former Rampart Division colleague Lawrence Martinez, whom he had accused of helping to frame two 18th Street Gang members on gun charges in April 1996. Perez testified under oath that the arrest was initiated by his meeting with a police informant on April 2 of that year. When Perez named the informant, Martinez's attorney, Darryl Mounger, promptly demonstrated that the man had been incarcerated on April 2, 1996, and could not possibly have met with Perez on that date. "I caught him with his pants down," Mounger said of Perez. "The problem with Perez," the attorney added, "is that he's told so many lies that he's confused. He doesn't know what the truth is anymore." Winston McKesson conceded that Perez had "erred," but once again defended his client's integrity. "He believes the informant is who he said it was," McKesson explained. "That's still who he pictures in his mind. But the identity of the informant is not what he considered important about this case."

Chief Parks and his right-hand man, Lt. Emmanuel Hernandez, both told reporters that "seventy to eighty percent" of what Perez had claimed in his "confessions" had been verified by LAPD investigators. Neither Parks nor Hernandez would provide any specifics, however, and their claims were hardly backed up by the performance of Perez as a witness against his fellow officers. Far later than it should have, and with considerably less prominence than the news merited, the *Los Angeles Times* reported that only three of the fourteen LAPD officers brought before trial boards in connection to the Rampart scandal had been dismissed from the department. What the *Times* did not mention was that one of those fired was Perez's former partner Nino Durden, and that the other two were Brian Hewitt and Ethan Cohan, both of whom had been convicted not on the basis of Perez's allegations against them, but by the testimony of Russell Poole. All eleven of the officers subjected to trial boards in which the main witness against them was Rafael Perez had been exonerated.

Finally, despite knowing it would essentially kill his career, at least as long as Bernard Parks or anyone associated with him ran the LAPD, Captain Roger K. Coombs, who had presided over one of these trial boards, told the *Times*, "Perez has not shown himself to be a credible witness." Many LAPD officers could scarcely restrain their cheers. "Coombs may have hurt himself in the short run," said Police Protective League vice president Bob Baker, "but most of the rank and file consider him a hero."

Los Angeles County District Attorney Gil Garcetti described Perez's problems as a witness in rather less ambiguous terms. "He's a liar," Garcetti said. "He tells the truth, too. But can you tell when he's telling the truth and when he's not telling the truth?" The short answer was no, and the enormity of the problem this created was just beginning to register with the powers that be.

The Los Angeles media, political establishment, and legal system had all committed themselves to what the *Times* now called "the admissions and allegations of Rafael Perez." Dozens of convicts had been released, hundreds of lawsuits had been filed, millions of dollars had been paid, and countless pages of newsprint had been invested in the claims of a man who didn't deserve to be believed about anything. A large part of the problem was that the media's coverage from the first had been driven more by ideology that by information. The *Times*, the *LA Weekly*, and the *New Times* all persisted in describing Perez as "Hispanic," even though he was half black. His own attorney had explained to them that "Puerto Rican culture is much closer to African American than to Hispanic, and that's why his closest friends were black." The *Times* had abandoned the link between Perez and David Mack, and between David Mack and Suge Knight, as soon as the Chuck Philips story on Amir Muhammed was published, while both the *Weekly* and the *New Times* had rejected the Mack-Muhammed theory without any investigation of it.

By far the most notable fact about the filing of Russell Poole's lawsuit against the LAPD was that the *Los Angeles Times* had declined to publish any serious investigation of the former detective's claims.

Poole's explanation for this carried truly dangerous implications. During the summer of 2000, Poole recalled, he had a series of conversations with Lait and Glover about his belief that Chief Parks had obstructed justice. "At first I said I didn't trust them," Poole said, "but then I agreed to cooperate if they told the story right this time. But the article I was expecting never ran. Finally I called them up to ask why. Scott Glover told me they had been getting pressure 'from upstairs.' When I asked what that meant, he said the publisher had made it clear that the *Los Angeles Times* was not going to help bring down an African-American chief of police."

Scott Glover and Matt Lait, along with their editor Jim Newton, all disputed Poole's claim. However, Deputy District Attorney George Castillo, now assigned to the Belmont Task Force that was investigating L.A.'s latest racially charged scandal, said he believed Russell Poole, and not the newspaper reporters. "I believe the *Times* refused to report this story because they're cowards," Castillo explained. "I've said that to the faces of Matt Lait and Scott Glover. And they've come up with the sort of whiny excuses that lead me to believe they probably said what Russ says they said. It's obvious to everyone that this is what's going on here. It's certainly the consensus of opinion within the Belmont Task Force."

Jan Golab, the freelance journalist whose reporting on Poole's lawsuit had made him a voice crying in the wilderness, agreed with Castillo completely. "The *Times* and the rest of the media in Los Angeles have ignored Russell Poole for one reason—liberal racism," Golab said. "You can't tell a story in which the good guy is a white detective and the villains are all black. That isn't allowed, even if it's true."

Golab, who found it difficult to sell his account of Poole's resignation from the LAPD (although Salon.com eventually did publish it online), was plagued by the unwillingness of those he interviewed to be identified by name. A "knowledgeable source in the Los Angeles legal community" had described Poole's lawsuit to Golab as "a mine in the water," while "a Los Angeles County official who asked for immunity" told the reporter that because of Poole's lawsuit "serious charges could result, including indictments for obstruction of justice." His sources all had been afraid, Golab said, that "the truth will never come out, because neither the media nor the politicians want it to, and that they'll be left holding the bag."

Some significant local figures were willing to speak in their own names on Poole's behalf, however. One was retired LAPD Deputy Chief Steve Downing, who described Poole's allegations to Golab as "appalling," then added, "Anytime you have leads in a case pointing to a cop, it's even more important that it be pursued to the absolute end. And you also have to ask the question: Who else is involved? Have any other officers been infected by these activities?" What Bernard Parks had done to Russell Poole's investigative reports was "an outrage," Downing later told *Rolling Stone* magazine. "The police chief's job is to produce the truth, not bury it."

Sergio Robleto, Poole's former lieutenant in South Bureau Homicide, was a man whom many of his fellow officers had believed would one day become Los Angeles's first Hispanic Chief of Police, until he resigned from the LAPD to take a job as an executive at "the corporate CIA," Kroll Associates. If Bernard Parks imagined he could discredit Russell Poole, Robleto warned, the chief had better think again. Poole was among the most honest and industrious police officers he had ever worked with, said Robleto, and possibly the most "thorough" detective he'd ever encountered. "Everything Poole does, he writes down," explained Robleto, scoffing at the suggestion that Poole might have exaggerated what took place in his meetings with Chief Parks and other high-ranking officers. "You're never going to catch Russ lying."

Proving that Rafael Perez was not a "credible witness," meanwhile, was becoming easier by the week. On September 26, 2000, the same day Russell Poole filed his lawsuit, the *Los Angeles Times* reported that a "jailhouse informant" said he had heard the ex-officer boast about being able to destroy anyone who crossed him. While he listened from the next cell, the man had told investigators from the Rampart Task Force, Perez bragged to his bunkmate, "If someone pisses me off, I'll throw their name into a hat, and they'll get investigated—innocent or not." The informant was an ex-LAPD officer named Hank Rodriguez who had been fired from the department in 1974. Rodriguez had been placed in the cell next to Perez's when he was arrested for a parole violation stemming from a drunk driving conviction. He observed that Perez had adopted "a gang member type of attitude" while in custody, Rodriguez said, regularly breaking into rap songs and crowing about his book and movie deals. Part of what made Rodriguez's claims newsworthy was that the LAPD had managed to "misplace" them for five months after they were made. This was explained to the Los Angeles County Superior Court by Dan Schatz, the LAPD commander whom Russell Poole blamed more than any other high-ranking officer (other than Bernard Parks) for the suppression of his investigations during 1997 and 1998. What Schatz called an accident, the *Times* described as "a potentially serious oversight" that could affect any court cases in which Perez was called to the stand as a witness.

"We're not done yet," Poole said. That much, at least, was certain.

CHAPTER THIRTEEN

By the autumn of 2000, more than a hundred felony cases had been overturned on the basis of Ray Perez's statements. None of his claims, however, had been tested in a court of law. Now, one finally would be. Prosecutors made what seemed an odd choice for the first criminal case brought to trial on the basis of Perez's story: four Rampart officers accused by Perez of framing 18th Street Gang member Allan Lobos on a gun possession charge. What made the prosecution's case so curious was that Lobos was a convicted killer serving a life sentence for first-degree murder. When the trial of those accused of framing the gang member on the weapons charge finally began, however, the decision made more sense: Three of the four officers were white, while ten of the twelve jurors who would pass judgment on them were minorities.

The legal drama soon would be overwhelmed by claims made outside the courtroom by a former girlfriend of Perez's named Sonia Flores, who told the FBI that Rafael and David Mack had shot to death a drug dealer named "Chino" and an older woman who appeared to be his mother. Mack and Perez wrapped the victim's bodies in garbage bags sealed with duct tape, Flores said, then drove to Tijuana, Mexico, and buried them in a ravine where the corpses of those killed in the border city's drug wars were dumped on an almost daily basis.

Flores told a story that was remarkably detailed. She met Rafael Perez in 1991 at the Pan American Nightclub near the Rampart Division station, Flores said. He had come into the club, Perez said, to check on underage drinkers. Flores, fourteen at the time, clearly qualified. Her age hadn't kept the officer from asking for her telephone number, however, said Flores, and soon after they began meeting for sexual liaisons at an apartment on Marathon Street that Perez shared with two other LAPD officers, David Mack and Sammy Martin. When she became pregnant with Perez's child, Flores went on, he took her to a clinic near the corner of Vermont Avenue and Fourth Street, where she aborted the fetus.

Sometime during either late 1994 or early 1995, Flores said, she was picked up at her home in Echo Park by Mack and Perez, who were driving Sammy Martin's black BMW. They drove her back to the Marathon Street apartment, then took her along when they made a delivery of cocaine to a man named Chino. Before leaving the Marathon Street apartment, Flores said, Perez and Mack put on their SWAT gear—black nylon jackets over full suits of body armor. She didn't find this unusual, Flores explained, because she had seen them wear their SWAT uniforms on other occasions when making cocaine deliveries. She was a bit concerned that Rafael had armed himself with three handguns, though, Flores said, and became frightened during the drive to Chino's apartment building on Bellevue Avenue, because Rafael began to instruct her in what to do if there was shooting.

All three of them went upstairs to an apartment with a four-digit number on the door, Flores said. Mack, who was carrying the cocaine in a brown bag, knocked. A Hispanic woman in her mid-fifties answered and let the three of them in. While she and the older woman sat in the living room, Flores said, Rafael, David Mack, and Chino adjourned to a back bedroom. She had met Chino a couple of times before at the Guatelinda Nightclub in Hollywood, Flores explained, and believed his name was Juan Cardoza. He was a small-time drug dealer who worked the Guatelinda on a regular basis.

The three men had been out of sight for only a few minutes, Flores said, when she heard their voices raised in argument. Only a moment later Mack stepped out of the bedroom and called for the older woman. The argument in the back bedroom continued, however, until Rafael pushed Chino into the living room and used one of his pistols to force the man face down on the floor. "Where's the money?" Rafael demanded, she recalled. When Chino said he didn't have the money, Ray placed his foot on the back of the man's neck and fired a single shot into Chino's shoulder. The older woman immediately came running out of the back bedroom and threw herself on top of Chino, Flores said, but Rafael simply shoved her aside, pulled Chino's head back, and fired another gunshot into his forehead. She felt the blood splatter her legs, Flores said, then watched in shock as Mack grabbed the back of the older woman's blouse and shot her in the head.

She was in hysterics at this point, Flores said, and Rafael had to carry her back to the BMW, which was parked in an alley next to the building. While Rafael drove to the Marathon Street apartment, Mack sat with her in the back seat and tried to get her to drink something from a bottle. When she refused, Flores said, Mack poured some of what was in the bottle onto a rag and covered her face with it until she lost consciousness.

She awoke in the bathroom of the Marathon Street apartment, fully clothed, but missing her tennis shoes and socks. Rafael was asleep in the bedroom and Mack was asleep on the couch. She remembered what had happened when she saw the blood on her shorts, Flores said, then immediately took them off and threw them into the trash. Rafael woke up a moment later and warned her that if she told anyone about what had happened, she would be prosecuted as an accomplice. Also, because Chino was connected to the Mexican Mafia, if it ever came out that she was involved in his death not only she, but her brother and children as well, would be murdered.

When she asked what had happened to the bodies, Rafael told her not to be concerned. She was fairly certain that he and Mack had dumped the corpses in Tijuana, Flores said, because Rafael had done that at least once before. They were headed south in his Ford Explorer, she recalled, when Rafael casually mentioned that there was a body in the back of the vehicle. She didn't believe him until he told her to look at the purse under her seat. She did, and inside she found the ID of a young Hispanic woman. "Just some puta from the El Panel," Rafael called her. The El Panel was a strip club at Florence and Western where Perez and Mack went on Wednesday nights, she explained, to enjoy the lap dancers. When they got to Tijuana that day, Flores said, they drove to a beauty salon owned by a friend whose brother owned another salon in Huntington Beach. To be sure that there really was a body in the back of the Explorer, Flores said, she unsnapped the cargo cover, pulled back a corner, and saw an obviously dead young woman lying on a plastic sheet.

She stayed at the beauty salon, Flores said, while Rafael and salon owner Rene drove off in the Explorer. When they returned, the body was gone. When she asked him to show her what he had done with the corpse, Flores said, Rafael without hesitation drove her to a field at the bottom of an embankment behind a row of houses and showed her exactly where he had dumped the woman's body.

She and Rafael broke up soon after this, Flores told the FBI, and she did not see him again until February of 1996, when she was at the McDonald's restaurant on Union Avenue. She was talking to an 18th Streeter named "Stymie," Flores said, who was on the lookout for a rival gang member he believed had killed one of his relatives in a drive-by shooting. She tried to talk him out of gunning for the man, Flores said, but Stymie refused to listen, so she called Rafael at the Rampart CRASH station. By the time Perez arrived, however, Stymie had shot and fatally wounded the man he was waiting for. Rafael drove her to the Rampart station on Union Avenue, Flores recalled, and showed her photographs of Temple Street Gang members. She picked out the picture of a man who had been sitting near her when the shooting occurred but Rafael said to ignore him and insisted that Flores point out two other men she did not recognize. She complied but at the same time decided she would not identify the two men under oath.

Rafael drove her to court on the morning of their trial, Flores recalled. On the way he showed her another photograph of the accused men, and said he would be sitting at the counsel table while she testified. After she said on the witness stand that she could not identify the suspects, Flores said, Rafael became furious with her. Yet the two continued their relationship for some months afterward.

During this period, she learned of several other serious crimes in which Rafael was involved with his "roommates" at the Marathon Street apartment, Flores said. One was the shooting of a man who had threatened to expose Rafael for extorting members of the Temple Street Gang. Rafael and Sammy Martin, while off duty, had tracked the man down and killed him on the street; Martin drove the car while Perez pulled the trigger, Flores said.

Rafael also had participated with Mack in a bank robbery, Flores said, along with two women whose names she didn't know, although she had been told that one of them worked at the bank. She had been present in the Marathon Street apartment while it was planned, Flores said.

Rafael actually had asked her to join them in the robbery, even offering to teach her to shoot a gun. She declined, but Rafael gave her $300 anyway, after the robbery, Flores said. When David Mack was arrested, however, Rafael became very concerned about what she knew, the young woman went on, offering her a sum of money and a house if she would leave the Los Angeles area. Her life was in danger, he told her, warning repeatedly that she would be killed if she talked to the police. She refused his offer of a house and money, Flores said, because she was convinced Rafael was setting her up to take the fall. She did stay in contact with him by phone, the young woman added, even after his arrest, but Rafael stopped calling in December of 1999.

On the morning of the first Rampart trial in Los Angeles, Mexican authorities were using a backhoe to excavate the ravine where Flores said the bodies of Chino and his mother had been buried. As courtroom observers studied a photograph of the site that ran under a banner headline at the top of the *Los Angeles Times* Metro section, prosecutors rose to inform the judge that they had refused to give Rafael Perez a grant of immunity in the "ongoing murder investigation," and probably would not call him as a witness. Attorneys for the four accused officers could barely contain their glee, and accused the district attorney's office of making "a deal with the devil" that had backfired on them.

"A bombshell," Erwin Chemerinsky called the prosecution's announcement. "It's hard for me to imagine the prosecution succeeding without Perez's testimony." The venerable defense attorney Barry Tarlow agreed. "It blows them out of the water," he told the *Times*. "It's probably the end of the Rampart cases and it's a sad day for the criminal justice system."

The D.A.'s office would not abandon its case, however. The ensuing trial was a bizarre but tedious affair, conducted by a judge who had written a letter of commendation praising Perez for his "professional" testimony during a kidnapping trial in her courtroom and driven by a prosecution team whose "victim" was a convicted murderer. Witnesses with names like Wicked, Rascal, Diablo, and Termite attempted to explain to the jury such subtleties as the difference between being a "tiny winy" (drinker) and a "tiny loco" (doper), while one police officer after another claimed not even to remember the incident in question. In their final arguments, defense attorneys ridiculed the prosecution's case as an "embarrassment" to the citizens of Los Angeles. What the lawyers did not recognize, though, was that they were talking to jurors every bit as inclined to believe career criminals as to put their trust in career cops.

Gil Garcetti, who one week earlier had been voted out of office by a nearly two-to-one margin (losing to a former underling, Steve Cooley, who called the Perez plea bargain the "worst of the century"), received what seemed consoling news on November 15th, when the jury delivered guilty verdicts against three of the four accused officers. The prosecution's victory celebration would be short-lived, however. Within a few days, a white alternate juror told investigators that she had heard the panel's Hispanic foreman say on the first day of the trial that the defendants were guilty. At almost the same time, five jurors signed affidavits stating that they had not been able to agree on whether the three officers told the truth when they claimed to have been struck by the gangbangers' car in the alley where the confrontation took place, but had found them guilty after agreeing that the cops did not suffer "great bodily injury." Problem was, the cops never made that claim, despite a report saying they had that was provided to the jury by the prosecution. Three days before Christmas, the convictions were voided and a mistrial declared.

Almost immediately, Sonia Flores confessed that she had made up the story about the murders of Chino and his mother. She had little choice, given that the FBI had located the alleged murder victims, alive and well. She had fabricated her tale, Flores said, to punish Perez for dumping her after she became pregnant by him, and wanted him to spend the rest of his life in prison. The feds, however, were troubled by a feeling that some of what Flores had told them was true. A number of things had checked out, such as her description of the black BMW driven by Sammy Martin and her recollection of the shooting outside the McDonald's on Union Avenue. Mack and Perez *were* fascinated by lap dancers, and Flores's description of the bank robbery had been spot on. The young woman also was able to lead the FBI to a garbage-strewn ravine in Tijuana just like the one she had described, but two days of digging by the Mexican authorities turned up no human remains. What to make of Flores was a subject of some debate at the U.S. Courthouse in downtown Los Angeles. One FBI agent suspected that Rafael Perez had persuaded the young woman to tell the story, then renounce it, so that he would not be forced to testify in court. When the FBI permitted Flores to plead guilty to a single count of making false statements to federal authorities, they insisted that she agree to at least two polygraph examinations intended to determine if anyone else had helped concoct her story. The results of those tests were never made public.

By this point, the truth had become a fragile fossil immured in sediments of deceit, cynicism, and sanctimony. Those few fragments that could be pried loose were too contaminated to trust, and the cost of clarification apparently was more than anyone wanted to pay. That spring of 2001, word around the Criminal Courts Building in downtown Los Angeles was that the state would not proceed with any more prosecutions related to the Rampart investigation, leaving further action to the federal government. A total of five LAPD officers had been fired by then, and another forty disciplined, but cop after cop were beating the charges against them at departmental trial boards. "The only real witness is Perez," Russell Poole observed, "and Perez becomes less believable all the time. Yet they're paying these gangbangers millions of dollars on the basis of what the guy says. Has anything like this ever happened before?" It had not.

By March of 2001 the last possible opportunity to separate simple truth from the complex of lies that surrounded the Los Angeles police-corruption scandal seemed to be the trial that might result from the lawsuit filed against the LAPD by Russell Poole. The federal judge who would preside over the case was admittedly impressed by what he had seen of Poole's documentation, while those who reviewed the entire file predicted that the case would explode on the city if it ever came to court. Poole's attorneys won virtually every early pretrial hearing, including one that resulted in the judge's order that Chief Parks and other senior LAPD officers submit to videotaped depositions.

He steeled himself, Poole said, with the knowledge that he could never do more damage to the police department than had already been inflicted. The LAPD by now was an almost entirely demoralized organization. The department employed nearly a thousand fewer officers than it had when Parks took over as chief, and a recent Police Protective League poll suggested that as many as two-thirds of current officers wanted to quit their jobs. Even with the substantially reduced requirements that had been implemented in the name of diversity, the department was unable to fill its Police Academy classes. Dissension within the LAPD had advanced to the point that the vice president of the PPL stated publicly that the entire Rampart scandal was the result of Chief Parks's determination to protect black officers, an assertion that would have been unthinkable one year earlier.

"We've come to the point where there are two standards in the LAPD now," said former Deputy Chief Steve Downing. "One for white officers and another for minorities. You can't possibly maintain discipline under those conditions."

The PPL's leadership had been warning for months that closing the LAPD's CRASH units would leave gangbangers feeling "they've been given a green light to go back and terrorize people." Such dire predictions were dismissed as police propaganda at first, but Los Angeles had seen a huge increase in violent crime during the past year, with murders up more than 25 percent, after eight years of steady decline, and gang members blamed for most of them. The key witness in one of the alleged CRASH frame-ups was arrested for rape, and in July 2000, after making a deal to collect $231,000 from the City of Los Angeles for the beating inflicted on him by Brian Hewitt, Ismael Jimanez was accused by federal prosecutors of conspiring to commit two murders during the previous year.

The investigation that Russell Poole had begun back in March of 1997, meanwhile, the one that Rafael Perez almost single-handedly turned into the "Rampart scandal," appeared to have subsided into terminal limbo. The murders of Tupac Shakur and Biggie Smalls remained unsolved, and Chief Parks continued to insist that they had nothing to do with the crimes by cops that had ravaged his department. "The racial politics of this city have become so ridiculous that the police department and the district attorney's office don't want to solve the Biggie Smalls case," asserted Downing. "They're afraid Johnnie Cochran will defend whoever is charged, and we'll have another O.J. situation."

Suge Knight, meanwhile, was about to be transferred to a federal prison in Oregon where he was scheduled for release in early August, meaning he would be back in his office at Death Row Records before the summer was over. The racketeering probe of Knight and David Kenner by the U.S. Justice Department recently had been described as "inactive" (in a story written by Chuck Philips for the *Los Angeles Times*), but the Biggie Smalls case refused to die.

On June 6, 2000, LAPD detectives Greg Grant and Brian Tyndall, along with Lt. Emmanuel Hernandez, made the trip north to the Cornell Correctional Facility, where Kevin Hackie was incarcerated on a weapons charge. The three officers were most interested in Hackie's claim that he knew what David Mack had done with the missing $700,000 from the Bank of America robbery in November of 1997. What Hackie first told the LAPD contingent, however, was that he had seen Mack and Ray Perez together at a number of Death Row Records functions "that were reserved for close friends of the owner or individuals considered to be in the owner's inner circle," and that Kevin Gaines had attended similar events. Hackie provided numerous places and dates where he had seen Mack and/or Perez with Suge Knight, beginning with the Black Image Awards show at the Beverly Hills Hotel in 1995. He was told then that Mack and Knight had grown up together in Compton, Hackie recalled. Mack had been without Perez at that event, but the two were together with Suge and his entourage at a Mike Tyson fight in Las Vegas during May or June of 1996, Hackie said. He saw Mack with Suge only a short time later at the MTV-sponsored "Toss It Up" event where Tupac Shakur made a guest appearance, Hackie went on. Hackie first met Kevin Gaines at Tupac's "California Love" video shoot, he said. The story that Suge Knight did not welcome Gaines's presence at Death Row events was a fiction, Hackie added. Gaines was at a second Tupac video shoot only a couple of weeks later, at a mansion in either Santa Ana or Anaheim Hills, and Suge had been present as well. Gaines also was at the Death Row Christmas party in December of 1995, and only a few days later was with the Death Row contingent that distributed frozen turkeys in Compton for the Brotherhood Crusade. He saw Gaines at several other Death Row events, Hackie said, the last being an awards ceremony in April of 1996.

Hackie also told the LAPD detectives that in February of 1999, shortly after his arrest on the weapons charges, he had been locked up at the Century Sheriff's Station in Lynwood for seven days with Ray Perez. The two of them never discussed the bank robbery, Hackie said, but Perez did say he still employed a street dealer named "Cadillac Willie" who was selling kilos of cocaine for him.

Hackie also told the LAPD trio that he had important information about the murder trial of Snoop Dogg. In January or February of 1996, Hackie said, Reggie Wright Jr. told him (during a conversation at the Death Row studios in Tarzana) that the case against Snoop was destroyed when important evidence disappeared from the West Los Angeles Police Station. Wright seemed to imply that one of his friends on the LAPD had taken care of this for him, Hackie recalled.

"I don't know what motivated Tyndall and Grant to go interview Hackie in prison," Poole said. "Hackie already had told us enough in our first interview with him that if we had just followed up on it all, we probably would have gotten to the bottom of all this. And if we'd had a picture of Perez at that first interview, we'd probably have ended up interviewing him, too, and who knows what that would have led to."

The story Hackie gave the LAPD paled in comparison, though, to the one that a Los Angeles jail inmate named Mark Hylland told to the FBI early in 2001. Hylland was a paralegal who had a history of practicing law without a license, often in the service of clients engaged in criminal enterprise. He claimed to have become involved with Ray Perez, David Mack, and two other LAPD officers back in 1992, when he met them at a strip club called Fritz's in Bellflower. Eventually the four hired him to launder the fortune they were earning as drug dealers, Hylland claimed, by secretly investing the money in real estate. According to Hylland, the main tactic of the four was to place the property in the names of the Hispanic gang members they arrested in the Rampart Division. "They'd wait until one of these guys went to prison," explained an investigator who had spent much of the past six months unearthing the paper trail left by these transactions, "then put the property in his name, rent it out, default on their mortgage payments, wait for the property to be repossessed, then buy it at auction for half of what it cost a year earlier." Behind a screen of phony transactions, he had discovered dozens of real estate deals that linked Hylland to Perez, Mack, and at least two other LAPD officers, said the investigator, who had become convinced that this part of Hylland's story could be proved.

It would be considerably more difficult to verify what Hylland had to say about the murder of Biggie Smalls, however. According to Hylland, he met Suge Knight for the first and only time in the parking lot of a Denny's restaurant in Bellflower where Knight was accompanied by Mack and Perez. After a brief conversation, Hylland said, Knight opened the trunk of his car, removed an envelope stuffed with hundred-dollar bills, and handed it to Perez, who then handed it to him. His job, Hylland said, was to fly to Arizona to hand this money over to a Phoenix cop who eventually obtained the weapon used in the hit on Smalls.

"The story sounds fantastic, I realize," said Hylland's Santa Monica attorney, W. Ronald Seabold, "but Mr. Hylland tells it very convincingly." While both the LAPD and the Los Angeles County district attorney's office dismissed Hylland's allegations, the FBI had interviewed him on four separate occasions, Seabold said. Hylland failed a FBI lie detector test in March of 2001, but a subsequent investigation turned up flight manifests and hotel records that showed the man had traveled to Phoenix on the dates he claimed. Seabold asked the U.S. Justice Department to take Hylland into federal protective custody.

The FBI and U.S. Attorney's office might have decided that they needed no new witnesses, however, after cutting a deal with Nino

Durden. In late March, Durden agreed to a seven-year, eight-month federal prison sentence and promised to testify against Rafael Perez and "other unindicted co-conspirators" for crimes not fully specified. Durden had been arrested by the LAPD back in July of 2000 and charged with attempted murder in the shooting of Javier Ovando. It was, said then D.A. Garcetti, "the most serious crime we can prove at this time." Shortly after Steve Cooley replaced Garcetti as district attorney, however, it was conceded that the evidence against Durden did not support an attempted murder charge. In his March 29, 2001, plea agreement with the U.S. Attorney's office, Durden admitted he was guilty of violating Ovando's civil rights and agreed as well to plead guilty in at least three other cases in which he and Perez framed, beat, or robbed criminal suspects.

It seemed obvious to the *Los Angeles Times* that the federal government intended to use Durden in order to charge Perez with the Ovando shooting, but this was not necessarily so. The deal Perez had reached with the district attorney's office would make it difficult to prosecute him for any crimes to which he already had confessed. Perhaps, some speculated, Durden was prepared to testify that Perez had committed crimes not mentioned in his "confessions," including those that involved David Mack and/or other LAPD officers associated with Death Row Records. Russell Poole regarded that as a dubious theory. "Durden knows as well as anyone that if he goes up against Suge Knight he'll have to spend the rest of his life either in protective custody or in hiding," Poole said. "Even if he knows who killed Biggie Smalls—and I doubt he does—I don't think he'd ever talk about it." What the feds might be able to do with Durden, though, Poole said, was persuade Perez to talk to them about those matters he had refused to discuss earlier. "If Perez believed he was facing serious prison time because of what Durden was prepared to say about him in court, I think he'd be willing to cut a new deal, this time with the feds, and tell them what he knows about David Mack and the rest of this," Poole said. "That's assuming the feds want to know. Whatever they do with Durden, though, it's going to open this all up again, and I welcome that."

In the meantime, the most startling revelation in the Biggie Smalls case had been produced not by the LAPD or the FBI or by the Los Angeles media, but by a documentary filmmaker based in West Sussex, England. Nick Broomfield was best known as the director of *Kurt and Courtney* but had become fascinated by the Biggie Smalls murder, especially after meeting with Russell Poole in Los Angeles. Early in May of 2001, Broomfield flew to New York to look for those who had been part of the Bad Boy Entertainment entourage on the night of Biggie's killing. He was especially interested in meeting with Eugene Deal, the New York State Parole Officer who had impressed LAPD detectives as the most reliable witness among those in the caravan of cars that had carried Puffy Combs and Biggie Smalls to the Petersen Museum party in March of 1997.

In his interviews with the police, Deal had been both first and strongest in denouncing the theory that Crips committed the crime, mainly because Keffy D and the other gang members he met at the Petersen Party had shown him "nothing but love" that night. And Deal's description of the "Nation of Islam guy," who seemed to be stalking Puffy Combs as they waited for their rides after the party, had always been the most intriguing statement provided by any of the witnesses to Biggie's slaying. The Muslim-looking fellow, Deal told Broomfield, had been dressed and groomed just like James Lloyd and Gregory Young said the shooter was: "He had the blue suit and bow tie and white shirt, peanut hair, receding hairline, brown skin." And after looking them all over very coolly, Deal explained, the Muslim walked away in the same direction that the killer's car came from just minutes later. Deal, by the way, believed that the assassin's prime target had been Puffy Combs, he said; if the first Suburban, the one carrying Combs, had stopped at the red light, Puffy probably would be dead today instead of Biggie.

When Broomfield asked him to describe the Muslim's face, Deal answered that he had looked "almost" like the composite drawing of the killer that an LAPD artist had made with the help of Li'l Caesar and G-Money. Only "this guy had a stronger cheekbone structure, where he looked a little sterner," Deal explained.

Broomfield then showed Deal both composite drawings of the shooting suspect done by the LAPD and photographs of a half-dozen individuals who had been linked to the death of Biggie Smalls in one way or another. Deal immediately pointed to one photograph and said, "That's him right there."

"That's him?" a startled Broomfield asked.

"Yeah," Deal said. "That's the guy who came up to me."

"That guy? That's him?" Broomfield asked again.

"Yes," Deal answered.

"Were you ever shown this picture before?" Broomfield asked.

Deal shook his head. The LAPD had never shown him a photograph of this man, Deal would explain a few minutes later.

"That's definitely him, though?" Broomfield asked again.

"Yep," Deal said, nodding his head vigorously.

The man in the photograph was Harry Billups aka Harry Muhammed aka Amir Muhammed.

When Broomfield told Deal the identity of the man he had picked out, the parole officer demanded to know why the police had not shown him a picture of Muhammed earlier: "I gave them my description of the individual which was far different from [the composite] because of his cheekbone structure and everything like that. Right? Why didn't they read my statement and look at this picture and put it to this? Knowing he had something to do with it?"

That was the same question he wanted to ask, said Russell Poole, when Broomfield sent him a transcript of his filmed interview with Deal. "I really want to hear what Fred Miller and Chuck Philips of the *Times* have to say when they hear about this," Poole said. "I wish I could see their faces when they read about it. But what I'd really,

really like to see is the expression on Chief Parks's face when this comes out. If I had a picture of that, I'd hang it on my wall."

Two weeks after Broomfield's interview with Deal, the frame placed on the "Rampart scandal" by the Los Angeles media was widened considerably by a pair of articles in national magazines. Published less than a week apart in *The New Yorker* and *Rolling Stone*, both articles placed the story of the Los Angeles Police scandal in the context of the Gaines-Lyga shooting, the David Mack bank robbery, and the Biggie Smalls murder investigation, something that no Los Angeles–based publication had done.

The local press answered with attacks on the magazine writers that mainly demonstrated how ignorant they were about a story they had been covering for almost three years now. The most lengthy diatribe was written by Charles Rappleye of the *LA Weekly*. Rappleye debunked the *Rolling Stone* article* with exactly one named source, Richard McCauley, who insisted he was the only LAPD officer ever to work for Death Row Records. Rappleye, who had been writing about the Rampart scandal since 1999, apparently did not know that Sharitha Knight had told the LAPD back in March of 1997 that Kevin Gaines worked for Death Row, or that at least three LAPD officers had told investigators during early 1998 that David Mack attempted to recruit them to work for the rap label, or that Reggie Wright Jr. had named three additional LAPD officers who did "security work" for Death Row when he was interviewed by the LAPD's Internal Affairs Division in May of 1997. That made five LAPD officers other than Richard McCauley who had been identified by the department as employees of Death Row Records prior to the spring of 1998, while at least a dozen others had been named by one source or another as LAPD officers suspected of working for the rap label. When the author of the *Rolling Stone* article cited the Internal Affairs investigation

---

*Written by Randall Sullivan, author of this book.

in which Reggie Wright Jr. was interviewed, then noted that Richard McCauley had resigned from the LAPD "in lieu of dismissal" shortly before a trial board hearing where he faced six potentially criminal charges, each one related to the lies he had told about his work for Death Row, a "humbled" Rappleye retreated into silence.

The *Los Angeles Times*'s strategy was to ignore the magazine articles altogether. While the San Fernando Valley's *Daily News* responded to the *Rolling Stone* and *New Yorker* articles with a front-page story, the *Times*'s only mention of the magazine pieces was a tiny item in which the newspaper reported on an absurd "racketeering" lawsuit filed by Kevin Hackie, who had accused *Rolling Stone* and *The New Yorker* of joining the LAPD in a conspiracy against him. The *Times*'s Chuck Philips promised to publish a story that would utterly vindicate Suge Knight in the Biggie Smalls murder, but no such article ever appeared.

Death Row Records itself did issue a "statement" that described the *Rolling Stone* article as "ridiculous and absurd," warning that Suge Knight was meeting with his lawyers (among them David Mack's former criminal attorney, Donald Re) "in order to ascertain any lawful and legal remedies that may be available to him." And only hours after his release from federal prison in early August of 2001, Knight granted an interview to Chuck Philips, who produced an article that read more like a press release than a news report. After noting once again that Kevin Hackie had sued *Rolling Stone* for exposing him "to immediate and imminent bodily harm" (while failing to mention that Hackie's attorney had agreed several weeks earlier to drop the magazine as a defendant in the lawsuit), Philips ended his article with a quote from Suge Knight: "I'm God's child and God always reveals the truth," Suge said. "Those stories are full of lies."

Not everyone thought so. Just a few weeks after the *Rolling Stone* article appeared, Russell Poole was visited by a pair of FBI agents who told him that, on the basis of "what had come out recently in the media," the bureau was launching its own investigation of Biggie Smalls's murder. "Just about every question they asked me concerned the involvement of LAPD officers with Death Row Records," Poole said. "I have to admit I was encouraged. I don't know for sure where the FBI is headed, but neither of these two guys seemed to be playing games."

At almost that same moment, attorneys representing a former Long Beach police officer critically wounded by a gang member armed with a gun that was officially in the possession of the Compton Police Department sat down to depose the Compton P.D.'s former deputy chief, Gary O. Anderson. His department, among several others, had been riddled with corruption, Anderson told the attorneys, much of it related to police officers who were in the employ of Death Row Records. "Read the *Rolling Stone* article," Anderson told the Long Beach officer's lawyers. "It's right on the money."

The loud rumble in the background, though, was the news that Voletta Wallace and the New York law firm that represented her son's estate were seriously contemplating a wrongful death lawsuit that would accuse individuals ranging from Bernard Parks to Suge Knight of responsibility for Biggie Smalls's murder. When Russell Poole flew back east for a meeting with Voletta Wallace in February of 2001, "I told her that I still believed the truth would come out," the former detective said, "but only if she took the lead in demanding it."

During the summer of 2001, a team of attorneys based in Louisiana and Colorado, each of whom had become involved after reading the *Rolling Stone* article, began preparing the rough draft of a legal filing that would grow to more than sixty pages by Thanksgiving. After struggling for months with the idea that all of those named as conspirators in the pending lawsuit were black, Ms. Wallace decided to proceed.

"People are afraid of all the skeletons in the closet," she explained. "But we have to let those skeletons out. I've been waiting more than four years. If we keep waiting, I'm afraid there won't be anybody left alive to talk by the time they finally open the door to that closet."

EPILOGUE

All through the spring of 2001, Russell Poole's lawsuit against the City of Los Angles had been delayed by a series of defense motions and requests for continuance. Then on June 6, one day after James Hahn was elected mayor of Los Angeles, U.S. District Court Judge Stephen Wilson dismissed Poole's suit on the grounds that the statute of limitations had expired by the time it was filed. This bad news was followed almost immediately by a U.S. Supreme Court ruling that the statute of limitations did not apply in cases where a timely complaint had been made to supervisors who failed to adequately investigate it. In such cases as those, the court ruled, the statute of limitations was effectively suspended.

Poole's attorneys promptly filed an appeal of Judge Wilson's dismissal of the suit with the Ninth Circuit Court of Appeals in San Francisco, which responded to the initial filings by urging Los Angeles city officials to sit down with Poole's attorneys and cut a deal. The city's attorneys, obviously shaken, replied that they would prefer to have a ruling from the court before deciding on a course of action. The Ninth Circuit is expected to rule sometime in early 2002.

No matter what the appeals court's decision, however, it seemed unlikely that Bernard Parks would be forced to submit to a deposition by Poole's attorneys before his term as Los Angeles Police Chief ends in August of 2002. "Parks must be one of the luckiest men alive," Poole observed.

The chief already was caught up in another controversy, however, this one created by his refusal to permit LAPD officers to wear an American flag pin that honored the victims of the September 11 terrorist attacks on U.S. citizens. The sheer folly and arrogance of the man had resulted in attacks on his character by journalists across the country. The *Los Angeles Times*, however, did not consider the matter worthy of even a brief article. The *Times* chose also to ignore the results of a survey of the LAPD's rank-and-file officers conducted by the Police Protective League that were published in late November of 2001. Asked to "grade" their chief of police, LAPD officers gave Parks a C- for integrity, a D for trustworthiness, and Fs for innovation, communication, and collaboration. Seventy-two percent of those who responded told the PPL that they did not trust Chief Parks. "By far and away, this is the most negative report card" ever given to a Los Angeles Police Chief by those who served under him, said PPL president Mitzi Grasso. "It exemplifies [Park's] lack of leadership qualities." L.A.'s new mayor, James Hahn, insisted that LAPD morale was "improving."

Racial politics continued to be the chief impediment to criminal investigations involving rap labels. In Texas, a federal drug investigation focused on the Houston label Rap-A-Lot and its owner, James Prince, was frozen after Rep. Maxine Waters sent a letter to Attorney General Janet Reno requesting that she intervene on behalf of an "African-American entrepreneur" who had been "harrassed and intimidated "by the Drug Enforcement Agency."

Prince's business dealings had been of interest to federal authorities since 1988, when a car bearing dealer plates from a used-car lot he owned was stopped near El Paso by police officers who found more than two hundred pounds of cocaine in a hidden compartment. Prince's cousin, who carried a card identifying him as a salesman for the car lot, sat in the passenger seat of the vehicle when it was stopped. While the salesman was released (because of insufficient evidence that he knew about the cocaine hidden in the vehicle), the driver was convicted and sentenced to federal prison. James Prince later helped the wife of the convicted man set up a bail-bond company housed in the Rap-A-Lot building. A federal task force formed in 1998 arrested several Rap-A-Lot employees, as well as a black Houston police officer convicted of using his patrol car to help one of the rap label's employees rob a drug dealer. The first federal trial of a Rap-A-Lot employee arrested by the task force ended with a hung jury in April of 2000 at the end of a proceding in which the star prosecution witness was threatened by a courtroom spectator while testifying and a juror complained that another spectator had attempted to write down her car's license plate number.

A month after Waters's letter was sent, Prince was interviewed by the DEA's Office of Professional Responsibility in the congresswoman's Washington office. Despite the fact that her congressional district was more than a thousand miles from Houston, Waters was present for that interview, an event DEA officials described as "unprecedented." Almost immediately afterward, the probe of the Rap-A-Lot label was suspended, over the strenuous objections of narcotics detectives in Houston, and the DEA agent who had been in charge of the field investigation was transferred to a desk job.

One year later, Prince's label released a CD in which rapper Brad "Scarface" Jordan boasted about the ability of the "Rap-A-Lot mafia" to stop a federal investigation, end the careers of agents involved in it, and kill those who became police informants.

"Our tax dollars at work," observed Russell Poole, who had followed the Rap-A-Lot investigation from Los Angeles.

Puffy Combs was proving no less adroit than Suge Knight at avoiding incarceration. Combs had been skating out of trouble with the law since 1991, when nine people were killed in a stampede at a celebrity basketball game he had promoted. While Combs was assigned 50 percent culpability in a civil suit, no criminal charges were filed. In 1995 Combs was convicted of criminal mischief for threatening a photographer, but he got off with a fine. That same year, he was arrested by the FBI in Washington, D.C., for menacing a man with a gun in a parking lot near Georgetown University. Puffy was released on his promise to appear later in a D.C. courtroom, but he never did and the charges were mysteriously dropped.

In 1998 Combs was investigated for firing a gun in a Cleveland hotel room, but no charges were filed. Puffy was arrested in early 1999 for an attack on record executive Steve Stoute in which Combs and his associates reportedly beat the man with a champagne bottle, a chair, and a telephone. Before the charge against Combs was reduced from assault to harrassment, Chuck Philips weighed in with a piece that ran on the front page of the *Los Angeles Times*'s Business section, writing "In a business where bare-knuckle tactics are common, Combs' alleged literal use of them on an executive at a rival corporation is an extraordinary event with no precedent." Suge Knight's criminal history apparently didn't count for much in Philips's mind.

Only a few months later, Combs, girlfriend Jennifer Lopez, and their entourage of approximately thirty people arrived for the weekly "Hot Chocolate" party at Club New York in Manhattan, where they spent most of their time in a roped-off VIP section. Puffy and his rapper Shyne at some point got into an argument with a man who allegedly tossed a wad of money at the pair. According to eyewitnesses, both Combs and his rapper pulled semiautomatic pistols. Shots were fired and three people standing outside the velvet ropes were wounded. Police later found shell casings from two separate weapons. Seventeen days later, Combs was arrested on charges that he had carried two loaded guns in his Lincoln Navigator as he fled the nightclub, one of which was thrown from the vehicle. Both pistols had been recently fired, according to police.

Despite the testimony of witnesses who said they had seen Combs fire his pistol inside Club New York, Puffy was acquitted at a trial in which his defense team included Johnnie Cochran.

In August of 2001, just as Suge Knight was preparing for his release from federal prison, Combs granted an interview to *Details* magazine, which was preparing a photo spread of Puffy and his new girlfriend, model Emma Heming, wearing diamond crosses, Chanel sunglasses, and nothing else. The interview ended quickly, however, when the magazine's reporter asked if Combs was concerned that the East vs. West rap feud would flare up again when Death Row's CEO was released from prison. "If y'all want to know bout East Coast–West

Coast, why don't you ask Suge Knight? Why don't you interview him?" Combs demanded, then stormed out.

Suge reportedly was much amused. His vow to "restart" Death Row Records (now known simply as "Tha Row") had been aided considerably by the success of an album the label had assembled from Tupac Shakur's outtakes and released in March 2001. Tupac's posthumous CD, *Until the End of Time* had gone triple platinum by the time Knight was released from prison. Suge struck new deals with both domestic and international distributors, and reportedly was in negotiations to sign Lisa "Left Eye" Lopes of TLC, the hip-hop bad girl best known for burning down her boyfriend's house. According to Suge's PR reps, Lopes would give up her "Left Eye" nickname to be marketed by Tha Row as "NINA," an acronym that happened to be gangsta-speak for a 9mm pistol.

Neither Suge Knight nor his renamed record label was free of the past, however. In December of 2000, a jury in Los Angeles had awarded $4.34 million in compensatory damages and another $10 million in punitive damages to record execs Lamont and Ken Brumfield, who claimed that back in 1993 Knight had persuaded the rapper Kurupt (Ricardo Brown Jr.) to break his contract with them and sign a new one with Death Row Records. David Kenner, who had represented Suge and Death Row in court, promptly vowed to appeal. And only days after Chuck Philips greeted Suge's return to L.A. with a puff piece that ran on page one of the *Times*'s Business section, the paper was obliged to report (in a story that ran on page six of the same section) that the rapper Daz Dillinger (Delmar Arnaud) had sued Knight and Death Row for cheating him out of more than $1 million in royalties.

Suge would profess both his religious faith and his patriotism in public statements made after the terrorist attacks of September 11, 2001. And when construction resumed on the 9,000-square-foot mansion in the hills above the San Fernando Valley that Knight had abandoned when he began his prison sentence back in 1997, Suge announced that he did not intend to live in the house, but rather would use it to create a "positive environment" for troubled youth. Only an outpouring of protests by outraged neighbors prevented the project from proceeding.

What a shame, remarked Suge, who insisted that all he ever wanted to do was serve his people.

The same month that Suge was released from prison, Afeni Shakur showed up in Georgia to attend groundbreaking ceremonies for the Tupac Amaru Center for the Arts, scheduled to open in March of 2003 with a studio space for the performing arts, and a gallery whose first showing would be of paintings and drawings sent to Afeni by fans of her son's music. An adjacent garden was to commemorate Tupac and other victims of gun violence. The Christopher Wallace Memorial Foundation, meanwhile, already had been operating for almost four years as a distributor of scholarships and grants to deserving students from inner-city schools. Voletta Wallace said the organization's goal was to make B.I.G. an acronym for "Books Instead of Guns." One had to wonder if either mother had ever listened to her son's records.

While it seemed certain that the murders of Tupac Shakur and Biggie Smalls would never be solved by the police in Las Vegas and Los Angeles, that did not mean the killers were in the clear. Two days before Thanksgiving 2001, a team of FBI agents arrived at the home of Russell Poole to collect copies of the investigative files he had kept in storage for more than three years now. The bureau had decided to proceed without asking for any assistance at all from the Los Angeles Police Department, the agents told Poole. "They said they didn't want their investigation to be 'contaminated,'" reported Poole. "I never thought I'd get satisfaction from hearing a word like that used to describe contact with the LAPD." Nearly everyone he asked for advice, including his own attorney, had warned him not to share his documents with the feds, Poole said. "I went ahead anyway," he explained, "because I figured, 'Hey, it's my government, too.' I don't want to end up feeling like there's nobody I can trust."

One week before Christmas 2001, the team of attorneys who now listed their clients as Faith Evans, Voletta Wallace, and "The Estate of Christopher Wallace" were still haggling over the language of a lawsuit they intended to file before the end of the year. The lead lawyers were Perry Sanders of Louisiana and Robert Frank of Colorado, nationally renowned litigators whose class-action lawsuits on behalf of United Airlines flight attendants and against the Schlage Corporation were already among the most closely watched in the country.

Earlier drafts of the lawsuit prepared by Sanders and Frank named not only Bernard Parks, but also David Mack and Amir Muhammed, as defendants in racketeering claims they intended to make against the City of Los Angeles and the LAPD. These versions of the lawsuit contained the specific allegation that "Defendants Amir Muhammed and David Mack conspired to murder Christopher Wallace."

After the New York attorneys respresenting the Wallace estate had signed off, however, the Los Angeles lawyers retained as "local counsel" persuaded Sanders and Frank to significantly reduce the scope of the suit, dropping the racketeering claims to focus on the LAPD's "deliberate indifference." Specifically, the suit would allege that the LAPD failed to properly supervise its officers, ignored or concealed the fact that officers were involved with Death Row Records, and deliberately chose not to investigate the probability that LAPD officers were involved in the murder of Biggie Smalls. David Mack and Amir Muhammed were still named as defendants on state civil-rights claims in the revised draft of the lawsuit, but attorneys had taken a tack that did not require them to prove that the two conspired to kill Biggie Smalls, only that there was probable cause to investigate that likelihood.

After they filed the lawsuit in early 2002, Perry Sanders said, the first witness they intended to depose was Russell Poole. Suge Knight and Bernard Parks would come later.

On January 9, 2002, the *Los Angeles Times* published a front-page article written by Chuck Philips that began, "A federal racketeering probe into allegations that Marion 'Suge' Knight and his Los Angeles label, Death Row Records, committed acts of murder, drug trafficking, money laundering and gunrunning has resulted in a pair of misdemeanor tax charges."

While federal authorities "have declined to discuss or even confirm the investigation," Philips reported, two anonymous "law enforcement sources" had told him the criminal probe of Suge Knight was "over." According to a pair of plea-bargain deals filed in the U.S. District Court one day earlier, Death Row Records and David Kenner would pay fines of $100,000 and $20,000, respectively, but no criminal charges in connection to the tax violations would be filed against Suge Knight. Kenner faced as much as a year in jail, but would file a request for probation, according to his attorney, Donald Re.

Philips's article also cited a letter from the U.S. Attorney's office in Los Angeles stating that Knight would not be prosecuted for money laundering. Knight hailed this news as a vindication. "I appreciate the fact that, after looking into these lies and finding nothing, [the government] had the integrity to say, 'OK, this guy broke no law,' and called it off."

Neither Knight nor his attorneys commented on the fact that the letter from the U.S. Attorney's office had not cleared him of murder, drug trafficking, or gunrunning, but Knight did attack *Rolling Stone* magazine and the VH1 television network for reports that linked him to the deaths of Tupac Shakur and Biggie Smalls. As had been his practice for more than a decade now, Knight accused his accusers of racism. "Do you think they could get away with publishing this kind of crap about a white executive?" he asked Philips. "No way."

The *Times* article briefly quoted Russell Poole, who told Philips, "I believe that Suge Knight was involved in the murders of Biggie and Tupac. In my opinion, neither Knight nor Chief Parks have been held accountable for what they've done."

On the morning the *Times* article ran, Poole took a phone call from two FBI agents who had told him they were launching an independent investigation of Suge Knight's possible role in the murders of Shakur and Smalls. "They told me they were happy about the *Times'* story," Poole reported. "They said, 'This is all good. We'd like Suge Knight to think that the federal government is no longer investigating him.'"

LABYRINTH ROSTER

DEATH ROW RECORDS

Marion "Suge" Knight, CEO Death Row Records
Tupac Shakur, rapper, actor
Calvin "Snoop Dogg" Broadus, rapper
Andre "Dr. Dre" Young, rapper, producer, record executive
David "DJ Quik" Blake, rapper and Bloods gang member
Tracy "the D.O.C." Curry, rapper
Michel'e, singer
David Kenner, criminal attorney for Suge Knight and Snoop Dogg, legal adviser
    to Death Row Records, executive of West Coast Management
Steve Cantrock, Death Row Records accountant and business manager, federal
    witness
Norris Anderson, brother-in-law to Suge Knight, Death Row Records executive
Sharitha Knight, estranged wife of Suge Knight, manager to Snoop Dogg
Kevin Lewis, studio manager for Death Row Records
Reggie Wright Jr., owner/operator of Wrightway Protective Services, director of
    security for Death Row Records, factotum to Suge Knight
Frank Alexander, bodyguard to Tupac Shakur
Kevin Hackie, bodyguard to Tupac Shakur

BAD BOY ENTERTAINMENT

Sean "Puffy" Combs, rapper, producer, CEO of Bad Boy Entertainment
Biggie Smalls aka Notorious B.I.G. aka Christopher Wallace, rapper
James "Li'l Caesar" Lloyd, rapper, associate of Biggie Smalls
Damien "D-Rock" Butler, friend and associate of Biggie Smalls
Gregory "G-Money" Young, friend and associate of Biggie Smalls
Paul Offord, director of security for Bad Boy Entertainment
Kenneth Story, factotum to Puffy Combs
Eugene Deal, New York State Probation officer, bodyguard to Puffy Combs

Faith Evans, singer, estranged wife of Biggie Smalls
Mary J. Blige, singer
Li'l Kim, singer, girlfriend of Biggie Smalls

RUTHLESS RECORDS

Eric "Eazy-E" Wright, CEO of Ruthless Records
Jerry Heller, business manager of Ruthless Records

BLOODS GANG

Jai Hassan Jamaal "Jake the Violator" Robles, Suge Knight's friend and favorite
   thug, shooting victim
Roger "Neckbone" Williams, identified by police as one of "Suge's thugs"
Aaron "Heron" Palmer, identified by police as one of "Suge's thugs," murder victim
Crawford "Hi-C" Wilkerson, identified by police as one of "Suge's thugs"
Ronald "Ram" Lamb, identified by police as one of "Suge's thugs"
Trevon "Tray" Lane, identified by police as one of "Suge's thugs"
Henry "Hen Dog" Smith, identified by police as one of "Suge's thugs"
Alton "Buntry" McDonald, identified by police as the most fearsome of "Suge's
   thugs"
Tim and James McDonald, brothers of Alton, identified by police as "Suge's thugs"

CRIPS GANG

Orlando "Baby Lane" Anderson, victim of beating by Tupac Shakur, Suge Knight,
   and assorted Bloods gang members, suspect in murder of Tupac Shakur,
   shooting victim
Duane Keith "Keffy-D" Davis, uncle of Orlando Anderson, briefly suspect in murder of Biggie Smalls
Jerry "Monk" Bonds, friend of Orlando Anderson, suspect in murder of Tupac
   Shakur

LOS ANGELES POLICE DEPARTMENT

Russell Poole, retired LAPD homicide detective
Bernard Parks, Los Angeles Police Chief
Willie Williams, former Los Angeles Police Chief
Daryl Gates, former Los Angeles Police Chief

Dan Schatz, LAPD commander

Jim Tatreau, LAPD captain, commanding officer of Robbery-Homicide Division

Pat Conmay, LAPD lieutenant, Robbery-Homicide Division

Emmanuel Hernandez, LAPD lieutenant, leader of Rampart Task Force

Fred Miller, LAPD detective supervisor, partner of Russell Poole

Kelly Cooper, LAPD detective, investigator of Kelly Jamerson beating death and Biggie Smalls shooting

Rafael Perez, former LAPD detective, liar, thief, and "cooperating witness"

David Mack, former LAPD detective, federal prison inmate

Kevin Gaines, LAPD officer, killed by Frank Lyga in March of 1997

Frank Lyga, LAPD detective cleared in shooting of Kevin Gaines

Derwin Henderson, LAPD officer, friend to Kevin Gaines and Sharitha Knight

Nino Durden, former LAPD detective, partner of Rafael Perez, federal witness

Sammy Martin, suspended LAPD detective, friend to David Mack and Rafael Perez

Brian Hewitt, former LAPD detective, dismissed from department for beating of Ismael Jimanez

Ethan Cohan, former LAPD detective, dismissed from department for failing to report beating of Ismael Jimanez

Richard McCauley, former LAPD sergeant who resigned "in lieu of dismissal" shortly before departmental trial board where he faced charges connected to his employment by Death Row Records

Kenneth Knox, LAPD senior lead officer who initiated original investigation of Death Row Records and police officers employed by rap label

Brian Tyndall, LAPD detective supervisor, Robbery-Homicide Division

John Iancin, LAPD sergeant and Internal Affairs Division investigator

Hurley Glenn Criner, David Love, and Kenneth Sutton, LAPD officers named by Reggie Wright Jr. as "security employees" of Death Row Records

LOS ANGELES COUNTY DISTRICT ATTORNEY'S OFFICE

Gil Garcetti, former Los Angeles County District Attorney

Steve Cooley, current Los Angeles County District Attorney

Richard Rosenthal, assistant district attorney, prosecutor of Rafael Perez

Lawrence Longo, former assistant district attorney, prosecutor of Suge Knight, fired from job in 1997

William Hodgeman, deputy district attorney, prosecutor of Suge Knight

George Castillo, assistant district attorney, friend to Russell Poole

LOS ANGELES CITY ATTORNEY'S OFFICE

James Hahn, former Los Angeles City Attorney, current mayor of Los Angeles
Corey Brente, assistant city attorney in charge of Gaines-Lyga lawsuit

LOS ANGELES COUNTY SUPERIOR COURT

John Ouderkirk, judge who sentenced Suge Knight to probation
Stephen Czuleger, judge who sentenced Suge Knight to prison

LOS ANGELES MEDIA

Matt Lait and Scott Glover, *Los Angeles Times* reporters
Chuck Philips, *Los Angeles Times* reporter
Rick Barrs, editor, *New Times of Los Angeles*
Charles Rappleye, articles editor, *LA Weekly*

LAWYERS

Johnnie L. Cochran, former O.J. Simpson attorney who represented estate of Kevin
    Gaines and assisted in criminal defenses of Puffy Combs and Snoop Dogg
Winston K. McKesson, Johnnie Cochran protégé and attorney for Rafael Perez
Charles Ogletree, Harvard Law School professor and attorney for Tupac Shakur
Oscar Goodman, Las Vegas attorney and self-proclaimed "Mouthpiece for the
    Mob" who provided legal counsel to Suge Knight, now mayor of Las Vegas
David Chessoff, former U.S. Attorney, partner of Oscar Goodman and attorney
    for Suge Knight
Donald Re, attorney for both David Mack and Suge Knight
Milton Grimes, former Rodney King attorney who later represented both Kevin
    Gaines and Suge Knight
Perry Sanders and Robert Frank, attorneys for Violetta Wallace in wrongful death
    lawsuit against City of Los Angeles

OTHERS

Violetta Wallace, mother of Christopher Wallace aka Biggie Smalls
Afeni Shakur, mother of Tupac Shakur

Jimmy Iovine and Ted Field, owners and operators of Interscope

Ralph Poole, former L.A. County Sheriff's deputy, father of Russell Poole

Gary Poole, brother of Russell Poole, missing since 1996

Harry Billups aka Amir Muhammed aka Harry Muhammed, friend of David Mack, suspected of involvement in the murder of Biggie Smalls

Kelly Jamerson, Crips gang member, beaten to death by mob at Death Row Records party, March of 1995

Mark Anthony Bell, friend of Puffy Combs, alleged victim of beating and robbery at Death Row Records Christmas party, December of 1995

Michael "Harry-O" Harris, South Central Los Angeles drug lord and businessman known as "Ghetto Godfather," provided start-up money for Death Row Records

Bruce Richardson, drug dealer, businessman, legendary street fighter, and murder victim

Corey Edwards, friend to Orlando Anderson, alleged member of Southside Compton Crips, police informant

Rev. Jesse Jackson, civil rights activist, friend to Afeni Shakur, delivered eulogy at Tupac Shakur memorial service

Maxine Waters, U.S. congresswoman, friend and supporter of Suge Knight

Omar Bradley, former mayor of Compton, California, friend and supporter of Suge Knight

Rob "Vanilla Ice" Van Winkle, rapper

Dick Griffey, CEO of Solar Records, producer of *Soul Train* TV show, mentor to Suge Knight

Andre Harrell, CEO of Uptown Records and (later) Motown Records, mentor to Puffy Combs

Quincy Jones, musician, producer, publisher of *VIBE* magazine

Kidada Jones, daugher of Quincy Jones and fiancée of Tupac Shakur

Mustapha Farrakhan, son of Nation of Islam leader Louis Farrakhan

George and Lynwood Stanley, music producers and victims of assault by Suge Knight

C. DeLores Tucker, director of Black Women's Caucus, anti-rap activist

Jacques Agnant, music producer and executive

Albert and Allen Hughes, filmmakers

Yafu Fula, member of Outlaw Immortalz, witness to murder of Tupac Shakur, murder victim

Reggie Blaylock, Inglewood police officer working security for Biggie Smalls on night of his murder

James Green, Compton police officer and Death Row Records "security employee"

Melissa Delgado, girlfriend of Richard McCauley

Jesse Vincencio, alleged drug dealer shot to death by David Mack

Veronica Quesada, nightclub singer, drug dealer, girlfriend of Rafael Perez

Carlos Romero, drug dealer and brother of Veronica Quesada

Sonia Flores, former girlfriend of Rafael Perez, FBI informant

Errolyn Romero, girlfriend of David Mack and accessory in Bank of America robbery

Dale Williams, accessory in Bank of America robbery, police informant

Javier Ovando, 18th Street Gang member, victim of illegal shooting by Rafael Perez and Nino Durden

Ismael Jimanez, 18th Street Gang member, victim of beating by Brian Hewitt

Carlos Oliva, victim of LAPD assault

Mickey Thompson, race car driver, former world land-speed record holder, murder victim

Mike Goodwin, promoter, suspect in Mickey Thompson murder

Erwin Chemerinsky, USC law professor and talking head

Tom Hayden, former California state senator, political activist

Jackie Goldberg, Los Angeles City Council member

Ramona Ripston, head of American Civil Liberties Union in Southern California

Gerald Chaleff, criminal defense attorney and former president of Los Angeles Police Commission

TIME LINE

1987   Suge Knight pleads guilty to battery with a deadly weapon in Las Vegas, sentence suspended

Andre "Dr. Dre" Young signs contract with Eric "Eazy-E" Wright of Ruthless Records

1988   Group N.W.A. (Niggaz With Attitude) records *Straight Outta Compton*

Suge Knight arrested for assault at Los Angeles International Airport

1989   Suge Knight cut from Los Angeles Rams football team

Ruthless Records reports *Straight Outta Compton* has sold 2 million copies

1990   Suge Knight pleads guilty to battery in Beverly Hills, sentence suspended

Suge Knight pleads guilty to battery in Hollywood, sentence suspended

Suge Knight arrested for assault with a deadly weapon in Las Vegas

Suge Knight pleads guilty to disturbing the peace in Van Nuys, sentence suspended

Suge Knight persuades the D.O.C. to join new label he will call Funky Enough Records

1991   Suge Knight convicted of giving a false name when arrested in possession of a deadly weapon in Beverly Hills, sentence suspended

Suge Knight persuades Vanilla Ice to sign over song rights to Mario "Chocolate" Johnson

Future Shock Entertainment files articles of incorporation, lists Marion "Suge" Knight as president

Suge Knight persuades Eazy-E to release Dr. Dre from his contract with Ruthless Records

David Kenner arranges meeting between Suge Knight and Michael "Harry-O" Harris at Metropolitan Detention Center in downtown Los Angeles; the three men negotiate a joint venture for record company Harris calls Death Row Records

Tupac Shakur releases first album, *2pacalypse Now*

1992   Suge Knight charged with assault with a deadly weapon in Beverly Hills, eventually pleads guilty to misdemeanor battery, sentence suspended

Suge Knight convicted of assault with a deadly weapon in Las Vegas, sentence suspended

Suge Knight convicted of carrying a concealed weapon in West Covina, sentence suspended

Suge Knight convicted of disturbing the peace in Van Nuys, sentence suspended

Suge Knight arrested for armed assault of George and Lynwood Stanley at Solar Records studios in North Hollywood

Jimmy Iovine and Ted Field of Interscope agree to invest $10 million in new rap label, Death Row Records, if Dr. Dre is signed

Death Row Records files articles of incorporation, Marion "Suge" Knight listed as president; no mention of Michael Harris

Dr. Dre releases his first record on Death Row label, *Chronic*; becomes biggest selling rap album of all time

Sean "Puffy" Combs, twenty-two, named vice president for A&R at Uptown Records

1993   Death Row Records releases Snoop Doggy Dogg's *Doggystyle*; album goes double platinum

Suge Knight, Dr. Dre, and the D.O.C. arrested after brawling outside Black Radio Exclusive convention in New Orleans; fifteen-year-old fan stabbed during melee

Andre Harrell fires Puffy Combs from Uptown Records

Puffy Combs incorporates Bad Boy Entertainment, signs distribution deal with Arista Records

Tupac Shakur releases second album, *Strictly 4 My N.I.G.G.A.Z.*, appears in film *Poetic Justice* with Janet Jackson

Snoop Dogg and two associates charged with the murder of Philip Woldemariam

Dr. Dre convicted of assault for breaking jaw of producer Damon Thomas

Tupac Shakur arrested for shooting an off-duty Atlanta police officer, charges eventually dropped

Tupac Shakur charged with sexually assaulting Ayanna Jackson at the Parker-Meridian in New York City

C. DeLores Tucker founds National Political Congress of Black Women to attack gangsta rap

1994 Bad Boy Entertainment releases first album of Biggie Smalls aka Notorious B.I.G., *Ready to Die*

Time Warner sells its half interest in Interscope back to Ted Field, who promptly sells it to Edgar Bronfman Jr.'s MCA

Dr. Dre sentenced for violating 1993 battery conviction when pleads no contest to drunk driving charge in Los Angeles

Tupac Shakur pleads guilty to assault of Allen Hughes in Los Angeles

Tupac Shakur shot five times during robbery in lobby of Quad Recording Studios off New York's Times Square; Biggie Smalls, Puffy Combs, and Andre Harrell present in studios

Tupac Shakur sentenced to prison in New York for sexual assault of Ayanna Jackson

U.S. Justice Department commences racketeering investigation against Suge Knight and Death Row Records

1995 Suge Knight pleads guilty to felony assault with a deadly weapon against George and Lynwood Stanley, given nine-year suspended sentence

Kelly Jamerson beaten to death at Death Row Records party in Los Angeles's El Rey Theater

Biggie Smalls arrested for attacking fans with a baseball bat in Manhattan

Biggie Smalls aka Notorious B.I.G. named rap artist of the year by *Billboard* magazine

Suge Knight insults Puffy Combs from stage at *Source* Magazine Awards show; East vs. West feud escalates

Shots fired at trailer being used to film "New York, New York" video of Snoop Dogg and Tha Dogg Pound

Biggie Smalls aka Notorious B.I.G. releases song "Who Shot Ya," taken by Tupac Shakur as a taunt

Tupac Shakur released from New York state prison at Dannemora, signs contract with Death Row Records

Suge Knight opens 662 Club in Las Vegas

Jake Robles is shot to death at Platinum Club in Atlanta; Suge Knight accuses Puffy Combs of responsibility

LAPD Officer Richard McCauley discovered manning front desk at Death Row Records studios in Tarzana; ordered to discontinue employment

Michael "Harry-O" Harris threatens Interscope and Time Warner with lawsuit, demands profits from Death Row Records

Death Row Records releases Snoop Dogg's *Dogg Food* album

Mark Anthony Bell assaulted at Chateau La Blanc mansion in Hollywood Hills

January 1996   Dick Griffey and Tracy "the D.O.C." Curry file $75 million lawsuit against Suge Knight to contest ownership of Death Row Records

February 1996   Snoop Dogg acquitted at trial for murder of Philip Woldemariam

Tupac Shakur forms own production company, Euphanasia

Tupac Shakur releases first album on Death Row Records label, *All Eyez on Me*; sells half a million copies first week in stores

March 1996   Dr. Dre informs Jimmy Iovine he wants to leave Death Row Records and start his own record label

Crips working for Bad Boy Entertainment clash with Bloods working for Death Row Records at Soul Train Awards show in Los Angeles

April 1996   Suge Knight announces Death Row Records will open an East Coast division in Manhattan

May 1996   Bruce Richardson murdered in Los Angeles

June 1996   Kenneth Knox of LAPD commences civil abatement action against Death Row Records studios in Tarzana

July 1996   Kevin Lewis assaulted in parking lot outside Death Row studios in Tarzana

Biggie Smalls's home in New Jersey raided by police who seize weapons and drugs

August 1996   Puffy Combs makes threatening comments in interview with *VIBE*

Kevin Gaines places 911 call reporting self as victim of shooting at Sharitha Knight's house; assaults officers who respond

Tupac Shakur fires David Kenner as his attorney

September 1996   Tupac Shakur shot in Las Vegas, dies in hospital

Police informant reports that Suge Knight has just delivered a load of AK-47 assault rifles to Bloods gang members in Nickerson Gardens housing project

Gang war breaks out in Los Angeles County between Bloods and Crips

Los Angeles County District Attorney's office removes Larry Longo as prosecutor of Suge Knight in assault on Stanley brothers

Las Vegas Police Department informs Kenneth Knox of LAPD that Richard McCauley was in Las Vegas at time of Tupac Shakur shooting and afterward was a guest in a Luxor Hotel room reserved by Suge Knight

October 1996   Larry Longo placed on administrative leave from D.A.'s office

Suge Knight jailed for failing drug test

Kevin Lewis agrees to cooperate with investigation of Death Row Records

November 1996   Death Row Records releases Tupac Shakur's posthumous *Makaveli*

Witness Yafu Fula shot to death in New Jersey

December 1996   *Los Angeles Times* reports that Death Row Records accountant Steve Cantrock has become a federal witness and is supplying the U.S. Justice Department with financial evidence against Suge Knight

February 1997   Los Angeles County District Attorney's office wins court hearing to revoke probation of Suge Knight and reinstate prison sentence; Knight sent away for "diagnostic examination" by California Department of Corrections

Biggie Smalls and Puffy Combs arrive in Los Angeles to shoot videos for the *Life After Death* album

Afeni Shakur files racketeering lawsuit against Suge Knight and David Kenner

March 1997   Biggie Smalls shot to death while leaving party at Petersen Automotive Museum in Los Angeles

Kevin Gaines shot to death in gun battle with Frank Lyga in North Hollywood

April 1997   Russell Poole, already assigned to investigation of Kevin Gaines, takes over as one of two lead detectives in Biggie Smalls murder investigation

May 1997   Russell Poole and Fred Miller travel to Las Vegas to meet with detectives investigating the murder of Tupac Shakur

LAPD Internal Affairs investigator John Iancin travels to Las Vegas to conduct investigation of Richard McCauley's employment by Death Row Records; leads to McCauley's resignation "in lieu of dismissal" from LAPD

Reggie Wright Jr. names three other LAPD officers who do "security work" for Death Row Records

Kenneth Knox ordered not to discuss investigation of Death Row Records without authorization from LAPD

June 1997   Suge Knight enters as inmate at California Men's Colony in San Luis Obispo

Aaron "Heron" Palmer, shot and killed on Compton Street corner

July 1997   *Los Angeles Times* reports that federal investigators believe Death Row Records started with seed money from Michael Harris

November 1997   David Mack, with help of three accomplices, robs Bank of America Branch in Los Angeles; gets away with $722,000

December 1997   David Mack arrested for bank robbery

January 1998   Dale Williams tells police what he knows about bank robbery

Russell Poole first learns of evidence that implicates David Mack in the murder of Biggie Smalls; investigation stymied by LAPD superiors

Poole learns that David Mack's first jail visitor was Amir Muhammed

February 1998   Poole first hears name Rafael Perez, identified as friend of David Mack

March 1998   LAPD presents final report on shooting of Kevin Gaines, exonerates Frank Lyga

LAPD discovers that two kilograms of cocaine checked out by LAPD officer are missing

April 1998   Rafael Perez becomes principal suspect in cocaine theft

LAPD learns of earlier theft of cocaine checked into evidence by Frank Lyga; Rafael Perez implicated

May 1998   Orlando Anderson shot to death in Compton

May-June 1998   Russell Poole engages in a series of public disputes with LAPD superiors over Biggie Smalls murder investigation, and suspected involvment of police officers working for Death Row Records

June 1998   LAPD Robbery-Homicide Task Force formed; Russell Poole assigned to focus on links between David Mack and Biggie Smalls murder

Russell Poole informed that he won't be working on Biggie Smalls case for task force, after all

July 1998   Russell Poole interviews Frank Alexander, Kevin Hackie, and Kevin Lewis

Rafael Perez photographed in "romantic embrace" with Veronica Quesada, who is later arrested when brother Carlos Romero shows up at her apartment with a quarter-pound of cocaine

LAPD detectives discover photograph of Officer Rafael Perez wearing a red sweatsuit and flashing West Coast gang sign

Russell Poole assigned to investigate beating of Ismael Jimanez by LAPD Officer Brian Hewitt

August 1998   LAPD raids and searches home of Rafael Perez; Russell Poole assigned to coordinate evidence

Russell Poole makes arrest of Rafael Perez for theft of cocaine from LAPD Property Division

October 1998   Russell Poole approaches prosecutors from Los Angeles County District Attorney's office to complain about administration of Robbery-Homicide Task Force

November 1998   Russell Poole asked to leave task force and transfer out of Robbery-Homicide Division

December 1998   Russell Poole takes sick leave from LAPD

Rafael Perez's first criminal trial ends with a hung jury

January 1999   Russell Poole returns to LAPD active duty, transfers to South Bureau Homicide

May 1999   Deputy District Attorney Richard Rosenthal negotiates plea deal with Rafael Perez, learns that Javier Ovando has been falsely convicted

Los Angeles City Attorney James Hahn, Police Chief Bernard Parks, and attorney Johnnie Cochran negotiate deal to settle Gaines family lawsuit

Suge Knight transferred from California Men's Colony to Mule Creek State Prison

June 1999 Rafael Perez details alleged corruption in LAPD Rampart Division

August 1999 LAPD disbands South Bureau Homicide; Russell Poole transfers to Harbor Division Homicide

September 1999 David Mack sentenced for bank robbery

Rafael Perez plea deal made public

October 1999 Russell Poole resigns from LAPD

December 1999 *Los Angeles Times* publishes "botched" account of Biggie Smalls murder investigation provided by Russell Poole

Rafael Perez fails all five lie detector tests administered by district attorney's office; Perez sentencing postponed

February 2000 Rafael Perez sentenced in Los Angeles Superior Court

May 2000 *Los Angeles Times* prints "veiled retraction" of earlier article implicating Amir Muhammed in murder of Biggie Smalls

June 2000 Kevin Hackie interviewed at Cornell Correctional Facility by LAPD's Emmanuel Hernandez, Brian Tyndall, and Gregory Grant; identifies David Mack, Kevin Gaines, and Rafael Perez as LAPD officers who attended Suge Knight's private parties

September 2000 Los Angeles City Council votes 12–3 to accept "consent decree" imposed upon LAPD by U.S. Department of Justice

Russell Poole files lawsuit against LAPD

October 2000 First Rampart-related trial of LAPD officers (four) begins in Los Angeles Superior Court

Media discovers that Sonia Flores has told FBI she was present when David Mack and Rafael Perez executed a pair of drug dealers; district attorney announces Perez will not be called as a witness at criminal trial

November 2000 Jury delivers guilty verdicts against three of four accused LAPD officers

December 2000 Convictions of LAPD officers voided on basis of prosecutorial error and juror misconduct

Sonia Flores confesses she made up story about murder of drug dealers

January 2001 Police Protective League poll indicates that two-thirds of LAPD officers would like to quit their jobs; LAPD unable to fill Police Academy class

February 2001	Jail inmate Mark Hylland tells FBI he was hired by Suge Knight, David Mack, and Rafael Perez to courier money to pay for murder of Biggie Smalls
March 2001	Nino Durden makes plea deal with U.S. Attorney's office, reportedly will testify against Rafael Perez and unnamed others in connection to criminal acts not specified
	"The Row" releases posthumous Tupac Shakur album *Until the End of Time*
May 2001	Puffy Combs's bodyguard Eugene Deal identifies Amir Muhammed as "Nation of Islam guy" he suspects of involvement in Biggie Smalls murder
June 2001	*Rolling Stone* and *New Yorker* magazines publish articles that link Rampart scandal to Biggie Smalls murder and involvement of LAPD officers with Death Row Records; majority of Los Angeles media either ignore or attack articles
August 2001	Suge Knight released from federal prison
September 2001	Attorneys Perry Sanders and Robert Frank begin preparing wrongful death suit against LAPD and City of Los Angeles

DOCUMENTS

GAINES-LYGA SHOOTING

Los Angeles Police Department Robbery-Homicide Division Report of Officer Involved Shooting DR #97-1511566 OIS# 029/97 20 pages

"Chronological Record" of LAPD Case DR #97-1511566, stamped "Confidential" Begins 3/20/97 Ends 5/27/97 31 pages

Fact Sheet, Gaines-Lyga Shooting, Internal Affairs Division, stamped "Confidential" and dated May 27, 1997 6 pages

LAPD Follow-Up Investigation, "Confidential DR #97-1511566," dated 5/27/97 21 pages

Los Angeles County District Attorney's Office, Bureau of Special Operations, Special Investigations Division report to Capt. William O. Gartland of the LAPD's Robbery-Homicide Division, regarding S.I.D. File # 100-8226/97-0211 LAPD OIS # 029/97, dated 3/19/98 7 pages

Legend for LAPD OIS DR #97-1511566 1 page

LAPD Property Report for DR #97-1511566, dated 3/18/97 3 pages (Kevin Gaines)

LAPD Property Report for DR #97-1511566, dated 5/1/97 1 page (videotape)

Photocopies of all evidence recovered from Kevin Gaines's vehicle and person 6 pages

List of numbers left on Kevin Gaines's pager on 3/18/97 4 pages

Government Tort Claim filed by the Law Offices of Milton C. Grimes "In the Matter of Kevin Gaines vs. City of Los Angeles" Case # C96-4857 stamped "Confidential" 5 pages

LAPD Robbery-Homicide Division "Clue Form" stamped "Confidential" (Statement of Sig Schien) 5 pages

LAPD Robbery-Homicide Division "Clue Form" stamped "Confidential" (Statement of Glen Vanevera) 3 pages

LAPD Robbery-Homicide Division "Clue Form" stamped "Confidential" (Statement of Robert Vanina) 3 pages

LAPD Interdepartmental Correspondence from Captain Paul H. Marks to Kevin Gaines, dated 2/25/97 1 page

LAPD Personnel Complaint, Internal Affairs Case #96-1295, stamped "Confidential" and dated 8/16/96 2 pages

Memo titled "Gaines Shooting" and stamped "Confidential" from Detective B. Farrar of the LAPD's Anti-Terrorist Division 2 pages

LAPD Six-pack photo lineup including mug shot of Kevin Gaines, stamped "Confidential"

LAPD "Statement of Earnings and Deductions" for employee Kevin Gaines, period ending 12/7/96 1 page

LAPD Employees Report, Subject: "Information on Death Row Records" in connection to Kevin Gaines, dated 3/31/97 1 page

LAPD memo dated 4/1/97 from Det. Inabu to Det. Poole requesting photo of Kevin Gaines for Wilshire Homicide "Gaines may be involved in their case. They need picture." 1 page

DEATH ROW RECORDS

"Statement Form" of Interview with Long Beach Police Officer L. A. Arnwine, assigned to "multi-agency federal task force" investigating Death Row Records Conducted by LAPD Robbery-Homicide Division Detectives McCartin, Martin, and Katz, dated 9/29/97 3 pages

LAPD "Follow-Up Investigation" report on DR# 95-07 14398, murder of Kelly Jamerson, dated 5/1/95 9 pages

LAPD "Preliminary Investigation" of DR# 95-0648425, assault and robbery of Mark Anthony Bell, dated 12/18/95 5 pages

LAPD "Follow-Up Investigation" report on DR# 95-0648425, robbery and assault of Mark Anthony Bell, dated 1/5/96 2 pages

LAPD "Follow-Up Investigation" report on DR# 95-0648425, robbery and assault of Mark Anthony Bell, dated 4/30/96 7 pages

LAPD "Statement of Henry Lee Smith," dated 10/9/97 2 pages

LAPD list of "Compton Blood Street Gang Members," compiled by gang intelligence unit, no date 1 page

LAPD list of "Compton Southside Crip Gang Members," compiled by gang intelligence unit, no date 1 page

LAPD "List of Suge Knight's Associates," compiled by Kenneth Knox during his investigation, no date 3 pages

LAPD list of "Vehicles Registered to Death Row Records, Marion H. Knight, Lessee," no date 1 page

TUPAC SHAKUR MURDER

New York Police Department "Arrest Report" on Walter Burns aka "Runner," dated 9/12/96 1 page

Las Vegas Police Department list of "Death Row Vehicles in Las Vegas," no date 1 page

LAPD memo on "Information Gathered from Search Warrant Affidavit Prepared on *9/25/96* by Compton Police Department" 5 pages

Orange (New Jersey) Police Department "Incident Report" on the murder of Yafu Fula, dated 11/10/96 3 pages

Las Vegas Metropolitan Police Department, Homicide Section, "Fax Transmittal" sent to LAPD Officer Kenneth Knox, no date (October 1996) 13 pages

LAPD "Statement Form" of Interview with Andre Luzano aka Paul Lewis aka "Lucky" by LAPD Criminal Conspiracy Section Detectives Kent Anderson and Kenneth Wheeler, dated 4/24/97 6 pages

LAPD "Statement of Corey Lamont Edwards," dated 6/9/97 7 pages

LAPD "Statement Form" dated 10/29/97 Statements provided by Detectives R. B. Griffie and S. J. Anderson, and Lt. A. J. Biello of the Atlanta Police Department, includes statement of Fulton County Sheriff's Deputy C. J. Howard 4 pages

Los Angeles County Sheriff's Department "Notice to Appear" issued to Calvin Cordozar Broadus on 5/1/98 1 page

Los Angeles County Sheriff's Department "Office Correspondence" from Lt. Brad Welker to LAPD Det. Russell Poole "Subject: Calvin Broadus Interview," dated 5/14/98 2 pages

Los Angeles County Sheriff's Department "Statement of Facts" File # 298-03037-0980-189 Arrest of Calvin Cordozar Broadus, aka "Snoop Doggy Dogg" Dated May 1, 1998 1 page

LAPD list of "Police Contacts" in connection to Tupac Shakur murder, no date 2 pages

BIGGIE SMALLS MURDER

LAPD "General Time Line" chronicling alleged criminal activities connected to Suge Knight, Death Row Records, Tupac Shakur, Biggie Smalls, Mob Piru Bloods, and South Side Compton Crips, dated 12/12/97 9 pages

LAPD "Report on Christopher Wallace Murder" prepared by Det. Russell Poole, Robbery-Homicide Division, in June of 1998 32 pages

LAPD "Notes by Det. Poole," handwritten interview and clue notes in four separate batches, written between 4/1/97 and 7/16/98 33 pages

LAPD "Tape Recording Log" of all interviews conducted in connection to DR# 97-0711963, Christopher Wallace Murder, between 3/9/97 and 5/20/98 8 pages

LAPD "Witness List" on DR# 97-0711963, Christopher Wallace Murder, no date
    14 pages
LAPD "Death Investigation," DR# 97-0711963, Christopher Wallace, deceased,
    dated 3/9/97 1 page
LAPD roster titled "Personnel at Scene, Christopher Wallace Murder," dated
    3/9/97 2 pages
LAPD "Statement (First) of James Lloyd," dated 3/9/97, 12:30 A.M. 1 page
LAPD "Statement (Second) of James Lloyd," dated 3/9/97, 4:45 A.M. 1 page
LAPD "Statement of Gregory Young," dated 3/9/97 2 pages
LAPD "Statement of Paul Offord," dated 3/9/97 1 page
LAPD "Statement of Kenneth Story," dated 3/9/97 3 pages
LAPD "Telephonic Statement by Det. Oldham, Major Case Squad, New York
    Police Department, to Det. R. Futami, Wilshire CRASH Detectives," dated
    3/9/97 1 page
LAPD photocopies of business cards of Det. Oldham, New York Police Department,
    and Timothy Reilly, Special Agent, U.S. Department of the Treasury, Criminal
    Investigation Division, with handwritten notes, dated 3/9/97 1 page
LAPD "Statement of Troy Albert," dated 3/10/97 1 page
LAPD "Statement (Second) of Gregory Young," dated 3/10/97 3 pages
LAPD "Statement of Inglewood PD Officer Rickey Sewell," dated 3/15/97 2 pages
LAPD "Statement of Damien Butler," dated 3/19/97 3 pages
LAPD "Statement of James Lloyd," dated 3/20/97 5 pages
LAPD "Statement of Sean 'Puffy' Combs," dated 3/20/97 4 pages
LAPD "Map of Shooting Scene, Christopher Wallace Murder" 1 page
LAPD "Log of 911 Tapes, Christopher Wallace Murder," no date 9 pages
LAPD "Report of Shooting Incident" outside Petersen Automotive Museum
    shortly before Biggie Smalls's murder 2 pages
Los Angeles Fire Department "Request for Dispatch Tape" from Arson Investi-
    gation Section to Commander, Operations Control Dispatch Section, dated
    3/9/97 1 page
LAPD "Murder Investigation Suspect Link Analysis, Christopher Wallace Mur-
    der," no date 3 pages
LAPD "Firearms Analyzed Evidence Report" on DR# 97-0711963, dated 3/12/
    97 2 pages
LAPD "Wanted Poster" requesting information about the murder of Christopher
    Wallace aka Notorious B.I.G., dated 4/2/97 1 page
LAPD "Reward Poster" offering $50,000 for "information leading to the arrest and
    prosecution of the person or persons responsible for the murder of rap en-
    tertainer Christopher Wallace," dated 5/15/97 1 page
LAPD memo from Det. Kelly Cooper of Wilshire Homicide to Det. James Harper
    of Robbery-Homicide concerning "people we know were here from the East

Coast or New York and have association with Bad Boy Entertainment," no date 2 pages

LAPD "Murder Investigation Progress Report" on DR# 97-0711963, Christopher Wallace Murder, written by Det. Kelly Cooper, dated 3/19/97 18 pages

LAPD "Six Month Progress Report" on DR# 97-0711963, Christopher Wallace Murder, dated 6/8/98, written by Det. III Fred Miller 2 pages

LAPD, Robbery-Homicide Division, "Chronological Record" of Christopher Wallace Murder Investigation, handwritten by assorted (five in total) LAPD detectives between 4/2/97 and 6/23/98 97 pages

LAPD "Statement of Reggie Blaylock, Inglewood Police Department," dated 4/28/97 7 pages

LAPD "Vehicle Configuration, Christopher Wallace Murder," prepared with assistance of Reggie Blaylock on 4/28/97 1 page

LAPD "List of Associations, Death Row Records," no date 2 pages

LAPD "Preliminary Investigation" into robbery of victim Gerald R. Scott (involving cell phone stolen on day of Biggie Smalls's murder and used in vicinity of Petersen Museum shortly before shooting) 2 pages

LAPD "Statement of Faith Evans," dated 7/1/97 2 pages

LAPD "Statement of [L. A. County Sheriff's Department Confidential Informant] taken at North County Correctional Facility," dated 7/10/97 2 pages

LAPD "Follow-up Investigation, Murder of Willie Jerome Clark," dated 8/5/97 6 pages

LAPD "Follow-up Investigation, Residential Robbery (RHD Handling)" involving victims Stormy Randhan (Suge Knight's girlfriend) and Capricorn Clark, dated 8/12/97 2 pages

LAPD transcript of phone conversation between "Devin" and Li'l Kim representative Hillary Weston, dated 9/10/97 2 pages

LAPD memo from Det. Russell Poole to Det. III Fred Miller concering "info from Ken Knox" involving murder charges against Patricia Wright, dated 9/29/97 1 page

LAPD "Statement of Dawan Dixon" dated 10/9/97 2 pages

LAPD, Robbery-Homicide Division "Information Control Forms," no date (April 1997) 3 pages

LAPD "six-pack" photo lineup (including David Mack) 1 page

LAPD "Photo Identification Report" by Damien Butler, dated 4/15/98 1 page

LAPD OFFICERS INVOLVED WITH DEATH ROW RECORDS

LAPD "Permit for Outside Employment" submitted by Officer Richard McCauley on 8/11/95 1 page

LAPD "West Valley Area Watch Commander's Daily Report" on investigation prompted by Sgt. Henry Robinson of the Compton Police Department, signed by LAPD Lt. Anthony Alba, dated 10/4/95 4 pages

LAPD "Employees Report" submitted by Officer Richard McCauley to Lt. Kenneth Hiliman, dated 10/4/95 2 pages

LAPD "Fact Sheet, Officer McCauley," prepared by Sgt. E. Payne of Wilshire Division, dated 11/7/95 2 pages

LAPD "Intradepartmental Correspondence" from Deputy Chief David J. Gascon, Commanding Officer, Human Resources Bureau, "Subject: Audit of Conflict of Interest Work Location—Wrightway Security, dated 11/8/95 1 page

LAPD "Intradepartmental Corresondence" from Commander Keith D. Bushey of Human Resources Bureau, Personnel Group, "Subject: Work Permit Revocation, Police Officer III Richard McCauley," dated 11/8/95 2 pages

LAPD report on "Gang Activity at Pacifica Industrial Park (Death Row Records Studios)" in Tarzana, written by Senior Lead Officer Kenneth Knox between 5/15/96 and 11/4/96 13 pages

LAPD "Off-Duty Employment Advisory" written by Commander David J. Kalish of Human Resources Bureau, Personnel Group (and approved by Deputy Chief David J. Gascon) to all LAPD Commanding Officers regarding concerns (prompted by the murder of Tupac Shakur) that LAPD officers "have been approached to work off-duty" at "several gangster rap recording studios," dated 11/6/96 1 page

LAPD "Special Investigation" report on IA No. 96-1408, complaint by "unidentified source" against Officer Richard McCauley and "possible others" made to Senior Lead Officer Kenneth Knox 15 pages

LAPD "Personnel Complaint Investigation" of Officer Richard McCauley by Sgt. John Iancin, dated 5/27/97 48 pages

LAPD "six-pack" photo lineup (includes Richard McCauley) 1 page

LAPD "Photo Identification Reports," dated 5/15/97, 8/18/97, 8/25/97 and 10/2/97 7 pages

LAPD "Witness List," Internal Affairs case No. 96-1408, no date 4 pages

LAPD "Deployment" Records, Wilshire Division, 3/31/96 to 4/13/96 and 7/7/96 to 8/3/96 6 pages

LAPD "Personnel Complaint Investigation" cover sheet for tape-recorded interview of Officer Richard McCauley on 8/20/97 1 page

LAPD "Wrightway Protective Services Activity Sheets," 1/10/96, 5/17/96, 5/23/96, 6/6/96, 6/13/96, and 6/20/96 6 pages

LAPD "Personnel Complaint Investigation" cover sheets for tape-recorded interviews with Lts. Ken Hiliman and U. Randall Quan on 10/15/97 2 pages

LAPD record of charges to Luxor Hotel room reserved by Marion "Suge" Knight, including payment on Mastercard issued to Richard McCauley 1 page

Las Vegas Police Department, record of charges on American Express card in name of James A. Green, September 1996 1 page

LAPD "Intradepartmental Correspondence" from Sgt. John Iancin and Det. Cindy Benes to Capt. C. L. Carter, Chief Investigator, Internal Affairs Division, "Subject: Personnel Complaint Investigation of Sergeant I Richard McCauley," dated 6/23/97 2 pages

LAPD "Notice of Proposed Disciplinary Action," issued to Sgt. Richard McCauley, dated 6/24/97 1 page

LAPD "Supplemental Investigation to Personnel Complaint Investigation IA No. 96-1408," resulting in "one additional allegation of misconduct against Sergeant I Richard McCauley," dated 6/25/97 5 pages

LAPD "Witness List," Internal Affairs Case No. 96-1408 3 pages

LAPD "Supplemental Investigation Witness List," Internal Affairs Case No. 96-1408 2 pages

LAPD "Personnel Complaint" against Officer Richard McCauley, Internal Affairs Case # 96-1408, dated 6/27/96 1 page

LAPD "Intradepartmental Correspondence" from Sgt. John Iancin to Capt. George L. Ibarra, Chief Investigator, Internal Affairs Group, "Subject: Supplemental Investigation, IA No. 96-1408," dated 10/31/97 33 pages

LAPD "Intradepartmental Correspondence" from Commander Gregory R. Berg, Internal Affairs Group, to Operations-Central Bureau, "Subject: Internal Affairs Group Review of Personnel Complaint Investigation IA No. 96-1408, Involving Sergeant I Richard McCauley, no date 1 page

LAPD "Intradepartmental Correspondence" from Capt. Jim Tatreau, Area Commanding Officer, Newton Community Police Station, to Deputy Chief Ronald Banks, Commanding Officer, Operations-Central Bureau, "Subject: Re-Skelly of Sergeant I Richard McCauley," dated 11/10/97 2 pages

LAPD "Notice of Proposed Disciplinary Action" against Officer Richard McCauley, issued by Captain Jim Tatreau, Commanding Officer, Newton Area, shortly before his transfer to the Robbery-Homicide Division 1 page

LAPD "Disposition of Complaint," informing Board of Rights members that Sgt. Richard McCauley has resigned "in lieu of dismissal," effective 2/17/98 1 page

DAVID MACK

LAPD "Affidavit of Det. III Brian Tyndall," dated 12/29/97 6 pages

California Department of Motor Vehicles registration papers on 1996 Chevrolet Impala SS in the name of David Anthony Mack 2 pages

LAPD "Permits for Outside Employment" issued to Officer David A. Mack in 1991, 1992, and 1995 3 pages

Federal Bureau of Investigation "Search Warrant on Written Affidavit" issued to search apartment at 1137 W. 25th St., Los Angeles, California on 12/29/97 3 pages

LAPD "Property Report" on items seized from purse, desk, and attic of Errolyn Romero, dated 12/16/97 3 pages

LAPD "Affidavit in Support of Search Warrant" filed by Det. Brian Tyndall with United States District Court, requesting permission to search safe deposit box of David Anthony Mack, dated 1/13/98 3 pages

Federal Bureau of Investigation summary of interview with Dale Chatman Williams, dated 1/17/98 2 pages

LAPD "Chronological Record" of links between Officer David A. Mack and the Christopher Wallace Murder, written between 1/13/98 and 1/30/98 by Detectives James Harper and Russell Poole 9 pages

LAPD memo related to above, reading as follows, "Russ, Lt. Conmay wants myself and Haro to maintain control of the Mack Clue Book until it's finished. Harper," dated 1/22/98 1 page

LAPD "Deployment" records, Wilshire Division, from 2/16/97 to 3/15/97 and from 6/16/97 to 10/15/97 6 pages

KEVIN LEWIS, FRANK ALEXANDER, AND KEVIN HACKIE

LAPD "Preliminary Investigation" of Assault With a Deadly Weapon on Kevin Lewis, dated 11/2/95 2 pages

LAPD "Declaration of Probable Cause" for arrest of Andre Eddie Pascal in the assault on Kevin Lewis, dated 7/30/96 4 pages

LAPD "Arrest Report" on apprehension of Andre Eddie Pascal for the assault on Kevin Lewis, dated 7/30/96 2 pages

LAPD "Follow-up Investigation" of Assault With a Deadly Weapon on Kevin Lewis, dated 7/31/96 3 pages

LAPD memo to Det. Russell Poole concerning information possessed by Senior Lead Officer Kenneth Knox, May 1997 1 page

LAPD notes of interview of Officer Kenneth Knox by Det. Russell Poole, May 1997 11 pages

LAPD "Chronological Record" (pages 57 and 58) of Robbery-Homicide Division investigation of Christopher Wallace Murder, concerning information passed to Robbery-Homicide Division by Senior Lead Officer Kenneth Knox, dated September 29-30, 1997 2 pages

LAPD notes of Det. Russell Poole's interview of Kevin Lewis, dated 5/20/98 12 pages

LAPD Robbery-Homicide Division "Information Control Form" concerning the interview of Frank Alexander by Detectives Russell Poole and Fred Miller, dated 4/28/98 1 page

LAPD notes of interview of Frank Alexander, written by Det. III Fred Miller, dated
4/28/98 2 pages

LAPD notes of interview of Frank Alexander, written by Det. Russell Poole, dated
4/28/98 7 pages

LAPD notes of interview by Det. Poole of Det. III T. Ball of South Bureau Homicide, regarding the murder of Darryl Cortez Reed in the home of DJ Quik,
dated 1/1/98 1 page

LAPD "Master Inquiry" results from computer records of Darryl Cortez Reed
murder, dated 1/21/98 6 pages

LAPD notes of interview of Kevin Hackie, written by Det. III Fred Miller, dated
5/12/98 2 pages

LAPD notes of interview of Kevin Hackie, written by Det. Russell Poole, dated
5/12/98 20 pages

LAPD "Notes by Det. Poole" chronicling his contacts with Lt. Pat Conmay, Capt.
Jim Tatreau, and Commander Dan Schatz regarding his interview with
Kevin Hackie, and as well conversations with Los Angeles County Supe-
rior Court Judge Mark Arnold on the same subject 5 pages

LAPD memo from Det. Russell Poole informing other Robbery-Homicide Division detectives that Kevin Hackie has implicated Reggie Wright Jr. in the
murder of Orlando Anderson, dated 5/30/98 1 page

LAPD notes of phone interview by Det. Poole of Robbery-Homicide Division with
Det. Bernal of South Bureau Homicide, regarding the murder of Bruce
Richardson, dated 6/10/98 1 page

LAPD notes of interview of Kevin Hackie at Cornell Correctional Institute
Facility in Baker, California, by Detectives Brian Tyndall and Gregory
Grant, accompanied by U. II Emmanuel Hernandez, dated June 6, 2000
7 pages

AMIR MUHAMMED

LAPD "Correctional Systems, Inc. Visiting Application and Approval List Form,"
dated 12/26/97 1 page

California Department of Motor Vehicles photograph submitted by Amir
Muhammed aka Harry Billups at Montebello City Jail on 12/26/97 1 page

LAPD composite drawing of suspect in Biggie Smalls murder by artist Marilyn
Droz, completed 3/10/97 1 page

LAPD Robbery-Homicide Division "Information Control Form" on DR# 97-
0711963,

Christopher Wallace Murder, concerning information from the FBI and the Federal Bureau of Alcohol, Tobacco and Firearms about "Nation of Islam hit
men" based in Los Angeles, dated 7/18/97 2 pages

LAPD notes by Robbery-Homicide Division Detectives B. Carr, T. Ball, Brian Tyndall, Gregory Grant, and Russell Poole on the links between the Christopher Wallace Murder, LAPD Officer David Mack, Amir Muhammed, and Det. Rafael Perez of the department's Rampart Division, numerous dates 12 pages

RAFAEL PEREZ AND RAMPART CRASH

LAPD "Notes by Det. R. Poole" concerning information provided by Det. III Brian Tyndall regarding the connections between Officer David Mack and Det. Rafael Perez, between Perez and Det. Trainee Sammy Martin, and between David Mack and Amir Muhammed, dated 2/2/98 3 pages

LAPD "Preliminary Investigation" of "unknown suspect" in cocaine theft from LAPD Property Division, dated 4/16/98 2 pages

LAPD notes of meeting between Russell Poole, Detectives Mike Hohan and Lou Segura, and U. Emmanuel Hernandez concerning the discovery that cocaine apparently stolen by Rafael Perez had been signed into evidence by Frank Lyga, dated 5/13/98 1 page

LAPD notes of surveillance of Rafael Perez and records of his phone calls, dated 7/30/98 3 pages

LAPD notes of interview with Det. Mike Hohan of Robbery-Homicide Task Force concerning tapes of the wire tap executed on the residence of Rafael Perez and of conflict between Detectives Russell Poole and Ron Ito, who has accused Poole of "trying to put a case on hardworking Rampart officers," August 1998 1 page

LAPD "Property Report" of items seized in search of Rafael Perez residence at 5904 Damask Avenue in Los Angeles, dated 8/7/98 14 pages

Los Angeles Superior Court "Rafael A. Perez BA 109900-01 File Index" 8 pages

Los Angeles District Attorney's Office "Points and Authorities" concerning basis of grand theft charges against Rafael A. Perez, written by Deputy District Attorney Richard Rosenthal 22 pages

Los Angeles County District Attorney's Office, Bureau of Special Investigations, Special Investigations Division, memo to Winston Kevin McKesson setting forth terms of agreement with Rafael Antonio Perez, dated September 8, 1999 3 pages

Los Angeles County Superior Court "Return to Petition for Writ of Habeas Corpus" filed "In re Felipe Enriquez Ordonez," dated 5/11/2000 20 pages

ROBBERY-HOMICIDE (LATER RAMPART) TASK FORCE

LAPD "RHD Task Force Time Line," from 2/3/98 to 9/30/98, written by Det. Russell Poole 40 pages

LAPD "Phone Request for New LAPD Personnel Assigned to Plaza Level" (first nine officers named to task force), dated 6/1/98 1 page

LAPD note from Det. Russell Poole reading, "Informed by Lt. Conmay that I will be a member of task force (on Biggie/Bank Robbery), dated 6/1/98, followed shortly by instruction to phone Commander Schatz's office 1 page

LAPD notes of interview by Det. Poole with Officer Armando Coronado, who accuses Rafael Perez and Nino Durden of "robbing dope dealers while on duty," dated 6/10/98 2 pages

LAPD notes of surveillance on Rafael Perez, Sammy Martin, and Nino Durden, as well as their relationships with David Mack, dated 6/12/98 2 pages

LAPD "Notes by Det. Poole" concerning relationships between Perez, Durden, Martin, and Mack, and the implication of other Rampart Division officers in wrongdoing 4 pages

LAPD notes on investigation of Rafael Perez, Nino Durden, and Sammy Martin, dated 6/17/98 2 pages

LAPD notes on links between Perez, Durden, Martin, and David Mack, dated 6/25/98 2 pages

Los Angeles Police Department "Rampart CRASH Roster" 2 pages

LAPD notes of Russell Poole's first conversation with Deputy District Attorney Richard Rosenthal, dated 7/20/98 1 page

LAPD notes by Russell Poole concerning his assignment to perform surveillance on the home of Rafael Perez, dated 8/25/98 1 page

LAPD notes on Property Division audit of missing cocaine, dated 9/1/98 2 pages

LAPD "Photographic Card Displays" of officers suspected of wrongdoing in connection to the investigation of Rafael Perez and his associates, no date 18 pages

LAPD Board of Inquiry, "Rampart Area Corruption Incident, Executive Summary," dated 3/20/2000 and signed by Chief Bernard C. Parks 27 pages

LAPD "Pitchess Information, Rampart Area Corruption Incident," dated 10/24/2000 8 pages

HEWITT/JIMANEZ INVESTIGATION

LAPD "Complaint Form" filled out by Ismael Jimanez on 2/26/98 3 pages

LAPD "Chronological Record" of complaint by Ismael Jimanez against Officer Brian Hewitt, from 2/27/98 to 3/5/98, compiled by Sgt. Brad Young of Rampart Division Complaint Unit 3 pages

LAPD "Chronological Log" of IA Case No. 98-1087, from 3/23/98 to 5/21/98, compiled by "Sgt. Staples" 2 pages

LAPD "Chronological Record" of investigation by Robbery-Homicide Division Task Force of assault on Ismael Jimanez, from July 1–9, 1998, compiled by Det. Poole's partner Det. Beatrice Cid

LAPD maps of Rampart Detectives building, interior and exterior 2 pages

LAPD memo with heading "Things to Do Today," filled out by Det. Russell Poole, with 21 entries, dated 8/31/98 2 pages

LAPD "Follow-up Investigation" report on pending charges of felony battery against Officers Brian Hewitt, Ethan Cohan, and Daniel Lujan, written by Det. Russell Poole, dated 9/30/98 37 pages

LAPD "Follow-up Investigation" report on charges of felony battery against Brian Hewitt, rewritten by U. Emmanuel Hernandez, dated 10/12/98 2 pages

LAPD report by Det. Russell Poole concerning information from Ismael Jimanez attorney Dennis Chang that the 18th Street Gang has offered "a prize" to anyone who kills a Rampart CRASH officer, dated 3/25/99 1 page

SONIA FLORES

Federal Bureau of Investigation report stamped "Confidential" dated September 7, 14, and 21, 2000 5pages

NINO DURDEN

United States District Court for the Central District of California, "Information" on charges pending in Case No. CR-01-256, United States v. Nino Floyd Durden, no date, 13 pages

United States District Court for the Central District of California, "Plea Agreement for Defendant Nino Floyd Durden, dated 3/29/2001 21 pages

RUSSELL POOLE

LAPD "Performance Evaluation Report" on Russell W. Poole, Homicide Detective, South Bureau Homicide, for period 3/1/89 to 9/30/89 2 pages

LAPD "Performance Evaluation Report" on Russell W. Poole, Homicide Investigator, South Bureau Homicide, for period 9/1/91 to 2/29/92 2 pages

LAPD "Performance Evaluation Report" on Russell W. Poole, Homicide Dectective, South Bureau Homicide, for period 9/1/92 to 2/28/93 2 pages

LAPD "Performance Evaluation Report" on Russell W. Poole, Homicide Detective, South Bureau Homicide, for period 3/1/93 to 8/31/93 4 pages

LAPD "Performance Evaluation Report" on Russell W. Poole, Homicide Detective, South Bureau Homicide, for period 9/1/93 to 2/28/94 3 pages

LAPD "Performance Evaluation Report" on Russell W. Poole, Homicide Detective, Wilshire Division, for period 10/1/94 to 3/18/95 3 pages

LAPD "Performance Evaluation Report" on Russell W. Poole, Homicide Detective, South Bureau Homicide, for period 11/1/95 to 10/31/96 3 pages

LAPD "Performance Evaluation Report" on Russell W. Poole, Homicide Detective, Robbery-Homicide Division, for period 11/1/96 to 10/31/97 4 pages

LAPD "Employees Report, Subject Commendation," dated 6/11/87 1 page

LAPD "Employees Report, Subject: Commendation," dated 10/11/88 1 page

LAPD "Employees Report, Subject: Commendation," dated 3/16/90 1 page

LAPD "Employees Report, Subject: Commendation; Outstanding Investigating Techniques," dated 9/26/91 1 page

LAPD "Employees Report, Subject: Commendation," dated 6/1/92 1 page

LAPD "Intradepartmental Correspondence" from Deputy Chief Mark A.Kroeker, Commanding Officer, Operations—South Bureau, "Subject: Commendation," dated 12/14/93 2 pages

LAPD "Intradepartmental Correspondence" from Lt. Sergio Robleto, Commanding Officer, South Bureau Homicide, "Subject: Commendation," dated 2/15/94 1 page

LAPD "Employees Report, Subject: Commendation," dated 2/28/94 1 page

LAPD "Commendation Report, Subject: Russell Poole," dated 3/24/94 1 page

LAPD "Intradepartmental Correspondence" from Lt. Victor M. Guzman, Assistant Commanding Officer, South Bureau Homicide, "Subject: Commendation," dated 3/31/94 1 page

LAPD "Intradepartmental Correspondence" from Deputy Chief Mark A. Kroeker, Commanding Officer, Operations—South Bureau, Subject. Commendation," dated 9/12/94 3 pages

LAPD "Commendation Report, Personnel Group," dated 7/25/95 6 pages

Los Angeles County District Attorney's Office, Bureau of Special Operations, Commendation for LAPD Det. Russell Poole, dated 12/21/90 2 pages

Los Angeles County District Attorney's Office, Bureau of Special Operations, Commendation for LAPD Det. Russell Poole, dated 10/29/93 1 page

Los Angeles County District Attorney's Office, Bureau of Special Operations, Commendation for LAPD Det. Russell Poole, dated 11/5/93 2 pages

United States Department of the Treasury, Bureau of Alcohol, Tobacco and Firearms, Commendation for LAPD Det. Russell Poole 2 pages

LAPD "Transfer Applicant Data Sheet," Russell W. Poole, dated 8/26/96 1 page

LAPD Board of Rights, Summons to Appear, dated 3/17/99 1 page

City of Los Angeles, Administrative Board of Rights, Subpoena for Detective Russell W. Poole, dated 4/14/99 1 page

City of Los Angeles, Administrative Board of Rights, Subpoena for Detective Russell Poole, dated 6/7/99 1 page

Superior Court of the State of California, for the County of Los Angeles, Grand Jury Subpoena, dated 9/27/2000 2 pages

LAPD "Murder Investigation Progress Report" on DR # 99-12-20691, dated 7/6/99 26 pages

Letter of "dismay" from Bernard C. Parks, Chief of Police, Los Angeles Police Department, to Detective Russell W. Poole (signed by Lt. John M. Dunkin, Officer-in-Charge, Harbor Operations Support Division), dated 10/25/99 1 page

United States District Court for the Central District of California, initial filing of Russell Poole v. City of Los Angeles, dated 9/26/2000 18 pages

LAPD, Media Relations Section, Office of the Chief of Police, "Press Release: LAPD Responds to Poole Law Suit," dated 10/2/2000 2 pages

BIBLIOGRAPHY/ RECOMMENDED READING

The definitive book on rap music and hip-hop culture is Steven Hager's *Hip Hop: The Illustrated History of Break Dancing, Rap Music, and Graffiti*, which provides a rich context for all its elements. An excellent book.

The most thorough and compelling consideration of Death Row Records in particular and gangsta rap in general is Ronin Ro's *Have Gun Will Travel*. What it lacks in narrative coherence, it makes up for in exhaustive research and vivid detail.

The only really significant examination of gang culture in South Central Los Angeles is Leon Bing's *Do or Die*, an earnest and courageous (if at times uncritical) engagement of both Bloods and Crips.

The best book about gangbangers (written by one of them) is *Monster* by Shanyika Shakur, a.k.a. Monster Kody Scott..

The Los Angeles Police Department has been the subject of numerous tomes. None of them are really excellent, but Steve Herbert's *Policing Space* is worth reading.

The deaths of Tupac Shakur and Biggie Smalls have been the subject of two books by *Las Vegas Sun* reporter Cathy Scott: *The Killing of Tupac Shakur* and *The Murder of Biggie Smalls*. Both were finished fast and dirty.

Tupac Shakur's bodyguard Frank Alexander published a book called *Got Your Back* (written with Heidi Siegmund Cuda). If you're interested in an encyclopedic chronicle of Tupac's sexual conquests, this is the book for you.

NOW YOU WILL KNOW THE TRUTH

A FILM BY
NICK BROOMFIELD

BIGGIE & TUPAC

THE STORY BEHIND THE MURDER OF RAP'S BIGGEST SUPERSTARS
AVAILABLE NOW

DVD additional features include unseen footage,
director's commentary and Nick Broomfield follow-up interview

Strong language

© 2003 Razor & Tie Direct LLC

www.biggietupacmovie.com